TRAVELLER'S TALES

BOOK TWO

ADVANCING YEARS WILL NOT STOP ME!

To Marian
What a wonderful world God has given us!

Rosemary

TRAVELLER'S TALES

BOOK TWO

ADVANCING YEARS WILL NOT STOP ME!

ROSEMARY LEE

Contents

Introduction	7
Still so much to see!	8
Ethiopia 2009	11
Patagonia (Chile and Argentina) 2011	27
Central Mongolia 2011	37
Uzbekistan 2013	51
Kyrgyzstan and Kashgar 2013	61
Southern Africa 2014	77
Bhutan 2015	93
Yunnan (South-west China) 2016	107
Caucasus – Armenia/ Georgia/ Azerbaijan 2016	121
Tibet 2016	141
Sri Lanka 2017	159
Iran 2017	169
Kham (Eastern Tibet) 2017	185
Japan 2018	201
Western Australia 2018	213
Pacific Islands 2018	229
Chile and Antarctica 2018	239
Northern Pakistan 2019	253
Himalayan India 2019	265
Western Mongolia 2019	281
The Amazon 2020	291
Atlantic and Caribbean Islands 2020	299

Introduction

LET'S GET THIS STRAIGHT. I am not an explorer nor an adventurer – I am just a holidaymaker who enjoys visiting unusual places, usually travelling as part of an organised tour and trusting local guides to show me the most interesting places to visit. Any one of you could do the same.

Yet in these unusual places, I try to seek out hidden corners and people who can help me understand the country I am visiting. And I keep detailed diaries to record my thoughts and impressions, which can transport me back into the scene at any time in the future. In this book, I intend to use those descriptions, and extracts directly from my diaries, so that you can travel with me to some amazing parts of the world.

Still so much to see!

THE NEW MILLENNIUM BROUGHT MANY changes in my life. After 25 years as a tour manager, escorting tourists on coach tours around Europe, I decided on a new career path. Already in the 1990s, I had become disillusioned with the attitude of the new owners of my company and had started teaching tourism part-time in Sheffield, alongside my touring. Now in 2001, I finally gave up tour managing (at the same time moving to Cornwall) to start full-time teaching at a local further education college. For a few years my own travels were limited by the financial constraints of a change in career, but by 2009 I was travelling again, though restricted to school holiday periods – and now with a digital camera, so that I have been able to include a few photographs with this volume.

Throughout my short teaching career, I tried always to inspire students with my own fascination for different cultures and landscapes. Especially memorable were 'residentials' to southern Spain, which allowed a day trip to North Africa – what an eye-opener for our inexperienced 17-year-olds, learning how to dress appropriately in a Muslim country and how to cope with hassling street-vendors. Even a couple of days in Amsterdam was an experience for them – I will not forget their faces as an elegant man wearing thick greasepaint and a tight Lycra bodysuit roller-skated past them! Nor the excitement of our 'country kids' when they first saw nose-to-tail buses on London's streets! There were new experiences for me too, as I had to extricate students from difficult situations (sometimes fuelled by over-indulgence in alcohol), as they made their first forays into adult life.

However, my freedom to inspire a love of travel in my students was gradually eroded by increased regulation of the teaching curriculum, and in 2007 I said a final farewell to my students. With only a few years of working life left, I took an undemanding job in a local supermarket, once again utilising the customer service skills which had stood me in good stead for so many years as a tour manager, until I decided to retire completely in 2013. For a couple of years I limited my travels, not sure whether I was financially secure enough to undertake expensive trips. Then came a revelation: all my life I had saved 'for my old age' … and now I decided that 'old age' had arrived! I started to use my savings to travel to any places I wanted to see, often multiple trips per year, aware that each successive year was bringing limitations to what I could physically achieve. As I write this, Coronavirus has stopped all travel, but I am hopeful that it will eventually be brought under control, and I will be off again … there is still so much to see!

Rosemary in Sri Lanka

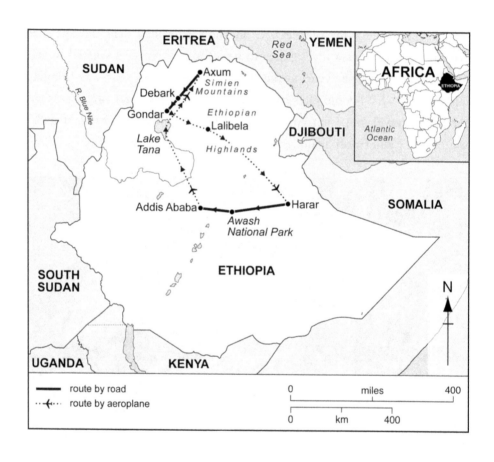

route by road
route by aeroplane

0   miles   400

0   km   400

Ethiopia (January 2009)

THE REALISATION OF A LONG-HELD dream! Back in the 1970s, friends who had lived for a time in Africa, told me about the rock-cut churches of Lalibela in Ethiopia, one of the wonders of the world. I was keen to see them, but it seemed impossible as one disaster after another hit the country: famine in the 1980s, war with Eritrea in the 1990s, fighting with Somalia in early 2000s. Finally in 2009, after more than 30 years of waiting, the situation stabilised enough for me to fulfil my ambition and travel to Ethiopia.

The capital city, Addis Ababa, was disappointing – just a crowded city made up of simple shacks mixed with modern concrete structures, and roads congested with traffic. In the cathedral compound we passed through throngs of worshippers, kissing the doorposts and kneeling outside the doors ... in the National Museum we saw the fossilised remains of 'Lucy' (at 3.2 million years old, one of the earliest humanoid relics ever discovered) ... tiny shops were selling everything imaginable in the Mercato, the largest market in Africa, crowded with donkeys and human porters – I was particularly taken by the sight of a mound of foam mattresses teetering along above a single skinny pair of legs! Our first evening took us to a local cafe to sample the staple food of the country – thin pancakes made from 'teff' grain (a type of local grass) ... an exceptionally boring foodstuff!

"Just as we arrive, the cafe is plunged into darkness, so we have to order by candlelight – a mixed success. We wanted 'injera' (pancake) with lamb, but end up with 'firfir' (shredded injera soaked in lamb juice, spread on another injera) – but at least the tomato & onion salad (served, of course, with injera) is good. We will have to be careful with our hygiene, though, since all three of

us are dipping into the mix with fingers which are all too easy to lick before reaching for more."

A change of plan next morning: the amalgamation of two flights meant we were hustled out of our hotel earlier than expected. I was fascinated in the airport to see a clock operating on traditional Ethiopian time – their day starts at 6am instead of midnight, so (at 8.15 on my watch) the clock read 2.15! I was not sorry to leave Addis, heading north to Bahar Dar beside Lake Tana, using the extra time to explore the lakeside:

"... walking beneath the burning African sun, beneath tall trees rustling with dry-season leaves, past clumps of papyrus growing thickly in the shallows. A group of fishermen are working their nets close to shore, perched in their narrow reed boats, turned up neatly at each end: one paddles his boat like a canoe, another stands up to punt along with a pole. White pelicans drift aimlessly, while overhead ospreys shout raucously at each other, their cries like shrieks of derisory laughter."

Next day we set out to view the Tissisat Falls on the Blue Nile, escorted down a steep rocky trail by three extra guides (perhaps overdoing the safety angle?) as far as a 17th century bridge across the river, densely packed with tourists trying to walk in one direction, local people driving animals to market in the opposite direction, and groups of stationary begging children. The view over the Falls themselves was impressive, though they were not huge at this time of year – a brown and cream swirl of water cascading over the main chute, with narrower gullies on either side. I decided I wanted to see more, so continued further alongside the river:

"... to a stony ford bustling with farmers moving herds of skinny goats, cows being washed to beautify them for market, and tourists being solicitously helped across the rough river bed. Our guides do not permit us to try to cross without assistance, nor allow us to query the price of this assistance (firmly fixed at 10 birr). Crowds of men are vying for the job of giving us a helping hand, and I am happy to entrust myself to a strong young lad who sees me safely through the rocks on the river bed."

The path took us along the opposite side of the river, passing through fields of the drug Qat (pronounced 'Chat') above a narrow rocky gorge. We stopped to view the Falls from this side, venturing down to the water's edge to feel the spray, then sat for a while at a 'pop-up cafe' – an enterprising young woman had built a couple of fires to brew her coffee and tea, filled a bucket with cold river water to cool bottles of soft drink, and arranged rocks as seating. The coffee was surprisingly good – but then, Ethiopia is the original home of coffee. One more crossing of the river was needed to get back to our coach – we could have chosen the jam-packed 'local' ferry (drifting with the current until the water was shallow enough for the boat to be punted manually into the shore) but instead elected to use the 'luxury' version specially provided for 'ferenjis' (foreigners) and wealthy Ethiopians – the same simple wooden boat, equally crowded, but with the addition of a motor.

The afternoon brought a tranquil excursion across the lake to Zegehi Peninsula for a first sight of a rural Ethiopian church building. We quickly learned that, in the Christian part of Ethiopia (the northern highlands), the Orthodox religion was an integral part of life – we visited innumerable churches, learning more about this complex faith all the time. This one was in the circular style of many rural churches, similar to the round thatched 'tukul' huts which formed the traditional village houses, though much larger. The interior was dominated by a huge square box (the 'Mekides' or 'Holy Place') which housed the Tabot (wooden or stone slabs representing the Tablets of the 10 Commandments) which every church in Ethiopia possesses: access here was only for the priests. A narrow passage ran between the Mekides and the church wall – here the men would stand for services while women stood outside, all clutching their 'chanting staffs' (useful to lean on during long services, but also to stamp the ground at set moments to punctuate the chanting). The Mekides was painted from top to bottom with brightly coloured scenes from the lives of Jesus and Mary, and with stylised images of Orthodox saints destroying the enemies of the faith. I quickly learned to tell good characters from bad – if you are a saint you are portrayed full-face (with two eyes) but if you are evil you are in profile (with one eye).

Back to the airport now – roads in Ethiopia were still so bad that the travel method of choice, for anyone with enough money, was by internal flight. We were travelling north again, almost to the Eritrean border, crossing range after range of brown, spectacularly eroded mountains dotted with white spots which indicated threshing grounds – even this arid landscape was cultivated by the diligent farmers of the north. Our goal was Axum, now a poverty-stricken, slow-moving village, but once (between 1st–8th centuries AD) capital of a kingdom which stretched from Mozambique to Egypt to Yemen – one of the 4 most important world powers of its time. Here we met another local guide, Seesi, who was passionate about the history of his country – he was almost in tears as he bewailed the modern international image of Ethiopia as a backwater of drought and famine.

He rushed us straight into sightseeing at the Stelae Ground, where graves of royalty and nobility were marked by massive stone obelisks (largest in the world) from the 3rd and 4th centuries AD. We visited two of the tombs, where I was impressed by precisely cut stonework – certainly as fine as Peru's Inca stonework. Obviously there was huge archaeological potential at this site, though Ethiopia could not afford any excavations and had to rely on foreign expeditions – 95% of the site was still unexplored. Seesi was proud to have worked with one German expedition which had uncovered a cross-shaped baptistery, built in the 3rd century by Ezana, the king who made his realm one of the first Christian countries in the world. Nearby were more royal tombs and the Ezana Stone (only found by accident, in 1981) with inscriptions in 3 ancient languages. I tried hard to absorb all this historical information, but could not help being distracted by the antics of a young girl at the site:

"A little girl arrives at the coach, breathless and panting having run all the way uphill to be first to greet us and offer her two paltry metal crosses for sale. We wave her away, but she refuses to give up and, as we move on to the next site, runs easily alongside the bus with a long loping stride (reminiscent of Ethiopian Olympic champions), rarely stumbling on the rough rocks we are bumping across."

I could not ignore such determination, so bought one of her crosses – which is now a treasured souvenir.

The history lessons moved into the realm of myth and legend as our sightseeing reached the so-called 'Palace of the Queen of Sheba'. Tradition holds that Ethiopia was the home of this queen 1000 years BC, and the Bible records that she travelled to Israel to meet King Solomon. Legend, mixed with history, continues the tale: the queen slept with Solomon, returning to her country pregnant with their son Menelik … in time he travelled to Israel to meet his father and was given (or perhaps stole?) the Ark of the Covenant, bringing it back to Axum – where Ethiopians believe it still resides, hidden in a tiny chapel in the town. The Ethiopian kings proudly claimed, throughout history, to be descended from Menelik – right up to the last king Haile Selassie, who was deposed in 1974. Seesi was convinced of the truth of these legends, though he had to acknowledge the archaeology of a French expedition which had discovered that most of the so-called 'Palace of the Queen of Sheba' dated from 600 AD (well after her time) ... but he was excited that his Germans had dug a small hole and discovered much older foundations beneath the walls: 'clearly the association with the Queen of Sheba must be true', he asserted! He had one final historical milestone to impress us:

"A rock-cut flight of steps plunges into a dark cavern containing just three niches hollowed out of the rock walls. Discovered in 1950 by the French, it has been documented by royal records (still held in Axum) to be the tomb of King Balthazar who ruled in the 1ˢᵗ century AD – and who was one of the three Magi to attend the infant Jesus in Bethlehem, making him one of the first ever Christians."

All this history was not the highlight of our visit to Axum, however. We had arrived in time to celebrate Timkat, one of the most important annual festivals of the Ethiopian church, marking the baptism of Jesus. All over Ethiopia, the priests would parade their 'Tabots' through their communities, before enacting a ritual baptism ceremony. We were in the town supposedly housing the real Ark of the Covenant, but there was no question of priests parading with that relic – it is hidden away, only ever seen by its guardian and his assistant. Even so, the procession was an exhilarating experience:

"The women's ululation reaches fever pitch, trumpets are blown, and musicians appear, leading the procession ... then the priests emerge from behind the shrine, gaudily dressed in jewel colours, shading themselves with equally gaudy umbrellas. One priest bears the Tabot on his head, draped in rich cloths ... ahead of them capers an elderly priest with hair as wild as John the Baptist himself. The crowd chants along to the music, clapping with complex rhythms at appropriate times, while bursts of ululation punctuate the chorus of sounds."

Having watched the start of the procession, Seesi hustled us through the crowds across to the other side of town to take up position to await the arrival of the swaying, chanting, white-draped mob (it is customary to wear white when worshipping) following in the wake of the priests. As they passed, we slipped into place among the faithful, walking and clapping with them, totally accepted without resentment among the worshippers. I walked with them into the compound where the Tabot was to spend the night in a special tent, already feeling a little uneasy at positioning myself so close to the precious relic – so I was horrified to see one guide actually ushering his (American) group right inside the tent, causing consternation among the worshippers who were themselves excluded, especially since none of the group removed their shoes before entering, and even more because the group included women. Talking to a shopkeeper later, I learned that this breach of etiquette had caused real distress among the worshippers – how insensitive some tourists (and their guides) can be!

The parade broke up now, returning later for a mass – though the priests continued to chant around the Tabot throughout the night. As the evening progressed, I returned to the compound around the tent – now calm after the frenetic celebrations of the earlier parade. Everyone was friendly and I received nothing but smiles and welcome:

"A group of older women shuffle in a tight circle in front of the priests – dancing, singing and ululating. A couple of wealthy Ethiopians are distributing huge bundles of candles to enthusiastically grasping worshippers – they insist that I take one too. After a while, the candles are lit and the compound is filled with tiny stars of light. Clearly these candles are significant – one boy blows his out so that he can relight it from mine."

Timkat was not yet finished, and next day we left our hotel at dawn to join the crowds of white-swathed people scurrying from every direction towards a huge cistern known as the Queen of Sheba's Bath, where the ritual baptism would take place. Our ever-solicitous Seesi organised the position of our coach among the crowds, negotiating with police who were trying to keep enough space for the ever-growing number of chanting priests, while also getting us as close as possible to the 'action'. Once he was satisfied, we clambered up to perch on the roof-rack with a fine view across the entire area, watching as more and more people arrived – a Biblical scene of white-shrouded figures taking up position on ledges of the rock face overlooking the pool. An outburst of ululation indicated that the main body of priests was moving, dressed in full regalia and carrying large elaborate crosses. Finally the bishop arrived – clad in shiny silver cape and hood, looking so modest amid the gaudy vestments of the priests. The busload of Americans arrived (late) and tried to force their coach into the crowd for a good view – this time, the police were on hand to drive them back to a safe position. The ceremony continued with chanting and Bible reading, drumming and jangling of the sistram (metal discs on a frame). Finally the bishop and his attendants staggered down the steps to the water's edge to lower their ceremonial crosses and bless the water … immediately the crowd, which had waited patiently throughout the hours of ceremonies, burst into movement:

"As soon as the last note of the blessing sounds, hordes of boys plunge exuberantly into the Bath, slithering down the steep sides or hurling themselves bodily out towards the water. They are clutching bottles, which they now fill and throw back up to the crowd waiting above so everyone can spray themselves with (now holy) water. The air is filled with shouts and laughter – their exuberance reflecting a grateful release from the long hours of solemnity."

Our next destination was not accessible by plane, so we launched into a 10-hour drive along an unsealed road through the mountains, originally created (with typical flair) by Italian engineers during their short occupation of the country. They actually left Ethiopia with a properly sealed road, but, when they demanded payment for it after they were driven out in 1941, the Ethiopian government destroyed the road surface so that they could refuse payment for an 'unfinished product' (or so our British escort told us!). As we bounced slowly across the stones and ruts, enveloped in a cloud of dust, we passed frequent gangs of local workers under the control of a few Chinese engineers – the road being rebuilt by (possibly) the next empire-building invaders? The journey, though wearying, was a wonderful way to glimpse the day-to-day life of the countryside. Early in the morning, and again at the start of the afternoon, we saw pupils (always in smart uniforms) making their way to school – with a shortage of school places, many rural schools were operating on a shift system with students attending either mornings or afternoons. We saw few pupils being transported to school – instead, streams of children were walking in immense crocodiles through the fields or over the hills, clearly valuing the opportunity to get an education in a way which western children rarely emulate.

As we drove further into the mountains, we stopped to stretch our legs in a few isolated villages where the school was too far away – only the older children attended, boarding or staying for the week with relatives, while the younger ones roamed the streets at home. They were excited when their day was enlivened by the rare presence of 'ferenjis', vying with each other to grasp our hands and walk with us through their village, chattering incomprehensibly. They were beautiful children with fine bone-structure and fascinating hairstyles:

"The men often twist their hair into many tiny balls, so their heads look like a massage ball, while little boys' heads are shaved except for a small topknot. The women and girls create tiny, very tight plaits, sometimes running across the head from front to back, sometimes pulling them across their foreheads in intricate patterns. A few prefer a mixture, with tight plaits at the front and a bush of uncombed frizz at the back."

In some villages we saw piles of charcoal by the roadside, a lucrative cottage industry in a country with few trees ... in others, we spotted white cups on a table outside a door – indicating that the house was selling Tella beer (it looked and tasted like muddy dishwater!). In small villages the homes were mainly cabins made of stone or mud, in larger villages there were single-storey concrete houses with shady verandahs where people were chatting and babies playing. The streets were full of goats and a few cows, lying in the shade of a tree – often in the middle of the road: the goats scattered when we approached, but we had to take avoiding action around the cows. There were always people walking, walking – Ethiopia seemed to be permanently on the move ... and always carrying something: jerrycans of water, sacks of grain or piles of wood balanced on their heads; babies or mysterious bundles wrapped in cloths on the women's backs; walking staffs resting on the back of men's necks when not in use.

Finally we reached Debark, once no more than a truck stop but, when we visited, in the process of developing as a hub for tourism in the Simien Mountains. Our hotel was basic, with bathrooms but no hot water ... and hopelessly overbooked (I eventually went out to find my own room at a nearby hostel). Breakfast was served by staff who were very keen to please, but had no idea of what to do ... on the second day our British escort took over, ordering the staff first to find tables, then cloths to cover them, then cutlery to put on them, and even disappearing into the kitchen to supervise the production of hot scrambled eggs (instead of lukewarm): I wonder if this simple 'training' has now produced efficient staff? Not everyone in the town was equally keen to please, however:

"A walk down the side streets is disturbing – not because of the poverty, but the attitude of the people. The children's begging is persistent and insistent, with no charm at all. More worrying are the teenagers, surly and even aggressive (some boys throw rocks towards me). Is it just because I am a woman wandering alone? The town is partly Muslim – should I have worn a headscarf? Do they resent me walking in their residential areas? Or has the town lost the gentle hospitality we have seen elsewhere, under the onslaught of backpackers?"

The Simien Mountains were worth the discomfort of Debark, however – volcanic plateaux studded with dramatic pinnacles of solidified lava. Our walk took us along the edge of the main escarpment, the air cool and fresh in the early morning with the scent of wild thyme; later in the day, swallows cruised overhead and lammergeiers soared effortlessly on the thermals. The highlight was our encounter with a troupe of huge Gelada baboons, just climbing from their overnight caves in the wall of the escarpment to the clifftops to catch the first rays of the sun:

"They are only just awake, warming up and grooming each other – the big males sit up, displaying their pink chests for adoring females to groom ... others lift their tails and expose genitals for cleaning. Suddenly a cacophony of harsh screams tells us that another troupe has caught the smell of local people and is running scared: our guide tells us that they can distinguish between the scent of harmless tourists and that of locals who persecute them because they eat the crops."

Next day we called at the village of Walaka, formerly a mixed community of Jews and Christians, though the last Jews left for Israel at the end of the 20th century. However, I met a 19-year-old girl (who spoke excellent English) and she sadly explained that Israel had accepted only those with a Jewish bloodline on their mother's side ... her Jewish father had taken a Christian wife, so she was not allowed to emigrate, and she was missing relatives and friends who had left. Such a courageous girl – her mother was working away from home, so she was looking after the rest of the family, while also selling baskets to earn money to pay piecemeal for an accountancy course which might bring her a better job in the future.

Now to Gondar, another former capital of Ethiopia – this time in the 17th century, when the kings had brought in Portuguese help to oppose the steady advance of Muslims from the south. Unfortunately, part of the price for this help was an acceptance of Catholicism instead of Orthodoxy, which led to civil war and the expulsion of all Catholics. We visited a complex of palaces, remarkably European in style (built under the influence of the Portuguese) and then the Debre Birhan Selassie church, one of many built by the king who expelled the Catholics, as a sign of his devotion to Ethiopia's original faith. One of the keys to Orthodoxy is its mystery – the priests encourage a deep sense of awe and respect in worshipping God, content to accept His inexplicable nature. However, I found myself increasingly confused by the symbolism which creates that sense of mystery:

"Nothing is simple: the walls around the church compound are studded with 12 towers (representing the 12 apostles) ... the facade is topped by 7 ostrich eggs (which are very strong, so represent the strength of Christianity) ... the chanting sticks can be raised (to represent the Resurrection), or lowered (to represent Christ's coming down to earth), or held horizontally (representing Christ on the cross). I switch off – it is all just too much!"

We abandoned the roads in favour of another internal flight, this time to Lalibela: till the airport was upgraded in 1997, the town was virtually isolated amid the mountains but by the time we visited, it was clearly developing fast with a lot of new buildings shooting up, including many hotels. Of course, the attraction was those 11 rock-cut churches I had waited so long to see – declared UNESCO World Heritage Sites in 1978. They were built in the 12th century by King Lalibela, who wanted to provide a substitute Jerusalem for pilgrims unable to visit the Holy Land because of Islamic aggression, cutting the churches deep inside the living rock so that they were invisible to potential attackers as Muslim armies moved in from the south. They were all still in regular use and some were fragrant with incense. I was enchanted by them:

"The building of the churches is amazing, though again our guide's explanations are beyond me. Everything has layer upon layer of meanings, adding to the sense of awe so beloved of the Ethiopian church. These are ideal churches for Orthodoxy, dark and mysterious with corners which never see the

light of day, and draperies which hide a multitude of treasures. They seem cluttered to us – rugs are hurled casually across the floor; benches are pushed against walls; piles of curtains, baskets and faded icons lie hidden in corners."

We scrambled around the first (best-preserved) group of churches, slipping off our shoes at the entry to each (we had been warned to wear socks to ward off the fleas living in the ancient carpets), entrusting them to a 'shoe-boy' who then carefully carried them to whichever exit we were using. With only tiny windows cut into the rock walls, the interiors were dim and mysterious – our guide shone a feeble torch beam into dark corners to point out dull frescos or ornate carvings. Each church had its own resident priest, sometimes dozing quietly but sometimes waking as we entered – one ambled across to collect his golden vestment and processional cross, then posed for our cameras:

"The first church is the largest, cut into the heart of an immense boulder. Descending to visit it, we find a maze of tunnels and ancient wooden doors which lead to a complex of 3 more churches, then on to more again. Everywhere the rock is smooth and polished by centuries of passing feet, and many of the steps are either impossibly worn, or so high and steep that I need hands as well as feet to climb them."

Most impressive of all was St George's Church, set apart from all the others, at first seeming to be just a bas-relief in the shape of a cross on the surface of a huge, rounded boulder ... then revealed as a 3-storey, free-standing church, hidden deep inside the rock. The final group of churches was less well-preserved, with one totally inaccessible because its roof was crumbling:

"From here, passages and stairs lead to the Tunnel – we pass through in darkness, feeling our way along the wall, holding on to the shoulder of the person in front (symbolic of the dark journey before emerging into the light of Heaven), to visit a tiny church supposedly built in a single day for King Lalibela's queen. Finally we emerge from the complex via a small hole in the lowest corner of the rock ... I feel as if I am being flushed out of a basin!"

Next day we mounted mules to parade in stately fashion through the middle of the village (to the amusement of the locals), then lurched off uphill on a rocky track through the fields. I was lucky to have an elderly and docile animal which gamely hurled itself at the ever-steepening path till we reached a grassy plateau. Now we continued on foot along a path clinging to the rocks beneath a bulging cliff, then up a flight of steps cut through the rock to reach a wooden door high in the mountains… in a patch of sun beyond the door lay yet another rock-cut church (Ashiten Maryam), carefully tended by a priest who climbed from the village every day. A memorable excursion, enhanced as we returned downhill, by a visit to the traditional 'tukul' home of a young family. They lived from a couple of fields producing peas and beans, bartered in market for 'teff' flour, so that their entire diet consisted of beans and injera – even their one-year-old baby was beginning to eat injera, as well as suckling. The young man told us that his dream was to buy a single ox to help with ploughing – the payment for our visit would help achieve his dream.

Lalibela had more than justified my long-held desire to visit, but there was one last treat in store: our hotel organised an open-air barbecue, bringing in a few local people to sing and dance for us:

"The dancing is amazing! Both men and women start by just swaying, but quickly move into the 'shoulder dance', snapping their shoulders, then their heads, back and forth so viciously that it seems they must break their necks. One tiny girl, though she has virtually no breasts, sends her beads bouncing up into her face by the violence of her movements."

I would have been happy to leave Ethiopia at this point, but our tour was designed to also give us a glimpse of the Muslim south of the country, so we flew on to Harar, only part of Ethiopia since the 1880s. The old town was nestled inside still-complete 16th century city walls, so our sightseeing took us on foot through the massive Showa Gate into a street market full of unusual products like coffee husks (used to make a type of tea) or sandals made of old car tyres. The people now had a more African look, lacking the fine bone-structure of the northern population, and the women were wearing more brightly coloured clothing – but there was little sign of the welcome and hospitality of the North:

"The streets are filthy, and both adults and children scream 'ferenji – money!' at us as we pass. In places, hordes of children come rushing down the alleyways to mob us, with none of the polite 'where are you from?' or 'what is your name?', which we are used to – instead, the demand is immediately 'gimme pen' or 'gimme money'. Men lie in doorways or gutters, chewing Qat – some already totally knocked out by it, in the middle of the day."

Harar was not a highlight of my trip, though my guidebook described it as 'a delight'. However, it was interesting to be taken inside a spotlessly clean, traditional Harari home, hidden in a courtyard behind high walls. Entering through a beautifully carved door, I found myself in a high-ceilinged living room filled with seating/ sleeping platforms on different levels (the highest for clerics and the head of the family, the lowest for the women and children), with the walls hung with colourful baskets and pots – the women's treasures. A little side room was filled with a huge bed – this was the 'honeymoon suite' where a new wife traditionally had to remain until she was pregnant (if she did not conceive, her husband could divorce her). That night we drove to a spot just outside the city walls, where an elderly man sat beneath an ancient fig tree – surrounded by a pack of hyenas, who traditionally were welcomed into the streets of the town at night, scavenging any edible rubbish and sanitising the streets:

"Our headlights illuminate a colourfully dressed elderly man with two buckets full of meat ... around him 10 or 15 hyenas circle nervously on the edge of the light, dashing in to grab a piece of meat held out on a short stick, then retreating again to the safety of the pack. The leaders of the pack are most courageous, taking the meat from a stick held in his mouth."

From Harar, we continued by road through a well-populated land with frequent villages and intensively cultivated land. Every home seemed to boast a few cows, firmly tethered by the road, as well as donkeys, goats and chickens – clearly a much richer region than the northern highlands. The road surface was good, though there was far more traffic: minibuses with roof racks laden with grain sacks, or clusters of yellow water-cans spilling down the minibus windows like bunches of yellow grapes; massively overloaded trucks pulling equally laden trailers crawling up the hills with engines labouring; trucks broken down, with blown engines or burst tyres, slewed across the road or turned on their sides – cargo usually already removed (perhaps illegally?) but taking days to recover the vehicle itself. The landscape looked more as I expected Africa to look: covered in prickly shrubs, dotted with flat shady acacias and studded with termite mounds, while the trees were hung with the brown 'basket' nests of weaver birds. Our last visit in Ethiopia was to be in the Awash National Park – however, there had been torrential rain which had turned the Park's tracks into mud baths, impossible for our minibus to traverse; all we saw was one startled warthog and a tragic lion captured in Somalia 3 years previously and imprisoned since then in a tiny cage:

"Tonight's hotel in a roadside service area, is by far the simplest of all. My room has a mosquito net (thankfully) but no toilet or shower, which would not be a problem except that the only toilet available is the one used by the entire resthouse ... and it has no flush – just a barrel of water and an old tin can. To wash we must all use the kitchen sink out in the courtyard, which offers only a trickle of water."

I would not have wanted Harar and Awash to be my last memories of this very special country. Fortunately, a church near our hotel in Addis Ababa was celebrating a holy day and I joined the crowds who packed the compound, standing quietly watching as people arrived to worship for as long as they could manage (the full mass lasted for hours), standing or kneeling on the hard ground as the priests intoned their liturgies over loudspeakers. Extra priests were wandering through the crowds with massive incense burners, wafting fragrant smoke over the worshippers wherever they were – one strolled through the compound carrying a cross for the faithful to kiss: he approached me too, hesitated as I bowed to him, then moved on with a smile and a blessing. The disappointments of the last few days of our tour were relegated to the pages of my diary, replaced by memories of the gentle piety of Ethiopian Christians.

Ethiopian Priest

Ethiopia - Lalibela

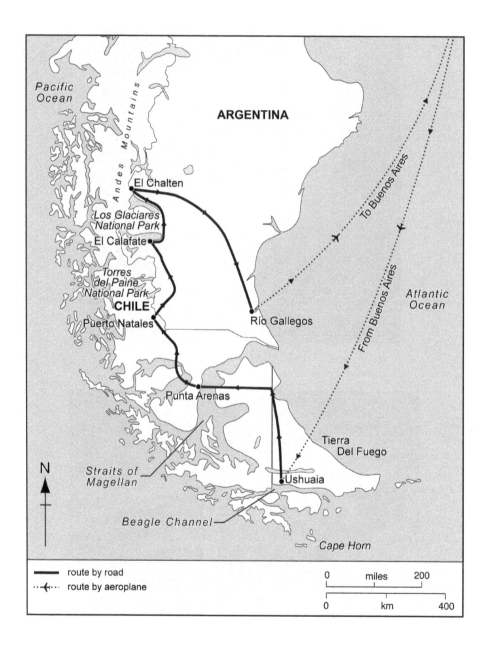

Patagonia – Chile and Argentina (March 2011)

I THINK I MUST HAVE forgotten how far away South America is from Europe, in the 11 years since I was last there – once again my diary bewails how long it took to get to Buenos Aires (16 hours) at the start of my tour to Patagonia (a region covering parts of both Argentina and Chile). I was looking forward to empty landscapes, but first we were bustled around the highlights of Argentina's capital: the elegant 18th century former Town Hall … Metropolitan Cathedral with its unobtrusive 19th century facade masking a cavernous baroque interior … towering 20th century Kavanagh apartment block, boasting balconies adorned with small trees. Sobering for me, being British, was the memorial to Argentinians killed in the Islas Malvinas conflict in 1982 (known to us as the Falklands War) – we repeatedly saw slogans declaring 'Las Malvinas son Argentinas' (once even on a tourist coach). We also visited the Monumental Cemetery, its narrow alleys lined with tombs of varying sizes and styles – including the discreet black marble tomb of Eva Peron. Finally into La Boca district, once the location of poverty-stricken tenements housing immigrants from all over the world, but now a vibrant centre of tourism, because this is where the Tango originated:

"One little street is full of cafes, many of which employ a couple of tango dancers who perform in the entrance to entertain existing customers and attract more. On street corners stand individuals dressed in sharp suits or tight dresses, offering high-priced photo opportunities in dramatic tango poses with passing tourists."

There was also time to travel by train and boat into the nearby delta of the

River Plate. I had hoped to find a region of isolated waterways and wildlife, but instead found a well-developed playground for the people of Buenos Aires, with a massive funfair full of screaming children, and a lively market:

"The whole train disgorges to join already milling crowds who are queuing at every ticket booth for ferries to different parts of the delta. The waterways are crammed with boats of every sort, from large catamaran cruisers to small launches, speedboats to jet skis, canoes to racing skiffs. A 'rowing school' moves up and down the channel – at each rudder sits an instructor constantly giving orders, while earnest, sweating students labour at the oars."

Next day we caught the early morning flight (another 5 hours flying time) to the furthest tip of South America, glimpsing a convoluted landscape of twisted ridges and sharp, snow-flecked peaks before we landed at the town of Ushuaia, proud to call itself 'Fin del Mundo' (the End of the World). A few tiny, corrugated iron shacks showed how it was until tourism arrived at the start of the 21st century – now the main street was lined with souvenir shops and restaurants. Rickety wooden stairways led up to homes perched high above the tourist town, though few residents remained here in winter, preferring to head north to Buenos Aires when the tourist season ended. My dreams of tranquillity and isolation were finally realised as we boarded a small boat to cruise out into the Beagle Channel, pulling away from the hordes of humanity into a world where Nature provided the crowds:

"A hubbub of activity draws my eye to a patch of sea where a shoal of fish has neared the surface – delicate terns are swooping and diving, whilst among them massive brown skuas also crash into the water with a flash of white wing feathers. One island is thickly painted with guano deposited by innumerable Imperial Cormorants, and at the tip of the island is a sealion colony – fluffy yellowy females rest quietly in an adoring mob around their two massive bulls."

Landing on one of the islands, we walked among weird round lumps of vegetation which our guide told us were Yareta plants, which grow only a few millimetres annually yet live for hundreds of years, allowing them to build into massive rounded 'boulders'. On the same island, we passed mysterious hollows in the ground, all that remained of shelters built here by the nomadic Yamana people – the sole native inhabitants of this remote part of the world.

They moved around the islands at the tip of South America in simple bark canoes (unclothed but covered in sealion fat to insulate them from the cold), fishing or hunting sealions and penguins, carrying a living flame in their canoes so that they always had a fire when they set up camp on land. In the late 19th century, English missionaries arrived, bringing with them diseases to which the Yamana had no resistance. They were further weakened when the missionaries encouraged them to wear clothing instead of (horribly smelly) fat – yet that clothing was constantly wet and provided no insulation. In less than 100 years, the Yamana were wiped out: how ashamed I felt as I later visited Ushuaia's small museum and saw their photographs, gazing into the sad, bewildered eyes of a people on their way to extinction.

Ushuaia lies in the south of Tierra del Fuego, an island divided between Argentina and Chile, so we were able to look across the water to the Chilean mountains as we explored Argentina's Tierra del Fuego National Park. Our guide pointed out gnarled and twisted deciduous Southern Beech and slim upright Canelo trees: clearly they had a very rough life in this region – unable to establish deep roots in the thin topsoil, so often toppled by vicious winds; attacked by life-sapping parasites, including 'Indian Bread' (which causes them to produce protective burrs) and 'False Mistletoe'. Another threat to Tierra del Fuego's trees was man-made: in 1946, 20 pairs of beavers were introduced in the hope of establishing a fur trade – it turned out that the climate was not conducive to growing top-quality thick fur, so the beavers were released to fend for themselves. They flourished so well that (when I visited) there were an estimated 80,000 animals on the island, damming streams and rivers to create ponds which in turn drowned the vegetation – we passed many valleys full of the white skeletons of trees:

"We pick our way cautiously amongst the ever-present tree roots, seeking footholds in cracks in the rock, to emerge on a stony beach, swept by chilly winds from the Beagle Channel. Everywhere the ground is covered with dead timber – trees felled by strong winds or drowned by changes in the drainage. It is all left to lie, drilled by woodpeckers as it rots, finally disintegrating into reddish dust where smaller birds peck for insects."

Next day we drove through the island's forested mountains, swathed in mist, to emerge on to grassy plains where we saw our first guanaco (wild llama) standing tall and stately on a ridge, ears pricked as he gazed down on the road. In order to reach the South American mainland, we first had to cross an international border – the Argentinian controls were simply a perfunctory stamping of passports, but the Chileans were far stricter, insisting on opening our suitcases to check for forbidden goods. As we moved off into Chile, the road was transformed from smooth tarmac to rough gravel, so rutted that it felt as though we were bouncing across a never-ending series of cattle grids – the window pane beside me dancing in and out, as if desperately trying to free itself of its frame.

Finally we reached the port of Bahia Azul to board a ferry for the half-hour crossing of the Straits of Magellan – a real sea-going ferry which rolled from side to side as its bows crashed through the surf, sending clouds of spray down the open car deck to soak the vehicles. I could well understand why the Straits of Magellan did not become the principal route between Atlantic and Pacific – how ever did the navigator Magellan feel as he explored the route (in 1520), his feeble sailing ship driven hard by these winds, not knowing even if there was an exit to the channel or whether he would be forced to sail back against the prevailing wind? In the Chilean naval port of Punta Arenas, we saw a modern replica of Magellan's tiny ship 'Victoria', no bigger than our ferry:

"I huddle in the shelter of the pilot's cabin on the top deck, listening to the wind howling around me and watching people trying to ascend the steps, being buffeted and battered before they can reach my refuge. Great rafts of kelp bob up and down on the waves, and small dolphins play in the surf."

We drove northwards across mile upon mile of treeless grassy steppe where only occasional cattle grids and gates by the roadside marked the access to 'estancias' – vast ranches, often boasting their own medical centre and school for the ranch-hands, raising cattle or heavy merino sheep. Far overhead we frequently saw soaring condors ... perched on fence posts were large falcons known as caracara ... right beside the road strode flocks of grey rheas (South American ostriches) – often a single male with a huge brood of chicks: the female leaves the upbringing of the chicks entirely to the male, who sometimes even kidnaps other chicks in an attempt to increase the size of his own brood. Also beside the road were frequent shrines housing images of Catholic saints, with offerings from passing truckers to protect them on these remote empty roads. In one place, I noticed a pile of plastic bottles and was mentally cursing whatever litterbugs had deposited them, when our guide Ani explained that in fact it was another shrine – this time to a local 19th century heroine who died of thirst here but was miraculously found days later still suckling her baby. Now passing travellers were leaving bottles of water for others to use to fill boiling radiators (or even to drink) – Ani left one on our behalf.

Our destination was the backpackers' town of Puerto Natales, full of hostels, internet cafes and mountain equipment stores, where we stopped for supplies before heading out towards the vast wilderness of Chile's Torres del Paine National Park. We approached the Park along bumpy dirt roads, damped down and speckled with muddy puddles from rain showers falling out of threatening clouds. The weather had not hindered our trip yet … was our luck about to change? Our accommodation for the next three nights was in cabins nestled beside Rio Serrano – in the evening, I walked by the river amid a silence and tranquillity broken only by the muted cackling of flocks of wild geese:

"Around me are multiple ranges of mountains – some serrated summits are clear, though painted a dusky blue by distance; others are mere flashes of white snow shining through gaps in the heavy grey cloud. Waterfalls cut narrow gashes in the solid green of mountainside forests, and open slabs of rock glisten with water."

Our guides tried to show us every part of this huge Park, starting before dawn by taking a boat along Lago Grey to its glacier (part of the immense Patagonian Icefield), watching the rising sun reflecting off the morning mists in a rosy glow. The mountains tantalisingly unveiled briefly, vanished again into the cloud, then revealed another glimpse of their serrated summits. Rounding a curve in the lake, the glacier appeared, a tiny patch of glistening blue ice beneath the massive snow-dusted rock of the Paine Massif, and small icebergs began to litter the lake's surface:

"We approach to within yards of the glacier, the water around us slushy with broken floes – some comprised of jagged layers of dark translucent green like a pile of broken bottles, torn from deep inside the glacier. The icy wall before us is pale blue, cut with gashes and holes which shine in a much deeper blue – a jumble of icebergs loosely held together. The glacier itself creeps down the rock-face in gentle waves, like a lightly baked meringue."

A burst of lunchtime sunshine briefly revealed the Paine Massif in its entirety – the black stone 'Torres' (towers) rising sheer from the sunburned grass of the plain below. Then we continued on deserted gravel tracks across the Park, past the achingly beautiful Lago Pehoe, a rich green lake surrounded by breath-taking mountains. We stopped to visit Salto Grande, where a deep green river rushed out of Lake Nordenskjold over a cliff into a cauldron of spray, then fought our way against powerful winds along the path to the lake itself for a view across the water to the Cuerno (horns) of the Massif, sharp peaks eroded from the cliffs.

Another full day in the Park visited three different lakes: first the lusciously turquoise Bitter Lagoon, with saline rather than fresh water – sometimes the lake is covered with flamingos, but on this day just a single bird was feeding. However, the hillsides around were covered in herds of guanaco with shaggy, brown and cream coats, loping away from us with an elegant leggy stride. We moved on, engine straining as we climbed over the pass leading to Laguna Azul (Blue Lake): as we approached, the clouds rolled back long enough to reveal all three of the Paine towers, their summits topped with (faintly obscene!) nipples of rock. Many of the (younger and fitter) members of our group had disembarked from the coach earlier for a strenuous walk on the Massif, so I wandered alone along the lakeshore, watching a wide variety of birds including a flock of over 30 condors circling overhead – a rare sight to see so many at one time, Ani told me. Our final lake was Sarmiento, strangely ringed by thick white bands of calcium (evaporated from the water), eroded into hollows and shallow caves which are reputedly a favourite lair of pumas – though we saw none:

"This has been an amazing day: it seems as though we have driven to every corner of the Park, yet we have seen few vehicles and even fewer tourists. On almost every trail we have walked and at every viewpoint we have visited, we have been alone in the vastness of this National Park. Wonderful!"

Torres del Paine NP would have been highlight enough for any tour, but Patagonia had more to offer. We crossed back into Argentina, travelling north on empty roads through flat arid grasslands, seeming lifeless after the abundant wildlife of Torres del Paine – the Andes steal all the rain from the clouds, leaving the Argentinian steppe dry and barren. Yet when we finally turned westwards, in no time the horizon was once again filled with ranges of mountains with lakes and rivers alive with birds. We arrived in the bustling tourist town of El Calafate, booming under the patronage of former President Kirchner and his (widely detested) wife Cristina, who succeeded him as President – they came from this region and had encouraged the rapid development of tourism here. In dramatic contrast to the tranquillity of Torres del Paine, coachloads and boatloads of tourists were swarming to visit Perito Moreno glacier, just outside the town ... but it was certainly worth the visit!

We boarded a sightseeing boat to cruise close to the wall of ice, a jumble of pale blue ice-spires rising up to 80 metres from the water. Once again (like Grey Glacier) part of the vast Patagonian Icefield, this glacier is up to 5km wide ... and is unusual in the world because it is still advancing, at the amazing speed of 1½ metres per day! This rapid advance means that it is actively 'calving' all the time – as we cruised past, we could hear constant rumbles and cracking from inside the ice-wall. After the cruise, we wandered along newly built raised walkways (designed to carry thousands of tourist feet safely across the rocks and delicate vegetation) to impressive wooden balconies located just across the water from the front of the glacier. From here we could watch as pieces of ice, and sometimes whole sections of the glacier wall, broke free with a crack like a pistol shot, cascading into the water to cause tidal waves and showers of spray:

"All is quiet and peaceful, the sun is warm, and I am almost dozing off when a huge 'crump' announces the breaking of a massive piece of ice which crashes into the water, causing the whole channel to echo with the sound of waves washing against the shore. Then another 'tower' explodes and showers the water with fragments. The tourists nearby explode too, bursting into activity with excited cries and the clicking of cameras. Then they move on and stillness descends again."

It was impressive enough for me to see these relatively small 'calving' events, but in the nearby museum I learned that every 3 or 4 years, the glacier advances so far that it blocks the flow of Lake Argentino – the water pressure builds up and then the entire ice-wall explodes. What a sight that must be (though the museum exhibit warns that people have been killed by pieces of flying ice).

El Calafate was our first stop in Los Glaciares National Park, but we moved further north within the Park to reach El Chalten, a tiny settlement only founded in 1985 to service visitors wanting to trek in the nearby mountains. Most of the population (and the visitors) were young people, which gave the community a relaxed and vibrant atmosphere, more backpacker than mass tourism. On our first day we were entrusted to the care of two mountain guides, who ushered us solicitously along well-made tracks overshadowed by high Andean peaks, including Mount Fitzroy (3300m), highest in Patagonia. Our guides were strict with us – I was rebuked for stopping to watch some birds, and there was no question of giving me time to write any impressions in my diary. We picked our way through gnarled forests (past a tethered group of llamas, being used as pack animals for long-distance trekkers), battered by strong winds and sprinkled with rain showers, searching the clouds for occasional glimpses of Mount Fitzroy. Not a really exciting walk, until our guide pointed out a black shape pecking at a dead log, which resolved itself into a female Magellanic Woodpecker:

"We creep on, and nearby is her mate, his bright red head a blur as he pounds at the trunk of a still-living tree, wood chips flying in all directions. How strong his neck must be, to peck so hard and so continuously without harm. Neither seems particularly disturbed by us – they are far more interested in the luscious bugs which they pull out at intervals."

Next day our guides arrived again (or at least, one guide arrived on time … the second had to be pulled from bed – a typical young man?) for a longer walk:

"Our guide assures us that today is 'flat', then amends it to 'a little up and down' … as we progress, we amend it again to 'Patagonian flat'. It's steeply up a dirt track at first, then a steady slog through forest on tracks ribbed with tree-roots. In the steepest places, rock and wood steps have been cut for us. In one especially difficult place, we have to scramble across a rock face using a chain for support – Patagonian flat?"

All morning we stopped at 'miradors' (viewpoints) from which we might have seen the notable peaks of the area, but they were always wreathed in cloud. By lunchtime, we were scrambling around the jumble of rocks which formed the terminal moraine of a glacier now retreated back up the mountainside, but there were still no glorious views (and the wind was strong and icy) so we quickly turned back down the mountain. Finally our guides relaxed their strict control, and I could walk at my own pace, stopping to look behind at intervals to see if the mountains would reveal themselves:

"Turning around ... WOW! The range is appearing! First the 3 towers of Cerro Torre, including the tallest (with its attached 'fungus' of ice clinging to the vertical cliff face). Then more and more of the range is uncovered – even Grande reveals its summit, though its glaciated slopes remain blurred by cloud. The sun emerges, and now I am walking in strong sunshine without a breath of wind. What a transformation!"

We had to leave El Chalten in the late afternoon, returning to El Calafate in time to catch an early flight back to 'civilisation' next day. Yet as we headed back into the steppe, Ani insisted on multiple photo stops to look back over the Andes, now totally clear, their black outline contrasting with the golden evening sky behind them – a view rare enough even to persuade our escort and driver to photograph themselves against this stunning backdrop. How blessed we were!

Patagonia - Torres del Paine

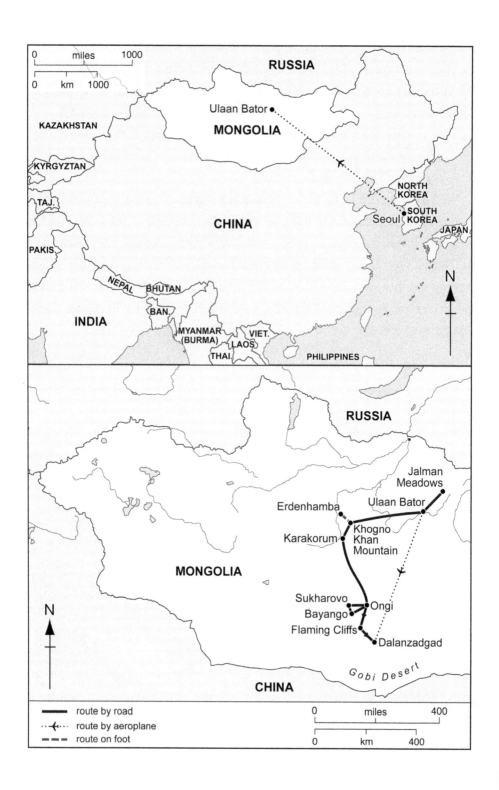

route by road
route by aeroplane
route on foot

Central Mongolia (July 2011)

I HAD NEVER FORGOTTEN THE wide open spaces of Mongolia which I had glimpsed 35 years earlier – so I was delighted to be able to undertake a much more intensive exploration of the country. The journey started smoothly in the ultra-attentive care of Korean Air, without a single hitch ... until I reached Seoul airport. I had expected a 6-hour layover here, with time to rest and read in the spacious comfortable lounges, before heading to the departure gate to check in for the onward flight to Ulaan Bator. However, when I reached the gate, I found an impersonal poster telling me that the flight had been delayed by serious storms in Mongolia ... for TWO DAYS! It was a bit of a shock at first, with frantic phone calls to the tour operator back in London, but then there was nothing to do but accept the airline's generous hospitality (bed and full board in a luxury airport hotel) and make the best of it!

In fact, the delay turned out to be a bonus, allowing me a glimpse of South Korea, a country I knew nothing about. I decided to try out the public transport into Seoul – excellently organised, with clearly marked stops and yellow-jacketed staff hovering everywhere, prepared to assist anyone who seemed to need help finding the correct bus. The journey took me across multiple bridges flying from island to island (Incheon airport is located on reclaimed land in the Yellow Sea), amid miles of muddy wastelands dotted with massive pipework and dredgers: South Korea was booming economically and building whole new cities where formerly there was only a shallow sea. All that I saw of Seoul and Incheon (a separate city), portrayed Korea as a vibrant modern state striding energetically into the future, advertising itself to the world by means of much-vaunted international sporting events (including the 1988 summer Olympics and the promise of winter Olympics to come in 2018). There was clearly a desperate desire to make foreigners welcome – whenever I hesitated anywhere, Korean citizens hurried to provide whatever information I needed; and in every tourist area, I encountered uniformed personnel offering both youthful enthusiasm and foreign language skills to help visitors. The cities were sparkling clean, and full of modern buildings supplied with all the cutting-edge technology for which Korea is famed (including large-screen televisions in bus and train stations).

Yet there was also a yearning for their past, though perhaps presented in a rather artificial and twee fashion. I visited the ornately painted Jogyesa Temple, and Gyeongbokgung Palace – former residence of the royal family, systematically destroyed by occupying Japanese troops in World War 2, but now being rebuilt like a miniature version of Beijing's Forbidden City. Here I stopped to watch a 'changing of the guard' ceremony amid milling groups of tourists, each escorted by a local guide proudly wearing a traditional (though impractical) costume of long, chiffony skirt and short jacket. Even in the airport itself, there were a range of cultural experiences available (free) to pass the time between flights, ranging from traditional painting or games, to regular parades by actors in full costume – entertaining us and at the same time making sure we were all aware of the long independent history and traditions of Korea, despite frequent invasions which had tried to swallow them up. I was impressed with Korea, but still glad when (after an additional 2-hour delay) we could finally take off for Mongolia.

First sight of Ulaan Bator was not inspiring – rows of Soviet-style apartments and pothole-strewn roads; broken pavements littered with dangerously deep holes; our hotel trying to offer modern facilities, but with electric sockets hanging loose, and leaky plumbing. Yet the grand buildings in Sukbaatar Square (the centre of the city) were imposing, and brightly floodlit by night. I remembered some of them from my last visit, but not the sparkling modern Parliament building (only erected in 2008, as an expression of the wealth newly flowing into the country from mining concessions). Another change from my last visit was the massive squat figure of Genghis Khan placed in front of the Parliament – the communist government had blacklisted him, but now he was once again the respected star of Mongolian history. Our guide confirmed that Mongolian traditions were once again being taught to schoolchildren, and a new sense of national pride meant that everyone now possessed at least one 'del' (the traditional silk tunic), worn regularly for special occasions and festivals. Continuing the tour, our driver forced his way through appalling traffic to the Bogd Khan palace – former winter palace of the kings, now housing museums of handicrafts and Buddhist relics. However, we could not dally over our visit – we had to allow time to fight through more chaotic traffic jams (another change from the empty roads on my last visit) en route to the airport, to fly south into the Gobi Desert.

The last vestiges of the severe weather which had delayed our arrival, were still hanging around Dalanzadgad airport as we landed – large thunderclouds patrolled the skies, dropping black fingers of rain in the distance, though we were standing in sunshine. We were quickly organised into our transport – a comfortable, though cramped, minibus for us and an ancient Soviet minibus for our baggage: we travelled in tandem throughout the country, with the two drivers assisting each other wherever the route became difficult. Those occasions were fairly frequent, since there were very few actual roads outside the settlements – instead, our drivers just selected the best route across the landscape, sometimes using the tracks of previous vehicles as a guide or following a line of telegraph wires … but sometimes just bouncing across trackless land, steered only by some inner sense of direction (when I asked how they navigated, they said simply 'they knew'):

"From the outset, the roads are no more than narrow gravel pathways across the steppe. We bump along at a slow and steady speed, though as we near the camp, the land is cut by innumerable gullies and our driver must circle back and forth, searching for a way past the deepest ruts to re-join the track."

There were few towns in Mongolia and only one city (Ulaan Bator, population one million – a third of the population of the entire country). 40% of the people were still nomadic or semi-nomadic herders, following their herds of horses (and camels, cattle or yaks, according to region) wherever they chose to graze, moving their homes (and large flocks of goats and sheep) when the herds travelled too far from the family's encampment. Only in winter (which is ferocious) did the nomads select a base to settle for a few months, usually in the shelter of the mountains, whilst the semi-nomads gathered their 'gers' together in one of the villages scattered across the land. Except in winter, these villages served only as 'service centres' (banks, shops, chemist, medical facilities, elementary school) with a few houses, mostly housing elderly people who also accommodated the children attending the school during term time.

Since there were few towns, there were also no hotels for tourists – so our accommodation throughout the tour was in special 'ger camps', using traditional 'gers' (often known by their Russian name of 'yurts') erected on permanent wooden bases for the summer season, and taken down again before winter. Our first camp was surrounded by wide open spaces of dry grassland, redolent with the scent of wild sage, alive during the day with the twittering song of larks and wheatears. At night the sky was filled with a mass of stars which tumbled all the way to the horizon, with no sound but the whisper of wind in the grass:

"The camp appears – a neat row of off-white felt gers flanked by wooden long-drop toilet sheds at each end of the site. Inside my ger are two brightly painted wooden chests, on top of which are thin cotton mattresses and warm blankets (definitely a 'firm' bed!); a solitary candle to illuminate the night; and a neat washstand with a tiny tank of water (filled each morning and evening with warm water) above a basin, which empties into a bucket. In the centre of the ger is a cast-iron stove, its chimney exiting through a hole in the roof – which can be covered over with a flap of felt in bad weather. It has all the facilities I need and looks so cosy and welcoming – I am delighted!"

Next day we travelled deeper into the Gobi Desert, leaving behind the golden grasslands to enter a land covered with sand and grit. In one place a spring was permitting a few families to grow vegetables for tourist camps in the area: the nomads themselves eat few vegetables, consuming mainly curds, cheese and milk from their sheep and goats, with some dried meat from the autumn slaughter of their herds. A sudden proliferation of tourist camps marked our arrival at the Flaming Cliffs – red sandstone cliffs where excavations in the 1920s had discovered fossilised remains of dinosaurs and their eggs. I was excited to find a stone which looked just like a piece of fossilised dinosaur skin – our wonderful guide, Handa, told me it was actually probably a 'Druse Crystal' (a natural formation), but I prefer my guess and still treasure it!

"Suddenly the ground falls away in a line of eroded sandstone cliffs, deep red in places not touched by the sun, though fading to a golden beige where sunshine has bleached the rock. Swifts soar on the up-currents, beetles bustle busily around us, a few clumps of thorn cling desperately to life in sheltered gullies. We wander up and down, slithering uncertainly on a surface of sand and loose stone of every colour and pattern."

The afternoon took us across typical desert landscape, driving over bumpy undulating dunes, coated in stone and rock which allowed the sand to form peaks and spires. The air was thick with dust blowing in the wind, making it ever harder for our driver to pick out the safest route through the mounds and gullies. Yet even in this desolate land, we passed occasional motorbikes (the favoured form of transport in the desert, where horses do not thrive) transporting goods or even herding groups of Bactrian (two-humped) camels. Finally we reached a dry riverbed where water, hidden below the surface, supported some sparse grazing for herds of camels, with their owners' gers clustered nearby. After all the desolation of the desert it was a shock to suddenly come upon this tiny settlement, but a much greater shock when we descended into the valley to find the 'Secret of Ongi' tourist camp:

"I had expected another isolated ger camp tonight, but instead our gers are in the compound of a huge temple-style hotel with every mod con – electricity points and lights in the gers, shower rooms (though admittedly only with cold water) in the hotel, even a sauna and massage room! And the camp is full – 45 gers in serried ranks, ringing with German, French and Italian voices. And I wanted to escape the crowds!"

Perched on nearby hills were the ruins of two monasteries, all that remained of an important monastic site built around the 'miracle' of Ongi – a flowing river in the desert. The monasteries were closed by the communists in the 1930s (and the monks forced into the army), while the river was diverted to supply nearby mines. Since the collapse of communism in 1990, three elderly monks had returned to re-establish worship in the area, so far rebuilding just one functioning temple. The guardian opened the building for us – a riot of colour in contrast to the drab desert outside, with furnishings and walls painted in red and gold, floors carpeted in red and green, the ceiling adorned with a huge red umbrella hung with streamers in the 5 colours of Buddhism. There were plans to rebuild more of the temples and perhaps even to restore the water in the riverbed – but Handa could not tell me where the money for these ambitious plans might come from. Mongolia was rich in mineral wealth, including coal, oil, emeralds, copper and gold – but lacked the infrastructure to extract these minerals themselves, so could only sell concessions to other countries (especially Canada) to exploit them.

Though it was interesting to see this rebirth of Buddhist faith in the desert, it was not our main reason for staying in Ongi camp – instead, we were going to use it as a base while we searched out a community celebrating the Naadam Festival (the most important annual festival in Mongolia) with the 3 traditional sports: archery, horse-racing and wrestling. Though many tourists choose to attend the huge festival in Ulaan Bator, I had elected to join village celebrations instead. We bounced off across the desert, first calling at the village of Sukharovo (where we summoned the pharmacist away from her personal festivities to open up the pharmacy for one of our group) to enquire where we might find a Festival, then leaving the desert for greener steppe land. Here, once again, we encountered abundant birdlife – a small lake thick with waders (including delicate Avocets and elegant Demoiselle Cranes), and innumerable falcons and buzzards cruising above us on the lookout for prairie mice (suslik). Finally we arrived amid bustling local crowds in the village of Bayango:

"Here Naadam has the feel of a district festival. Everyone is dressed in their best clothes, whether sparkly party dresses or traditional silk 'del' and felt boots. Piped music blares from the official grandstand, where 'local heroes' adorned with medals (for everything from animal breeding to motherhood – one lady mimes to us that her medal was awarded when she bore her eighth child) are installed with a large vat of 'airag' (fermented mare's milk)."

After medals were awarded for this year's achievements, the competitions began: no archery in this particular village, so the first action was wrestling – the sport I had most wanted to see. My initial impressions focused on the wrestlers' costumes: heavy leather boots, a neat pillbox hat, a tiny silk jacket covering only the man's shoulders ... and oh-so-tight brief panties! However, as I watched, I gradually worked out the principles of the wrestling, clearly encompassed by layers of tradition. Each wrestler presented himself to the crowd by dancing with raised arms, then slapping his thighs to show his readiness to wrestle. His first opponent was a young boy, usually felling him easily, celebrating his win by running with flapping arms around the wrestling area (there was no fenced arena, just a piece of beaten earth where multiple matches were taking place). Now came the real wrestling match, pushing, pulling and twisting, trying to hook a knee or simply to flip his opponent on to his back. The victor again celebrated with much flapping of his arms (in imitation of an eagle's wings), before he returned to his opponent to duck under his arm, in a sign of respect for the loser.

I was fascinated to watch match after match, until eventually we moved on to see a horse-race just about to finish on the hills above the village. The jockeys were all young boys, aged just 4-12, so that they were small and light enough to be a minimum burden to the horses; the races ranged from 15km for young horses to 28km for adult stallions, making these competitions more a question of endurance than of speed. The jockeys wore no protective clothing or helmets – the only concession to safety was a car which followed the racers in case someone was thrown:

"A few distant puffs of dust announce the arrival of the riders – this has been a 24km race and it shows! The first arrivals are still just about running, lathered in sweat, but successive horses struggle past, some barely walking, some just about trotting under the jockey's enthusiastic flailing with a plaited rope. There is little applause, except from us, and the horses are quickly unsaddled and led off to be walked to cool them."

Back in the village, the 'airag' was flowing freely among the adults, while the children were racing from place to place screaming and giggling. The wrestling continued, though now only contests or lessons for boys. Later there was to be a concert and games of 'ankle-bone flicking', but it was time for us to leave, returning to Ongi camp for another night. And what a night it turned out to be, for me!

"In the middle of the night, I am turning in bed and moving my pillow, when a sharp intense pain stabs my finger, as if I have caught it on a huge thorn. I fumble for my torch and turn it on, to see a pale, coffee-coloured scorpion sitting in a fold of my sheet – its sting raised and twisting back and forth. A few moments of panic ensue, as my room-mate traps the creature in

her glasses-case for further inspection and my finger continues to burn with pain. We set out to seek someone who can tell me whether Mongolian scorpions are poisonous. Finally a member of camp staff assures me that the answer is No, though I spend the rest of the night alternating between nervousness at every twitch of the bedclothes, and periods of tearful shock."

Next morning, we opened the spectacle case to reveal our scorpion (now named Genghis) for Handa's inspection – she called it a 'goat-tail' and did not seem impressed (further research called it a Giant Hairy Scorpion, confirming that its sting is only mildly venomous), so Genghis was released to burrow safely back under a stone, his coffee-colouring camouflaging him into the sandy soil. Since we were so far from any medical facilities, it was just as well that his venom was not potent!

Our tour now continued out of the Gobi Desert back into the rolling grasslands of the steppe – mile upon mile of sandy gravel greened by clumps of sage, chives and other wild herbs which never seemed to have quite enough water to grow into each other and form a meadow. Still there was enough grazing for occasional flocks of sheep and goats wandering freely across the land, only herded back to their owner's camp when it was time for milking. As we drove deeper into the grasslands, the numbers of birds of prey increased, including a rare Saker Falcon sitting quietly on a hummock watching for prey, and a magnificent Golden Eagle which soared into the air as we drove by. The ground was littered with the holes of susliks and marmots – though we rarely saw either, as they disappeared down their holes on our approach. Of course, there were no convenient 'service areas' for refreshment:

"Morning break is just a stop in the middle of the track (we've seen no other traffic yet today) in the midst of the vast steppe. A couple of low sandy hummocks give the illusion of privacy while we 'water the horses' (as Handa calls it), but in truth you just have to assume no-one is watching you – after all, with only 2 million people in a country the size of Europe, there is unlikely to be someone about!"

Eventually the grasslands became richer and greener, now dotted with frequent herds of horses (and our first yaks) grazing near clusters of gers which were clearly more well-to-do, with small portable solar panels and satellite dishes. In the midst of them was our next camp – fortunately not as busy as Ongi. The land around it was alive with flying and crawling insects, including a huge variety of grasshoppers which whirred and clicked around us, and I was delighted to see a pair of red-legged choughs (symbol of Cornwall, but so rare back home) cawing loudly from a rooftop. Strolling in the environs of the camp next morning, I stopped to chat with a woman who was laying trays of new-made curds and cheese on the roof of her ger, to dry in the sun. She offered me a taste (deliciously tangy), then invited me to come inside (taking care not to step on the threshold, which Handa had warned us would be a major social gaffe):

"It is all very tidy, but crowded with possessions. There are two beds, and a young man sleeps like a log on the floor in front of a row of brightly painted cupboards – where a small TV and a transistor radio stand among a row of family photos. The stove in the centre is burning brightly, pouring out smoke via the pipe to the roof, while a large basket of dried dung sits alongside as fuel."

A short distance from camp lay the remains of the once-vast city of Karakorum, founded in the 13th century by Genghis Khan as his capital, its stones later used to build a huge Buddhist monastery complex, in turn devastated by the communists in the 1930s. When we visited, there was little to see of Genghis Khan's city – just a few ruinous walls and a squat stone turtle sitting all alone in a weed-ridden field. The monastery, however, was beginning to function again, with multiple temples in a series of separate compounds across the site. One of the compounds had been protected in the 1930s purge, by the efforts of the local people themselves – inside, numerous worshippers were bowing to pray, then giving a resounding slap to a cymbal at the door as they left, to draw attention to their prayers. 200 monks were already living permanently on site and we saw some of them gathering for prayers as we arrived:

"A loud horn summons them and they approach the temple, chatting and joking like the young men they are. Mongolian worshippers are also arriving, prostrating themselves repeatedly on special sloping boards in front of the main stupa (shrine). Then the ceremony begins, with monks seated at desks in the centre of the temple gabbling the mantras at high speed."

Returning to camp for lunch, Handa took the opportunity to tell us more about Mongolian husbandry, which I found fascinating: cows were used for milk, meat and hides for leather ropes and bags; sheep produced milk and meat, and their wool was used to make the felt used on the gers; camels were mainly used for transporting goods, though they were also milked and their wool was used for ropes; goats produced milk, but also precious cashmere wool (Mongolia was one of the top producers of this luxury product, in the world). Finally horses: used for riding, racing and milk (to make the alcoholic 'airag') – the most honoured of all the nomads' animals, so that their skulls were often placed on one of the shaman 'Ovoo' mounds after their death. We were frequently seeing these mounds, mostly located at road junctions or the summit of passes to enlist the aid of the spirits to keep passing traffic safe. Though the communist regime had tried to eliminate all religion in the country, there had been a resurgence in Tibetan-style Buddhism since 1990 – a faith which also respects the gods and spirits of nature, so is easily able to exist alongside Mongolia's older shamanistic faith.

We were driving back in the direction of Ulaan Bator, stopping briefly beside a large reed-fringed lake where the water was thick with the tadpoles of Natterjack toads, and the reeds filled with the chuckling sound of birds. Being close to the city, the banks of the lake were busy with families picnicking and paddling – I would have liked to stop too, especially to investigate the birdlife, but we turned off the main track at this point to drive into the mountains. We climbed up to a high valley between ridges of heavily eroded rock, in places piled one on top of the other like a Dartmoor Tor – and at the foot of one cliff-face was our camp:

"What a site! Filling the horizon in front of our gers is a dark and distant mountain range, frilled at its base by a line of golden sand dunes, whilst behind us tower these great piles of rock. This is a simple camp again, with stirrup-pump shower and long-drop toilets – but who can complain in a setting like this!"

As we prepared for bed, a huge black cloud appeared above us, dropping a little rain. The camp staff leapt into action, covering the roof-holes in the gers so that we slept the night in total darkness (gers have no windows) – and were woken next morning by a novel wake-up call as the holes were uncovered, bathing us in morning sunshine: perfect for a walk up the slopes of Khogno Khan Mountain, surrounded by unpolluted Nature:

"Swarms of grasshoppers and crickets leap or fly away from us; brilliant orange, blue or white butterflies flit around the path; bright yellow lilies, tiny

wild onion flowers and purple thistles surround us. Suddenly our escort taps my arm and points up at the rocks. I can see nothing, so he flaps his arms – OK, it's a bird, but what...? WOW! At the same height as us, perched on a rock on the other side of the gully, is a huge pile of branches – the nest of a Black Vulture ... and in the middle of it sits an almost fully-grown chick, its feathers still fluffy and soft but its cruel white beak clearly visible."

In the afternoon, Handa took us to visit a family living close to our camp, where we were able to watch the children milking the goats – first making an undignified grab between the goats' back legs to see if the udder was full, then grasping the animal by the horns to hold it while another child squatted to milk it, also from behind. Inside the tent, we were entertained with 'milk tea' (actually just hot milk, with no taste of the powdered tea supposedly added to it) and yoghurt. Nomad tradition dictated that no visitor was ever permitted to leave without being given food and drink.

Reluctantly, next day we had to pack up and leave this idyllic spot, travelling for a few hours back into the bustle of Ulaan Bator. I needed to change some money – not an easy task, since all the banks were shut! Instead I headed into a large department store advertising a bank in its basement, but found only a few cash machines, so I approached a young man to see if he spoke any English and could help. He understood my problem but did not know how to help, so called up his supervisor who suggested somewhere I could try. When it became clear that I was not understanding where to go, he escorted me out into the streets – striding along for 15 minutes to take me to a bank which was open. What kindness to drop everything to help a visitor – I was impressed!

In the evening came another highlight, when we were taken to a folklore show. I had escorted innumerable coach groups to innumerable folklore shows in Europe and so was expecting a typical tourist venue. At first, it seemed that was all we would get: over-polished versions of traditional dances, and music played on unfamiliar instruments. But then a 'throat-singer' began to perform, using two different voices at the same time – an amazing sound like a combination of high-pitched Jewish harp and deep vibrating hum. I was entranced, managing to record his song with my camera, so that I have been able to replay it at home on many occasions.

More sightseeing next day before leaving Ulaan Bator, starting with an early morning walk by myself to try to understand this strange mixture of a city – a few historic temples crouched amidst examples of pompous Soviet architecture, yet now all dominated by cranes and the concrete shells of new buildings under construction. As I stopped for a photograph, a slightly drunk Mongolian man approached me, offering me (by gestures) a 'drink at his place' … when I feigned incomprehension, he changed his offer (still by gesture) to 'sex at his place'. I remained impassive and eventually he wandered off, leaving me more amused than threatened – I had not been propositioned like this since my youth!

Joining the rest of the group again, we were taken out to visit Gandan Monastery – the only monastery in the country which was allowed to function (under strict supervision) during communist times … and the only monastery I had visited back in 1977, though I could barely recognise it. In 1996 it had been re-established with a Japanese donation of a huge, gilded Buddha statue and a large new temple to house it. Since its re-establishment, the monastery had flourished, now possessing 10 temples and housing 900 monks. The 8-storey Buddha was surrounded by double lines of prayer wheels, whirling in constant motion as pilgrims frantically swiped each one during their progress around the statue.

Now we could leave the city behind us, travelling once again out into the grassy steppe. We stopped briefly at the incongruous sight of a massive, polished steel, mounted statue of Genghis Khan – built to commemorate the anniversary of the Khan's birth by a Mongolian millionaire (later to become the country's President). Then it was onwards into hills forested with coniferous trees – at first following a broken tarmac road, but then turning off on to a completely unmarked sandy track (again, how did the driver know where to turn?). Our coach struggled up a steep climb, stopping beside another large Ovoo at the top:

"A vast panorama of grass opens up, criss-crossed by a network of tracks and ringed by smooth hills. Below us is a pastoral idyll – the meadows are filled with huge flocks of goats and sheep, plus smaller herds of cattle, horses and yaks. A large gathering of gers, split into family groupings, sits close by the herds. It's a perfect picnic spot, but lunch is in the other van – and we've lost it!"

After (eventually) having lunch, we crossed another pass to enter the Khan

Khentee Protected Area, driving through a landscape carpeted with wild flowers, to our camp at Jalman Meadows. As soon as our gers were allocated, I launched out for a walk through a wonderland of flowers such as I have never experienced anywhere on my travels. There were so many that I felt as though I was trampling through someone's flower-beds – edelweiss, yellow potentilla and rosy pinks, yellow vetch and tiny blue-eyes. Higher on the hillside, the colour palette changed to the striking pink of fireweed and the rich blue of harebells. There were also hundreds of butterflies flitting around me and crickets leaping at my feet, but unfortunately they were joined by hordes of tiny flies – so many that we had to cower in a netted pavilion to read and later eat our dinner, swathing ourselves in coverall clothing (including face-masks and hoods) whenever we emerged. However, the flies vanished in the evening – and we were treated to the sight of an amazing orange moon rising over the hills.

Next morning there was a brief respite from the flies as fog covered the meadows – but as soon as the sun burned through, they were back! Many of the group headed off to the river for an adventurous morning of rafting but instead, I walked along a muddy riverside track: the mud was a magnet for butterflies which danced together in huge numbers by the path, while the occasional areas of marsh were alive with iridescent dragonflies. The flowers I had admired the previous day were now joined by light purple geraniums, deep purple larkspur, red sorrel and grasses – such a feast of colour that I hardly knew where to look next! Sadly, this was our last night in the Mongolian countryside:

"At midnight, I rise (to 'water the horses') and emerge from my ger to find the whole site bathed in the light of a full moon. The air is totally still, without a breath of wind. The only sound is the distant rush of water from the river – the clattering crickets and buzzing flies are now silent, camp noises all hushed in sleep. This is what I came to Mongolia to find – total peace and tranquillity!"

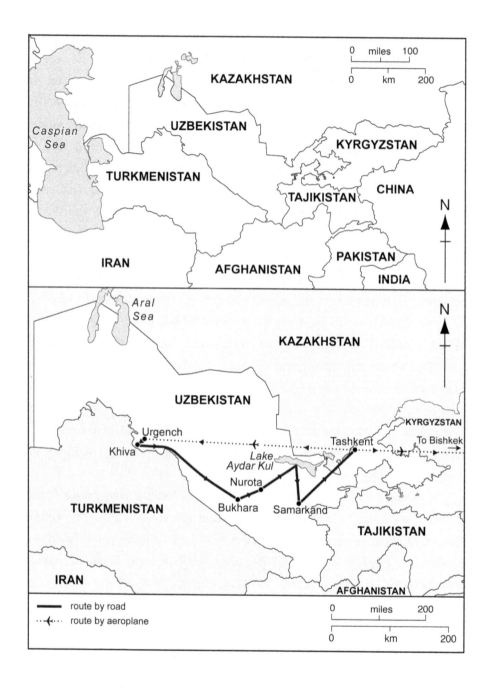

Uzbekistan (August 2013)

THERE WAS A BIG BIRTHDAY on the horizon – I was due to turn 60 and had decided to retire. So where could I spend this special birthday? I studied the brochures and eventually found a tour precisely timed so that I would be in the legendary city of Samarkand on my birthday ... what could be better?

I flew via Turkey into Tashkent (capital of Uzbekistan) – not a good start to the tour, since the airport was jammed with hordes of local people laden with plastic-wrapped bundles from their shopping trips to Istanbul. My suitcase was pulled off the conveyor belt by officious porters and buried underneath those bundles – I only found it during one last search around the customs hall, before reporting it as lost. Already late, I was further delayed by Uzbek customs men who were determined to check every bundle being imported, resulting in massive queues. Finally I attached myself to the back of a group of French tourists being waved through without any checks, arriving at my tour bus as the last of our group to board. However, all my harassed frustration was soothed when I met our Uzbek guide, Marat – calm, efficient and full of information. He immediately solved our first problem, money changing (we arrived on a Saturday, with banks not due to open till Monday), by producing multiple thick 'bricks' of Uzbek banknotes for each of us: only the 1000 cym (pronounced 'sum') note was in regular use (each worth just one US dollar) so our money belts were constantly stuffed to bursting with currency.

Ancient Tashkent was no more than a small trading town until the mid-19th century when Tsarist Russians occupied it, building a 'New Town' in typical grand Tsarist style alongside the mud-brick 'Old Town'. In 1930 it was declared capital of Uzbekistan, a country newly created as borders in the USSR were redrawn. The city sits in an active earthquake zone, and a terrible earthquake in 1966 destroyed much of the Old Town. The USSR sent immediate aid and rebuilt the destroyed part of the city in monumental socialist style – resulting in total confusion for our tourist minds: the 'Old Town' was mainly built in the 20th century … though the 'New Town' was built in the 19th century! Only a tiny section remained of the ancient settlement:

"The spotlessly clean, narrow alleys are lined with forbidding and windowless walls, studded with heavily carved wooden doors – yet when I peer through an open doorway, I see a sunny courtyard where two ladies sit at their tea-table. Their table is groaning with food, together with a beautiful porcelain teapot and cups. They wave me to join them, but sadly I have no time to accept their invitation."

Next day we took an early flight to Urgench, sitting amid barren desert lands yet on the banks of the Amu Darya River (renowned in ancient history as the River Oxus) which rises in the Pamir Mountains and flows the length of Uzbekistan – originally disappearing into the landlocked Aral Sea. However, in one of the ecological tragedies caused by the USSR, so much water is being taken out of the river for irrigation of the desert along its route, that it is totally drained before it ever reaches its destination, leaving the Aral Sea desiccated. As we drove from Urgench to Khiva, we passed many shallow, inefficient canals running from the river to fields growing melons and especially cotton (a crop which causes ecological damage because it needs huge quantities of water and uses harsh chemicals during the harvest). Alongside the roads were mulberry trees, grown for Uzbekistan's silk industry. The land was all still owned by the state, so farmers were given seeds, fertiliser and insecticides by the government in exchange for growing compulsory quantities of wheat, cotton and mulberry leaves (sent to other farmers who specialised in producing the silk cocoons): all permitted only to be sold to the state. Other crops of fruit and vegetables were allowed to be sold in the markets.

Our destination was the ancient Silk Road city of Khiva, where completely intact city walls (made of mud-brick) rose serenely out of the jumble of concrete homes and wires which formed a modern Uzbek town. The skyline was studded with tall minarets (though only 15 of the original 80 remained), which were once used as lighthouses, with a fire on the top to guide the trading caravans of Silk Road merchants as they travelled across the desert by night, avoiding robbers and burning heat. We bounced along a dirt track beneath the walls till we reached a huge building, beautifully decorated with blue tiles yet forbidding in its lack of windows … this was our hotel, a former madrasa (Islamic college). To reach its entrance we had to leave our coach and walk into the pedestrianised old town. Inside, all the rooms were located around a peaceful courtyard:

"I clamber up twisting, narrow and high steps, then along a stone-flagged, whitewashed corridor to my room: first a bathroom built into the thickness of the madrasa wall, then a few steps down into a neat little cell – very dark until I throw open the door at the far end to find a tiny balcony looking out over the old town. What an exciting place to stay!"

The city of Khiva was once capital of a powerful empire reaching from Baghdad to China in the 11th century. It was devastated by Mongol armies and the kingdom finally disappeared when it joined the Uzbek Soviet Republic in 1924. The USSR immediately began to 'sanitise' the old town, demolishing houses to build modern replacements – but fortunately in 1990, UNESCO stepped in to preserve what remained by declaring the entire old town a Museum City. Now, inside the ancient walls was a maze of alleyways lined with plain mud-brick walls, splashed with the brilliant turquoise and blue tiling of mosques and minarets. We visited the royal Winter Palace, exploring the once-hidden, elaborately tiled courtyard of the Harem, and the Fortress with its tall watchtower and magnificently tiled reception hall. For me, the most fascinating edifice in town was the 10th century Friday Mosque, its ceiling supported by 213 wooden pillars – many still original:

"The mosque is amazing: a forest of carved wooden pillars, many resting on wooden stalks nestled in camel wool (to prevent any damp rising to rot the wood) inside a cup (so they can safely rock in earthquakes, without falling). 2 square holes in the roof allow light to reach almost everywhere, though the furthest corners fade into gloom. The rich warm colour of the wood makes you feel that you are entering a forest glade to worship, cocooned safely beneath a carved ceiling illuminated by sunlight."

Just outside the old walls was the market, where knots of ladies in colourful headscarves were squatting beside cloths spread with luscious locally grown fruits and vegetables and, in the car park, mounds of melons of many different types were piled up beside the tailgates of small trucks. In one small shop, I noticed a lady with a mouthful of splendid gold teeth – tradition says that the ladies coat their teeth in gold, so that they have a treasure they can use if they are divorced (a simple procedure for men in Islamic society). By noon it was just too hot to do anything more than retreat to a courtyard restaurant to drink tea while reclining on a carpeted dais beneath shady trees, but as the afternoon cooled a little, I explored the atmospheric rabbit warren of dusty streets, twisting back and forth around the walled courtyards where Khiva's residents lived.

Next day we were off early, crossing the Amu Darya River on a fine new bridge only two years old: Marat told us that before it was completed, light traffic could cross on a floating pontoon bridge at this site, but coaches and trucks had to either enter Turkmenistan to find a bridge, with huge border delays, or else drive along the tracks of a railway bridge, timing their crossing to avoid trains! We followed the course of the river all day, always surrounded by the featureless barren desert which makes up most of Uzbekistan's landscape, in places passing massive pipelines carrying gas (an important export for the country). Eventually we drew into Bukhara, once another major trading centre on the Silk Road and now also declared a UNESCO World Heritage City – though far larger and more complete than Khiva.

Sightseeing here showed us innumerable architectural treasures, starting with the 9th century mausoleum of an early Persian ruler, built of unadorned pale bricks laid in such intricate patterns that the whole building resembled a woven tapestry. There were many madrasas – most glorious of all was the Kalon complex comprising a madrasa (still in use to educate 100 boys) and a mosque, both with domes covered in rich turquoise tiles. We trudged on (in steadily increasing temperatures) behind our guide, climbing the ramp into the Ark fortress, dutifully photographing the carved and painted portico of the Friday Mosque … but it was such a relief to escape the heat in an air-conditioned shop offering toilets, tea and a display of the carpets for which Bukhara has been famous through the ages:

"We see lovely carpets made of sheep or camel wool, so fine that they

shimmer in the light – though all are made in Afghanistan, sold as 'Bukhara carpets' only because they were made specifically to be sold by the merchants of Bukhara. On the other hand, the silk carpets are actually woven in this city. The assistant waves a top-quality Uzbek silk carpet at us, so soft and supple that it flaps and ripples like a blanket. Such a temptation ... but costing up to 5000 US dollars. Perhaps not!"

Sightseeing in the heat of the day was a strain, but in the cooler evening air the population of Bukhara gathered in the heart of the city around the pool of Labi Hauz:

"As dusk approaches, the families come out to play. Clearly the children are the apples of their parents' eyes (and the eyes of grandparents, uncles and aunts), dressed to the nines in smart shirts or frilly dresses. They are treated to balloons and whistles, ice-cream and cola, and to rides in child-sized, radio-controlled cars."

Next day we had a free day to explore on our own, so I started as early as possible to avoid the heat, rejoicing in the vibrant life of this Museum City, unlike the carefully preserved but atmospherically dead city of Khiva. The streets were full of people staggering along with armfuls of shopping or carrying large plastic bottles to fill with water from standpipes. Bukhara's 'trading domes' (bazaars clustered beneath high domed roofs with multiple entrances to catch breezes and keep them cool) were still functioning as they had since they were built in the 16th century – now offering examples of fine Uzbek crafts, including colourful ceramics, musical instruments, embroideries and delicate Persian-style paintings. I made my way along shady suburban streets, greeted by every child with a friendly 'hello' and by most adults with a respectful 'salaam' or touch of hand to heart, until I finally tumbled back into the world of mass tourism at Kalon Mosque. The madrasa, being a functioning school, was closed to the public, but the mosque was open to visitors (used for worship only on special occasions):

"What a fabulous mosque this is! A vast courtyard with colonnaded arches topped with mosaics of coloured tiles, every arch offering a different design and a different palette of colours – some predominantly blue and turquoise, others green and red. Looking back along the length of the courtyard, the view encompasses the facades and cupolas of both mosque and madrasa, and the minaret – a surfeit of glorious architecture!"

By now, the day was once again too hot for serious sightseeing, so I spent some hours sitting in various cafes watching the parade of tourists and local people, eating lunch on a breezy rooftop overlooking the multiple domes of the city. Then I strolled on into silent alleyways lined with adobe walls, peering into pleasant courtyards where residents were reclining on their daybeds. I was half-heartedly aiming to find the tomb of Turki Zhandi, so asked a passing lady for directions – she in turn attached me to another lady walking home past the tomb. After a brief stop at the tomb (merely a marble stone set in a small garden), this lady insisted that I return home with her:

"She produces grapes and melon from her fridge, and a cup of (hopefully bottled?) water, then brings me a fan and a facecloth to wipe my sweaty face. As I nibble at the grapes and melon, she fetches family photos to show me. We communicate for an hour or so (though we have no language in common), before she allows me to leave – but only after she has given me a hand-embroidered bag, refusing anything I could offer as a gift in return. Such hospitality!"

Of all the places we stayed in Uzbekistan, I have the fondest memories of Bukhara. Despite the fact that its buildings were often crumbling, and its streets broken and smelly, it was a real, living community where I felt truly at ease: the hosts at our little family-run hotel who were delighted to chat with us; the smiles and greetings from passing Bukharis in the streets; the hospitality of the lady who took me to her home … no beggars or tricksters, just a warm-hearted welcome. But we had to leave, driving back into the desert alongside battered, hardworking trucks from Turkey, Iran and Afghanistan. By lunchtime we had reached the town of Nurota, isolated enough for its ancient Islamic shrine to remain venerated throughout Soviet times. Marat allowed us just enough time to visit the sacred Spring, its deliciously green water (full of trout) lying deep below elaborate marble balustrades – but we seized the opportunity also to run up slippery dust paths to a fortress ruin high above the town, supposedly built by Alexander the Great in the 4th century BC (though there had been no archaeology to confirm it).

We had a longer stop for swimming at Aydar Kul (lake), artificially created in Soviet times when a dam (currently in Kazakhstan) regulated its level twice a year by releasing water into a depression in Uzbekistan's desert. Since the establishment of separate countries at the end of the Soviet era, the lake was gradually decreasing in size. At the end of the day we reached a small village, inhabited by ethnic Kazakh people – formerly nomadic shepherds who were encouraged to settle during Soviet times (to make them easier to monitor and control). Here we moved from our coach into two ancient Russian minibuses (minimal comfort, maximum reliability) to bounce along a rutted sandy track to a fixed yurt camp where we would spend the night. The yurts were covered with canvas, rather than Mongolia's felt, insulated inside by walls of colourful carpets – with thin mattresses on the floor where we could lay our sleeping bags. A group of Bactrian (two-humped) camels awaited us, plodding silently among the dunes for a 20-minute ride – time enough to set my hips into the wide straddle necessary to sit astride a camel, so that for some time after dismounting, I could only walk with a John Wayne swagger!

"Dinner tonight is enlivened by the arrival of 15 or so hedgehogs (regularly fed from the camp kitchen), scuttling under the table amid our legs so fast we can barely see them at first. They are different from British hedgehogs: a little smaller, with longer legs, softer prickles and very large ears."

Next day we returned to the main highway, increasingly jammed with traffic and sometimes blocked by police checkpoints as we approached the city of Samarkand. This was the destination I had dreamed of, its romantic reputation well-known throughout the world. Yet it was actually just a bustling modern city, pleasantly clean and fresh with lots of greenery … though enhanced by a few spectacular buildings, especially the group of mosques and madrasas which surround Registan Square in the heart of the city. After settling into our hotel, a group of us set out for the Registan, arriving to find the entire square brightly floodlit in honour of a Festival of World Music, due to start in a couple of days. Even better, a full dress rehearsal of the performance was underway in the square: police prevented anyone approaching too close, but we were able to find a spot where we could see the stage (between all the TV cameras and booms):

"Troupe after troupe of dancers whirl and glide across the stage in a riot of colour, ladies swaying in unison and energetic men leaping high, twirling bolas in the air. A variety of singers perform in front of them, singing popular Uzbek songs to the delight of the watching crowd. Once the show is over, we move on – drawn this time by more catchy music emanating from a huge

wedding feast taking place in a nearby hall, where a band raps out a foot-tapping tune using keyboards and traditional drums."

What an introduction to the city, and what a way to celebrate the last day of my 50s – it was my birthday next day!

Sightseeing in Samarkand meant learning another tranche of Uzbek history, this time introduced to Temur (also called Tamerlane) who (in the 14th century) laid waste to large areas of Central Asia as he tried to re-create the empire of Genghis Khan ... and to his highly educated grandson Uleg Beg – we visited the partially reconstructed astronomical observatory which he built. There was nothing left of the ancient city, totally destroyed by the armies of Genghis Khan, so the monumental city we visited was largely created by Temur and his successors. I was impressed by the Necropolis – a huge cemetery which had grown up around the tomb of an important Islamic saint, with imposing mausoleums built for Temur's family and a vast Soviet graveyard beyond:

"The complex we have visited has blown our minds – magnificent mausoleums with facades tiled in elaborate patterns: the finest workmanship bestowed on the dead by kings, princes and wealthy merchants, all striving for glory in death at the side of Mohammed's cousin. Do all the atheist Soviet faces on the tombstones in the modern graveyard, have the same desire to enter the gates of Paradise alongside Kusam Ibn Abbas?"

Temur's own mausoleum was located in the city centre (shared with several holy men and his grandson Uleg Beg) – this time decorated both inside and out in breath-taking patterns of blue and gold, topped with an unusual ribbed dome. The actual graves were opened by Soviet scientists in 1941, wishing to find Temur's skull and create an accurate image of his face. Local people feared that opening the tomb would release 'the spirit of war' (which they believed had possessed Temur) and, sure enough, the very next day saw World War 2 reach Russia. Stalin ordered everything closed up again and, as soon as it was done, Russia won a great victory at Stalingrad ... a coincidence?

Of course, the star of all Samarkand's sights was Registan Square, surrounded on three sides by the magnificent tiled facades of two madrasas and the Golden Mosque:

"I thought we were 'wow'ed' out after all the architectural riches we have seen, but this is something else! The decoration of the walls is light and

elegant in pale blue with red and gold leaf, but the mihrab is covered in so much golden calligraphy that the blue background barely shows through, crowned by a beehive of tiny niches where white designs are set into a rich golden base. What a shock, when my eyes can finally leave this glorious (if gaudy) decoration, to find that one side aisle of the mosque is laid out as a souvenir shop!"

Our official sightseeing finished at the Registan, so (once the heat of the day decreased) I set off to explore the 19th century 'Russian town' where I found the huge, solid and heavy-looking Orthodox cathedral. Inside the priest was saying Mass, a disembodied voice emerging from behind the iconostasis, while a handful of women stood to listen, scattered across a wide expanse of marble floor. Nearby I strolled in a local park where a Siberian-style log church and a colonnaded mosque had both been transformed into cafes. The park was full of people – young couples kissing and cuddling, families strolling and children playing:

"One little boy, dressed up (for his circumcision ceremony?) in a pure white suit, is thrust at me by his parents so that they can photograph us together. I am hardly presentable, with sweaty locks escaping from an old sunhat, hung about with bag and camera – yet to them, I suppose I'm a 'unique photo opportunity'?"

Next day, a few of us left the main group to return to Tashkent for our flight to Kyrgyzstan:

"It's a 4-lane highway, but the driver needs to be alert! Pedestrians dash (or hobble) across the road in every village; cars reverse into the traffic if they miss their turn – some even drive the wrong way along the carriageway if it is closer than finding the next gap in the central barrier; donkey carts and even handcarts stop suddenly; flocks of sheep stray from the verge into the road. And of course, there are potholes and deep ruts where overladen trucks have sunk into the tarmac."

Goodbye Uzbekistan!

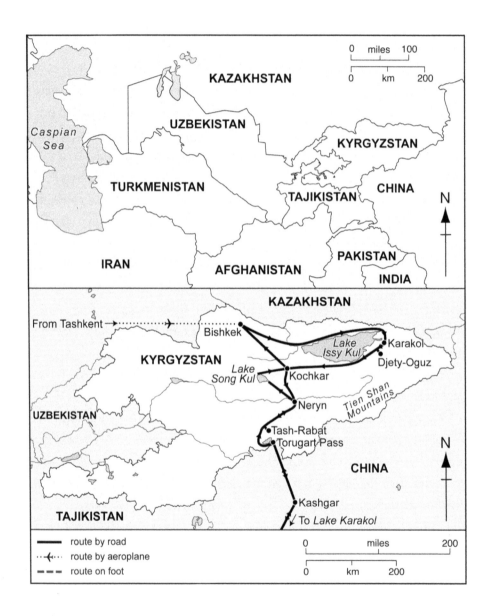

Kyrgyzstan and Kashgar (August/ September 2013)

THE TOUR TO CELEBRATE MY 60th birthday continued ... but what a contrast between Uzbekistan and Kyrgyzstan! Our first sight of the country was in the capital city Bishkek (called Frunze until independence in 1991) – clean but broken streets, filled with chaotic traffic generating a hubbub of hooting; people mostly wearing informal western-style clothing, unlike the distinctive long sparkly dresses and headscarves of Uzbek women; lots of trees and greenery, instead of desert dust; functional but rather run-down buildings, with none of the dramatic tiled facades we saw in Uzbekistan.

Why was there such a lack of historic buildings? Our new guide Olga explained that Kyrgyzstan actually had little tradition of buildings at all. Through history, the country was inhabited mainly by nomadic tribes from a range of ethnic groups – still there were over 60 different ethnic groups in the country, and the name Kyrgyzstan means 'land of 40 tribes' ('40' being their way of expressing the concept 'many'). In the 7th century, the nomadic tribes struck a deal with the Chinese to exchange horses for silk, establishing Kyrgyzstan as part of the Silk Road, so a few merchant settlements grew up along the route, but these were all devastated in the 13th century by Genghis Khan and were never rebuilt, leaving the country to revert to its simple nomadic way of life. Tsarist Russians arrived in the 19th century and founded the city of Bishkek, but by 1916 Tsarist Russian rule had become oppressive – hundreds of thousands of Kyrgyz people tried to flee across the mountains into China, but they were not allowed to settle and had to return in the depths of winter: many died, leaving Kyrgyzstan chronically depopulated.

The country was absorbed into the USSR in 1924, and Olga spoke of Soviet times as a Golden Age for the country. The Soviets encouraged the nomads to settle, providing jobs and social support for large families which helped to repopulate the land. They also established education and health services, bringing the people into the modern age. However, the period since the collapse of the Soviet Union had brought one disaster after another, with unemployment running at up to 45% in some areas. Kyrgyzstan has very few natural resources – mainly water (sold to Uzbekistan for irrigation) and some minerals (including the 5th largest gold reserves in the world), though without the infrastructure to extract them efficiently. Most doctors and teachers had been Russian, so they returned home after Kyrgyzstan became independent in 1991. Corruption was rife, with poorly paid teachers happy to 'sell' good grades. To make things worse, their 2nd President was deeply corrupt – when he was finally ousted from power, he took the majority of the country's financial reserves with him. Whereas in Uzbekistan I had the impression of a country energetically building a new economy for the new century ... in Kyrgyzstan there seemed to be mostly lethargy: a people who could not see how to forge a new path into the future, preferring to yearn for a time when 'Big Brother' Russia looked after them.

We set off on a highway alongside the fast-flowing River Chu – another of the strange Central Asian rivers which never reach the sea, rising in Issy Kul (lake) and disappearing into the deserts of Kazakhstan. It led us into Boom Gorge:

"Suddenly the fertile valley closes in, dropping away below us. The road twists and winds near the bottom of the valley, crossing back and forth over the rushing river, thick green in colour and topped with rolling white waves. Everywhere are wires – electric pylons, telegraph poles, signs for road users and railway. In a layby, an elderly metal caravan painted with a red cross offers medical aid to victims of accidents (frequent on this busy road)."

As we emerged from the gorge, a strip of vivid turquoise water appeared ahead of us, flanked by the snow-flecked Tien Shan Mountains – we had reached Issy Kul, largest lake in Kyrgyzstan (182km long). Our long day's drive took us the entire length of the lake – through farmland where harvesters were bringing in crops of corn and hay; by villages of small houses with large gardens filled with apple orchards; past clusters of hotel complexes catering to rich Kazakhs and Russians who came here to swim and fish. At one point, our drivers turned off the main road to stop beside a field of huge black boulders, enclosed within a railing: a sign declared it to be a 'historical state museum' – but what were we supposed to see? Olga walked with us further into the field, pointing out faded images etched into the rock – Scythian petroglyphs dating back to 2000 BC, representing deer, ibex, snow leopards and even a few hunting men (all probably intended to ask the Spirits of the Sky for luck at hunting).

By nightfall, we had reached the end of the lake (and almost the eastern end of the country): there were few tourist facilities in rural Kyrgyzstan, so we spent the night in a family guesthouse located in a small community outside the town of Karakol. As soon as we arrived, I was out exploring, watching as the village settled down for the night. The dirt roads were busy with little children playing and adults strolling, while older children brought down their livestock from pasture on foot or horseback: every household kept a few cows at home for fresh milk, taking them out each morning to common pastureland outside the village, where a professional cowherd watched them throughout the day until they were fetched home again. Meanwhile the calves spent the day tethered in the village, so that they did not drink all the milk before the householders could collect it:

"I reach the last house in the village, where one of the cows brought down by the children is now tethered in a pen and a man is preparing to milk her. He calls to ask if I am American, then if I speak Russian – when my answer to both questions is 'No', he loses interest and crouches to the milking. He quickly fills a small bucket, then unties the calf which hurls itself at its mother to feed."

Next day we visited the 'sights' of the town of Karakol (once a thriving industrial town, but declining since the collapse of the USSR), including the wooden Orthodox cathedral where mass was underway, attended by members of the Russian ethnic community – mainly women in headscarves and a few heavily bearded men. A hidden priest muttered prayers quietly behind the iconostasis, while the sound of a women's choir floated down from a raised balcony. As we left, the bells suddenly burst into a cacophony of sound to mark the end of the first set of prayers. Karakol's population was officially only 15% Christian and 85% Muslim, yet the mosque seemed underused and rather run-down – set in a beautiful garden of roses and apple trees, but in dire need of a coat of paint, with a wooden minaret topped by a very wonky metal dome. Our final visit was to the museum surrounding the tomb of the Russian explorer Przhevalsky who explored much of Central Asia and Mongolia in the 19th century, striving in vain to reach the forbidden city of Lhasa – he died in Karakol as he prepared for one more attempt to travel into Tibet.

Now we headed directly into the mountains, entering Djety Oguz Gorge (where Yuri Gagarin, first man in space, came to recuperate after his flight). The road was transformed into a rutted track taking us (amid clouds of dust) through tall conifers alongside an increasingly enticing, sparkling mountain river. The drivers of our two minibuses (both called Sergei) hurled themselves with enthusiasm across the torrent on a bouncing plank bridge, then tackled the rocky road beyond, littered with stones fallen from the cliff face above. There was a short delay as our road was blocked by a herd of horses being driven to pasture ahead of us, though they soon scrambled away up the hillside and we clattered on:

"Finally, at 2000m, we bounce through a ford to emerge into the sunlit summer pastures at the head of the valley. A flock of sheep and goats grazes peacefully beside a stand of conifers. In the distance, the herd of horses arrives to settle down to serious grazing close by two small groups of yurts. The pastureland stretches invitingly up the valley to a tree-lined gorge amid jagged rocky peaks. The air is filled with the roaring sound of the river and freshened by a cool breeze."

We continued along the southern shore of Issy Kul, with another brief stop to paddle in its refreshing water. I would have loved to overnight in the mountains but there was nowhere to stay so we had to continue driving as the sun began to set – our drivers ever more alert to avoid hidden potholes and slow-moving cattle obstructing the road as they were driven homeward. To add to their worries, heavy rainclouds began to build up over the hills (though the light-show of rainbows and sunbursts was another delight for me). Finally we reached the western end of the lake, re-joining the valley of the River Chu and the highway to China, driving the last miles into the village of Kochkar. Here our group was split between three private homestays – their ethnic Kyrgyz owners moving out into yurts in the garden to hand over their rooms and facilities to us. Tonight one of the families cooked for us – Kyrgyz meat soup ('shorpo') and stuffed dumplings, then fruit, biscuits, bread and home-made raspberry jam.

A leisurely start to the next day began with breakfast in the family's yurt, kneeling at a low table on thick furry rugs, eating slightly salty rice porridge and tea. Then we were joined by our hostess, her round face and oval eyes typical of the ethnic Kyrgyz (comprising 70% of the country's population). She oozed serenity, rarely smiling but radiating calm tranquillity as she told us about some of her people's traditions (though she admitted that many were now being lost) – most notably relating to babies:

"When a woman is expecting, she wants to assemble all the best characteristics for the baby – so she collects small pieces of fabric from a clever man, a wealthy man etc ... then sews them together into a shirt for the newborn. The new baby is not shown to anyone outside the home for 40 days, to protect it from evil, and even those in the house try not to look into its eyes. After 40 days they hold a feast to show off the baby, especially to wise old men who traditionally gave the child its name."

Kochkar village was clearly trying to establish a low-key tourist industry based on Kyrgyz traditions, with many houses displaying the 'homestay' symbol. When we returned to the village near the end of our trip, we were given a display of traditional felt-making, involving soaking raw wool with boiling water and then rolling it back and forth on the ground for 30 minutes, stamping on it to compress the different colours together ... then we were invited to view the finished products in the showroom of the Golden Hands co-operative. We descended on their wares like addicts deprived of our 'shopping fix', pleased at last to find typical Kyrgyz handicrafts for sale – I still delight in my felt rug!

However, for me Kyrgyzstan was mainly about the mountains and now we were heading again into the Tien Shan range, this time planning to continue right through to China. At first the road was smooth and fast, well-built by Chinese engineers who were still at work: improving the surface, straightening the bends (often by blasting a cutting through the rocks) and widening the lanes to accommodate huge trucks carrying Chinese goods through to the West. We climbed steadily up to Dolon Pass (3038m) on a road surrounded by summer pastures already almost empty of animals, as winter approached. On the far side of the Pass, green pastureland was still dotted with herds of horses, cattle and sheep. Clusters of yurts sat near the herds, and also a few old caravans and railway carriages – the only railway in the country (running from Bishkek to Moscow) now carried only freight, so the passenger carriages were being recycled as summer accommodation for nomads. Further down the hillside, we stopped at a family yurt where they were selling 'kumiss' (alcohol made from mare's milk, partly fermented and partly fresh). Olga bought a cupful so that we could sample it – I took a sip, but it was intensely sour and had such a strong alcoholic kick that even that tiny amount set my eyes rolling!

"Our road descends steeply, following a tiny sparkling stream between the cliffs, passing the scene of a drama: a heavily laden truck has slipped into the ditch. Another unladen truck is present, but the abandoned towrope indicates that it is too heavy to be towed out. Now 2 men stand in the ditch, debating the situation. We pass a police car on its way up towards the site of the accident – but what can HE do?"

Descending to the town of Neryn, traversing one last rocky gorge, we suddenly emerged into a wide open valley – the temperature rose dramatically, and the landscape was transformed into a patchwork of green and golden fields. This was our last chance to eat lunch in a restaurant and to buy picnics for the next days – from here onwards there were no more permanent settlements until we reached China. We climbed to Kyzyl-Bel Pass (2484m), learning to recognise the character of the passes from their names. The Kyrgyz language was relatively simple in some ways, suited to the needs of a pastoral society (for example, there were only 3 words for birds – large, medium and small, with no names for individual species), yet there were 3 different words for 'Mountain Pass': 'Art' meant a pass which climbed straight up and down again; 'Ashuu' meant a pass which climbed in a series of hairpin bends; 'Bel' meant a pass which climbed steeply uphill then flattened off into a plateau:

"Wow! It seems that now just one valley divides us from the range holding the highest peaks, all capped with glaciers and snowfields – filling the entire horizon. They look to make an impenetrable barrier between us and China, yet the presence of Chinese trucks labouring up the pass in the opposite direction show that there is a way through – and tomorrow we will cross it! Just below this awe-inspiring range, normal domestic life goes on: elderly

combine harvesters cut the grain and overloaded trucks carry home the hay – each vehicle almost buried beneath its load, as if wearing a huge shaggy cap."

Before we continued to the border, we turned into a side valley, following an unsurfaced track beneath towering cliffs till the rocks closed in to block any further advance into the mountains. In this remote isolated spot stood the 15th century buildings of Tash Rabat – called a 'caravanserai' in all the guidebooks (as suggested by Kyrgyz authorities, perhaps wanting to attract some of the Silk Road's tourist trade?), though I agreed with Olga that it could not have been a resting place for traders, since this was a dead-end valley with no through route. Instead she suggested that it had been a monastery for heretical Nestorian monks, hidden away from persecution in the country's coldest valley:

"Tash Rabat is such an interesting surprise. I can see where the 'caravanserai' idea comes from – on approach, we see only a strong gateway and wall, with a dome. But the interior is full of dark and mysterious passages with low doorways – more conducive to prayer than to trade. The main hall is uplifting, with light streaming through cleverly situated windows in the dome, but I find the monks' cells even more inspirational: each one has its own secret dome, not visible from outside – a personal glimpse of heaven for each monk alone."

Our minibuses dropped us at Tash Rabat then returned to a small seasonal yurt encampment (at 3000m altitude) where we were to spend the night, leaving us to walk at our leisure back down the valley to join them. It was an enchanting walk between rocks bathed in golden evening sunlight, the only sounds being the rush of the stream and a few invisible birds in the bushes. As I walked, a herd of horses moved cautiously past me under the leadership of the dominant mare, joined eventually by a Kyrgyz man (wearing his traditional white felt hat) who drove them a little closer to his yurt – there were foals among them ... and wolves in the mountains. Close by the camp, the hillside was pockmarked with the holes of a marmot colony where great blobs of golden fur were crawling awkwardly around, almost dragging their stomachs on the ground – the marmots were already so fat in preparation for their winter hibernation, that they could barely move. What a delightful place to spend the night, beneath a sky carpeted with stars:

"We have to squeeze the whole group into 3 yurts (one for the married couples, one for the men, one for the women), and there are only two long-drop toilets and just one washstand for the entire 7-yurt complex (wet wipes will be needed here, I think!) ... but the setting makes everything else worthwhile. We sit beneath a large rocky outcrop with eagles circling overhead, choughs calling harshly from nearby rocks and marmots whistling their alarms. Camp dogs introduce themselves, friendly and ingratiating – one even brings her puppies to meet us."

The journey to the border began with a return to the smoothly surfaced highway, imperceptibly moving from rolling hills (where horses, sheep and cattle were being gently ushered to pasture by horseback shepherds and their dogs) into ranges of higher snow-capped mountains, looming ever closer to the road. Already 90 minutes from the actual border, we were stopped by a first checkpoint: this whole area was a restricted zone (historically tense when the USSR and China were testing each other's strengths along this border) and still we had to show our passports to be admitted. We climbed up to a high pastoral plateau, now empty of livestock with the advance of winter, and on to Tuz Bel (3500m). Here the road surface deteriorated into a building site, transforming the golden pastureland into a grey wilderness, coated with dust rising from our wheels. Beside the road we spotted a large cluster of portacabins – year-round homes for the Chinese workers who were building this high-altitude road. Olga told us that they came from China's ethnic minority groups, who were normally deprived of a full Chinese passport – they were willing to work here (paid only with their bed and board) until the road was finished (due in 2015 – 2 years hence) with the promise of full Chinese citizenship in return for their work, and all the privileges which that would bring.

Finally we reached the Kyrgyz border controls – disembarking for a friendly and efficient check of our passports, before bouncing through the potholes to the top of the Torugart Pass (3750m/ 12,300ft) and the actual border – a simple gate across the road, firmly closed in our faces. Our Kyrgyz minibuses were not permitted into China, so we were to cross on foot to join our Chinese coach, which had not yet arrived ... we nibbled our lunch, and waited:

"The Pass is impressive – a rocky ridge cut by a narrow gorge carrying

the road. The air is chilly and thin, making my heart pound and my breath gasp, so we wait in the minibuses until finally our coach appears beyond the fence. Now the guard permits us to wheel our cases through the gate to board it, bouncing down S-bends on a rutted road until a line of trucks announces the Chinese immigration post – it is closed for lunch, so a huge backlog of trucks has built up. Finally the trucks start to move, and we are taken through a special gate, all our baggage unloaded for X-ray and manual checks, and slow inspection of passports – the officials cannot read our names in the Latin alphabet and must search for a face which matches the photo inside."

Finally we were released to descend the appallingly surfaced road through an arid desert landscape (here we were in the rainshadow of the Tien Shan Mts), caught up among convoys of second-hand trucks – many still bearing the names of European companies which originally owned them. In places we were delayed by large flocks of fat-tailed sheep (trotting along with such a sexy wiggle of their huge bottoms!) being driven down from the high pasture. The valley was so narrow that often there were no alternative tracks and the flocks had to share the road with forceful Chinese trucks – in one place we were moved by the tragedy of a group of dead sheep laid out side-by-side on the roadside: one shepherd's annual profit wiped out by an overly impatient driver.

We had left our Kyrgyz guide Olga back at the border gate and had now picked up a new guide (Nur) – a member of the main ethnic minority in this Xinjiang province: the Uighurs. Like the Tibetans, Uighurs have not settled comfortably under Chinese rule and our road down to Kashgar passed in a welter of resentful commentary. Nur told us about the city of Kashgar, once one of the most vital hubs on the Silk Road, ruling its own affairs for much of its 3000-year history – until the (Han) Chinese arrived in 1939 and imposed limitations on free trade and movement, rewriting the history books to erase Uighur history (I said the commentary was heavily biased!). In 2006 there had been an uprising in the city of Urumqi, partly caused by Muslim radicals but partly by Chinese persecution of Uighurs – since then, persecution had increased. Any Uighur men wearing their traditional square cap (the 'doppa') were likely to be detained on the slightest excuse, and no Uighur working for the government was allowed to wear the doppa, grow a beard or attend a mosque. Since 2012 (just one year before my visit) children were receiving most of their lessons in Chinese (officially because they would need this language if they wanted to go to university or work in one of the professions), with only 2-3 hours of Uighur language lessons per week. I had heard some of these stories of oppression when I visited Xinjiang in 1986 – clearly things had not improved in the interim: China was trying hard to assimilate their multiple minorities into the mould of the dominant Han ethnic group.

First sight of Kashgar was a disappointment. I had expected an ancient Silk Road city, on the lines of Bukhara in Uzbekistan, but was presented with a modern city, heaving with traffic – especially hordes of scooters and scooter-trucks. There were still parts of the old city remaining, mud-brick houses perched on the hills, but huge areas were being demolished, leaving only mounds of rubble and isolated walls revealing glimpses of destroyed interiors. The government was concerned by the lack of modern sanitary conditions in these mud-brick homes and had built new apartment blocks instead – though these were so shoddily built that word was spreading among the Uighur residents of the old town, and they were refusing to move out of their homes. In 2006 Kashgar's old town was used as the backdrop for the popular film 'The Kite Runner' (instead of Afghanistan, where the story is set), bringing western journalists to Kashgar. They were horrified to find the traditional houses being destroyed and made such an international scandal that the Chinese government was forced to preserve a small part of the old town for posterity – though when I visited, demolition was still proceeding in most other areas. On principle, Nur refused to pay the entrance fee to enter the 'official' part of the old town – instead, he took us into one of the areas earmarked for demolition but still inhabited by long-time residents of the city:

"The streets are narrow and a bit smelly, with crumbling walls in places and wires strung above us, but well-paved and clean. We call in at a hat shop which is also a home, with a cool balcony adorned with flowers for summer use and cosy indoor rooms for the cold winters. In a way, the Chinese are right that the living conditions here are poor, yet the Uighur are also right that it is a good way to live in this climate – cool in the alleyways and on the terraces, warm indoors in winter with tiny rooms which are easy to heat."

Below the hillside remnants of the old town, rich Uighurs were constructing modern homes in traditional style, with beautifully carved window frames and doors. All around them, a Uighur heartland was developing – full of the sound of hammering and sawing, the streets lined with ladies stitching embroidery and traditional hats, and a Uighur food market was filling the air with the fragrance of roasting meat and spices. Nearby was the 15th century Idkah mosque, largest in China, and already men and boys were arriving for prayer (women prayed at home). Nur pointed out cameras recording how long worshippers remained at prayer: Chinese authorities did not permit anyone to stay longer than 30 minutes. Later I wandered for a while in the bazaar, then decided to find a cup of tea and watch the world go by:

"Sidewalk cafes are not common here, but finally I find a tiny coffee shop with a single outdoor table, where my green tea is served elegantly in a glass kettle set on top of a tealight to keep it warm. I watch the parade of people passing by – ladies swathed in thick brown cloth, their heads and faces entirely covered (Uighur style); ladies in sexy tight dresses; ladies in flip-flop sandals or teetering on super-high heels. Men in Uighur 'doppa' hats or round white skullcaps, boys in t-shirts and jeans. Scooters clatter noisily through the crowds, each carrying up to five people at a time."

Next day was to be the highlight of our stay in Kashgar – a visit to the famous Sunday market. For me, the livestock market was most interesting – even as we approached, we passed innumerable scooter-trucks where whole families squatted in the back, clutching sheep, goats, calves or occasionally magnificent bulls. On site, vehicles were arriving continuously, some small trucks with just a few animals but some double-decker transporters carrying up to 50 beasts. In the sheep/ goat section they were unloaded by the simplest means – one man climbed up to grab each animal and throw it over the side (even from the upper deck of the large transporters) – a good job that they are agile! Willing hands caught the more wilful animals (usually goats) if they tried to escape once their feet touched the ground, but most trotted easily into chicken-wire pens, from which they were extracted one by one to be tied to long ropes for display to potential buyers. In the cattle section, unloading was more difficult since cattle were less willing to jump from the vehicles – though eventually they were persuaded, and fastened to metal railings for inspection, with much poking and prodding of flanks, bellies and balls:

"The buyers wander up and down, squeezing (fat-tailed) sheep's bottoms

and goat's udders. Owners frantically clip the sheep's wool on their behinds, to emphasize the fatty pads. A few knots of activity indicate a sale going on: sale complete, the purchased animals are manhandled unwillingly away from their flock and loaded back on to the trucks, bleating miserably."

We had one more day in Kashgar, but I had seen enough of the city and jumped at the chance to take an excursion along the Karakorum Highway towards the Afghan and Pakistani borders. At first, we travelled through irrigated land producing maize, cotton, sunflowers and vegetables – the villages along the way were full of stalls piled high with all manner of seasonal fruits. As soon as the irrigation ceased, however, the land was transformed back into arid desert – dry eroded hills striped with red, beige or yellow rock. In one place a coachload of Chinese tourists had stopped to fossick beside a river – apparently 'river jade' (a highly prized stone) had been found there. We entered the restricted border zone – easy for us to enter with our full national passports, but Nur told us that Uighurs are not normally permitted to enter sensitive areas (or even other Chinese provinces): he had a special permit for this day only, to escort us:

"An enticing jumble of steep eroded ridges soars above the narrowing river valley, where small herds of camels graze on barren hillsides. The broken tarmac is littered with stones, and piles of rock by the roadside show where landslips have been cleared – a large landslide a few weeks ago temporarily closed this road. We turn a bend ... and there before us, rises a wall of gleaming white snow peaks – the Pamir mountain range. Almost at their foot is the checkpoint into the restricted border zone, an insignificant trace of mankind totally dominated by the imposing finger-like peak of Kongur (7700m / 25,000ft)."

The journey was ever more dramatic from this point onwards, our coach grinding in low gear up serpentine bends surrounded by huge fields of boulders which had fallen from the vertical rock faces above us. Up at this altitude we began to see familiar felt Kyrgyz hats – the Chinese authorities were encouraging ethnic Kyrgyz people to settle their mountainous border areas (even building communities of houses for them, instead of spending the winter in their yurts), trusting them to guard the borders more reliably than local Uighurs. All the way we were disputing the road with heavily laden trucks often lurching to the wrong side of the road as they cut corners or struggled to overtake each other – the Karakorum Highway is known as one of the most dangerous roads in the world ... with justification!

"The vehicles perform their own particular ballet, swerving from side to side to find the smoothest surface or straightest line, hooting energetically with two or three-tone horns, to force other traffic to one side and allow them to pass (even when they are on the wrong side of the road). Our own journey is accompanied all the way by the plaintiff wail of the coach air brakes."

We climbed ever higher, the camels grazing on occasional sparse patches of greenery now joined by herds of yaks. Finally we passed through an incongruous Chinese dragon gateway to our destination, Lake Karakol, lying at 3600m. Ahead of us towered Muztag Ata (7549m), its rounded summit polished and shining with a glacier, which turned into a massive ice-covered cliff as it slid down the mountainside; behind us Kongur was still visible despite drifting banks of cloud obscuring part of the otherwise blue skies. Across the lake were the red roofs of another new Kyrgyz winter settlement, though their summer yurts were still scattered around the shores of the lake close by their grazing herds of yaks:

"At the far end of the lake, an area of pastureland is dotted with a large herd of yaks, whilst beside the yurts near the road, four yak calves are tethered, bellowing mournfully for their mothers' milk. A ferocious klaxon from a passing truck alerts the family to the fact that a group of adult yaks are responding to the cries of their calves, steadfastly making their way along the road towards them with loud reassuring honking grunts. It takes much energetic stone-throwing to turn them again, then the oldest son escorts them all the way back to their grazing area."

I was excited by my first foray into the Pamir Mountains (might I ever get the chance to explore more of them?), but not sad to leave Kashgar, retracing our steps through the arid dusty landscape to the border. This time there were minimal checks by both Chinese and Kyrgyz officials. We walked back through the gate at the top of the Torugart Pass into the welcoming arms of Olga and our two Sergeis again – they had spent the past days waiting for us at the yurt camp in Tash Rabat Valley. We spent one more night there too, noticing the increasing chill in the air – the camp was only open for a couple more weeks before the yurts were dismantled for the winter and returned to the local families who owned them. We returned again through the town of

Neryn, this time visiting the unusually shaped, gaudily decorated mosque (built in 1985 with Saudi money) – but it was clearly not well-used nor well-maintained: only 4% of Kyrgyzstan's population were practising Muslims (though 93% were nominally Muslim), and traditional respect for Sky and Earth spirits was more common (we often saw juniper bushes being burned in front of homes to protect against evil spirits).

We climbed again into the mountainous west of the country, ascending Moldo Ashuu Pass (its name indicating that it would be a series of hairpin bends):

"This Pass is an absolute stunner, and it is not even marked on the map! At first, we climb gently through an increasingly narrow Alpine valley with grass meadows still studded with flowers, and rocky outcrops dotted with tall fir trees. Suddenly we are on to a series of hairpins, our minibuses scrabbling up the rocky track, recently dampened by a shower of rain which lays the dust. All around, the peaks are clear and sharp against the pale blue sky. We leave the vehicles to walk the last part of the road, amid deep blue gentians and waving grasses. It's completely silent, no sound even of wind or water, until our playful drivers start rolling rocks down the mountainside, cracking and bouncing in an avalanche of scree."

Safely arrived on the high plateau, the drivers picked us up again and we drove on towards the huge Song Kul Lake (80km long) – far from being a soft pretty Alpine lake: a cold wind howled along it and its waters were steely grey, ruffled and rippled by the wind and dotted with rafts of ducks. It seemed a scene of utter desolation, yet cattle were grazing contentedly by the lake, totally at home there. Our accommodation was a cluster of yurts (at an altitude of 3100m) surrounded by meadows thick with edelweiss flowers. We were woken next day by a raucous squawking chorus from the ducks and geese on the lake (an important halt on their migration route), then we spent the morning walking in the hills around the camp. In some ways the scene was reminiscent of Mongolia, though here there were few insects at our feet and no hawks soaring above us – but the land was not empty. Kyrgyz shepherds on horseback were ushering their flocks gently across the pasture: one came to meet us and rode alongside us as we walked, unspeaking but clearly appreciating a bit of variety in his otherwise monotonous day. As we turned again for the valley, he whipped his horse over towards his flocks, whistling and calling commands to his young dog, driving the sheep dramatically towards us before turning them at the last minute – proudly demonstrating his skill before waving goodbye to us.

One last steady climb from Song Kul Lake led us up to the top of Kalmak Ashuu Pass (3446m), descending the hairpin bends on the far side, back to the valley of the River Chu and the main highway. My sadness at leaving the mountains was reflected in the weather – after dodging the rain clouds through most of our journey, we descended back into Kochkar amid torrential rain, with hailstones rattling on to the minibus roof. By next morning, the mountains behind us were dusted with fresh snow. We stopped to visit Burana Tower, the remains of a minaret which once stood in a wealthy merchant city on the Silk Road: it surrendered to Genghis Khan in the 13th century and was spared damage, only to be destroyed by earthquakes in the 14th and 15th centuries and abandoned. Now the brick tower stood alone in the middle of acres of flat farming land. It almost seemed incongruous to be admiring Silk Road architecture again, when in my mind Kyrgyzstan was all about its glorious mountain scenery and peaceful rural lifestyle – actually far more to my taste than the intensive culture and history of Uzbekistan.

Kashgar - fat-tailed sheep

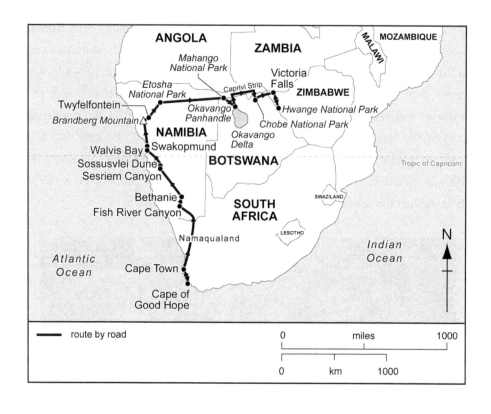

route by road

Southern Africa (September 2014)

FOR MANY YEARS, I HAD been hearing tales of the magic of Africa and the wonders of safari – but there seemed to be so many different destinations offering so many different types of safari experience, that I had never known which to choose. I also still wanted to visit Namibia (the Millennium destination which I never reached) and finally I discovered a tour which offered both – but again there was a choice to make: to stay in comfortable lodges or to camp? I decided that I wanted to fully experience Africa and its animals ... I wanted to hear lions roar by night! So the decision was made – I would camp my way around Namibia's National Parks, touching on South Africa, Botswana and Zimbabwe on the way.

We started in Cape Town, though I only managed to spend a few short hours visiting the city itself. My impression was a pleasant city, with gardens and imposing buildings like the Tuynhuis and Parliament (Cape Town is the legislative capital of the country). Everywhere was dominated by the massive bulk of Table Mountain, though it was constantly draped in cloud (its 'tablecloth') until finally, on the day we were due to leave the city, we were treated to a stunningly sunny morning with clear skies: all plans for departure were hastily re-arranged and we hurried to join the first queues of the day at the cable car station. Even the cable car was an experience, one of the few in the world which revolves slowly to allow everyone to see the entire view as it ascends the mountain:

"We have limited time, but there's enough to get a flavour of the summit: it really is remarkably flat, with a stone and concrete path leading around it.

There are low shrubs and plants between the rocks, and a few 'dassies' (rock hyraxes) are chewing the greenery in a seeming stupor – but the highlight is the view over the city and coastline. "

We were also taken for a tour around Cape Peninsula to the Cape of Good Hope (by the way, <u>not</u> the most southerly point of Africa!). Most of the route followed a rocky shoreline, with occasional white sand beaches – though the sea was rough and grey, the views thick with mist and spray ... and I was surprised by the chill in the air on the western side of the peninsula, caused by the Benguela Current (coming directly from Antarctica). On Boulder Beach we visited a large colony of African (formerly called 'Jackass') penguins – the world's only penguins to tolerate the high temperatures of the African mainland. The adults could swim out into the chilly sea to cool off, but we were told that the land-bound chicks regularly died in the heat, and we watched as adults crouched over their offspring to try to shade them. From Houts Bay we took a boat ride to see the nearby seal colony:

"The boat ride is exhilarating as we move quickly out of the calm harbour into the open waves of the sea – 2 years ago they had a record 30m high wave here, though today the highest is just 2m: still impressive as our boat rolls deeply from one side to the other. The waves crash against the flat-topped rocks where fur seals are dozing, enjoying the shower as spray drenches them. "

Now loaded into our tank-like safari truck, we left Cape Town to head northwards to our first campsite among the vineyards, orange groves and Rooibos (Redbush) tea plantations of the Olifant Valley – and a lesson in how to erect the tents which would be our home for the next three weeks. Fortunately they were easy to manage, since next day was one of the longest on the trip and we had to dismantle and pack up everything in the dark! We traversed the arid plains of Namaqualand, seeing only a hint of the acres of wildflowers which cover the region in spring, then crossed the Orange River into Namibia – from 1884 until 1920 a German colony, then until 1990 a Protectorate of South Africa (still with close links, including using the Rand as their currency). Now it was finding its way into the future by exploiting large reserves of copper and uranium, as well as the rich fishing off its coast ... and some tourism.

At this campsite we were treated to hot showers, a swimming pool ... and lush grass pitches – though they were not typical of Namibia. Next day we left behind us the well-watered landscape of the Orange River Valley and the tarmac roads which had brought us out of South Africa, instead hitting 'The Dust' – 75% of Namibia's roads were unpaved, and most of the land was hard-packed, yellowish-grey earth dotted with boulders (in fact, 16% of the country was covered by the Namib Desert):

"A cloud of dust ahead of us announces the start of the dirt roads – well-maintained and fairly smooth where the graders have been at work, but otherwise deeply rutted with sideways serrations which set our vehicle vibrating. There is little traffic, though, so we can travel with windows open until a cry of 'windows!' from those in the front seats, warns of the approach of another vehicle and its dust cloud."

Very soon we were entering the Ai-Ais NP (15% of Namibia was protected in National Parks), winding through ancient sandstone hills towards Fish River Canyon (2nd largest canyon in the world). Now our Zimbabwean guide Malvin was in his element, stopping the coach at intervals to show us some of the native plants: a large silvery bush of the Euphorbia family which contains a deadly poison yet is edible to zebra, kudu and rhino; huge Kokerboom trees, also known as Quiver trees, because Bushmen used to cut their branches, scraping out the spongy centre to make quivers to carry poisoned arrows safely. He also picked up zebra droppings, breaking them open to show us how dry they were (zebras re-absorb all the precious moisture before releasing their droppings).

As we drove on, we began to see lines of dry cliffs marked with horizontal strata till finally we arrived at the Canyon itself. It reminded me of the Grand Canyon, not a single deep gorge but instead convoluted and complicated as the original tectonic rift in the ground has been eroded, slipped and eroded again into innumerable hanging valleys and miniature ridges. We had no time (and no permit) to descend into the gorge, but instead walked along its rim as the air cooled into evening, finally settling to watch the sunset, sipping beer and eating a stroganoff cooked up for us by Malvin (the advantage of carrying our kitchen with us) – how jealous the other (non-camping) groups were!

"All is still. The wind has dropped for the moment and I am too far above the river to hear the water: only an occasional chirp of birdsong breaks the utter silence. A large cricket startles me by jumping up in front of me in a massive leap before he crashes back to the ground with a thud. He sits

unmoving, eyeing me cautiously till I move closer, then hurls himself over the edge of the cliff. The sun sinks lower and we watch the canyon walls glowing red in the setting sun before fading into a soft powder grey."

Now we were really out in the African bush – in the night I was disturbed by the yipping sound of jackals and the scuffling of oryx wandering past my tent. Next morning our driver (Jabo) stopped repeatedly to allow us to photograph animals grazing on vast expanses of wispy golden vegetation: first a herd of oryx ambling through the scrub, then a 'dazzle' of zebra fleeing panic-stricken across the road (yes: a zebra crossing!), and our first giraffe. We made a brief stop in the little town of Bethanie, chatting to friendly locals as we stocked up on supplies in its mini-supermarket and drank coffee in the attached cafe. The land became more and more arid, though in places we crossed low concrete bridges over streambeds which clearly ran with water in the wet season. Wildlife was ever more sparse, though I was fascinated by the immense communal nests built by Sociable Weaver birds, often enveloping an entire tree in a jacket of golden straw, some nests so heavy that they had actually broken the branch from which they hung.

Finally the flat, featureless land was broken by the ridges of a mountain range, its slopes dramatically striped with different coloured strata, cut into peaks and gullies – including our next destination: Sesriem Canyon. After exploring its depths, we gathered on the rim of the canyon to watch the sun set in a brilliant red ball, joined by a troupe of baboons absorbing the last traces of heat from its rays, and swifts which swooped and soared to catch the insects rising from the valley floor:

"It looks nothing as we approach, but suddenly the canyon opens up at our feet – a deeply eroded river channel cut into conglomerate rock which is thick with embedded pebbles. A few straggly trees thrust roots into cracks in the rock walls and lean out towards the light. I scramble over the boulders, dodging sandmartins hunting their supper right in front of my face, to reach a massive rock fall where a whole section of the gorge has collapsed, trapping a green pool of clear water."

Next day our entire campsite was up before dawn, but Malvin's strict discipline and Jabo's determined driving managed to get us off first, bouncing across the sandy terrain, initially still silvered by the light of the moon but then glowing bright red as the sun rose. As daylight increased, we could see that now we were surrounded by ridge after ridge of rich red sand, the Sossusvlei Dunes. This was clearly one of Namibia's tourist hotspots: to protect the dunes, only 50 vehicles were allowed to enter in each of the four daily visiting periods, though those who camped inside the National Park (like us) were allowed an hour's extra time between 6.15am and the Park's general opening time of 7.15am. How lucky we were to experience the dunes in the clear light of dawn (they became hazy as the day's heat built up) ahead of the mass of other tourists! We drew up at Dune 45, one of the highest at 170m, delighted to be the first group of the day to climb it:

"Ours are the first footprints ascending the spine of the ridge, though hordes are climbing behind us. I try to keep in the footsteps of the person ahead of me, firmer than the soft fine sand alongside, but still they often break under my weight and slide my foot backwards as my muscles try to push me forwards. The first part is steep, but then it evens out and becomes a gentle rhythmic plod to reach the highest point, looking out over a sea of sand."

Now we transferred to Jeeps for a mini-expedition deeper into the Namib Desert – described as hyper-arid land since it receives only 20mm of rain annually but experiences 300mm of evaporation. Yet even here plants had adapted themselves to survive, like the Nara plant which wastes no moisture on growing leaves and instead wraps its seed in juicy fruits which encourage animals to eat them and thus distribute the seeds. Most interesting of all was the Ice Plant which grows huge leaves in season to catch every drop of dew, but in the dry season (when we were visiting) looks completely dead – Malvin picked a single dry seedhead and added a couple of drops of water: before our eyes it turned from grey to brown, and began to open up to release its seed, assuming there was now enough water to germinate. Amazing! There were also creatures choosing this terrain as their home: the Fog-basking (Stenocara) Beetle which, in the early morning, channels droplets of fog (formed by the juxtaposition of chilly ocean currents and hot desert air) into its mouth by standing on its head with its back facing the ocean breeze; the Shovel-snouted Lizard and stripy Dune Ant both have extra-long legs so that they can lift their bodies off the burning sand.

Hidden among the dunes were flat valleys (known as Vlei) virtually paved with a layer of calcium left behind when water from flash floods was captured by the development of a new dune, allowing the growth of acacia trees, some living for 300 years ... but then dried out, killing the trees. Malvin told us that some of these trees probably died 500 years ago – yet they were still standing since there was no water to either rot the wood or encourage termites to eat it:

"It's an eerie feeling to stand on this long-dead lake floor, without any breeze to cool the burning air. A few flies buzz, lizards skitter in the shade, a crow caws in the distance, but otherwise the only sound is the chatter of tourists, strangely muted by the depth of the silence. Dry remnants of acacia trees twist and stretch their blackened boughs to the sky, though some have collapsed with the effort and now lie prostrate, with branches reaching horizontally across the baked white ground."

Another early start next morning, this time to try to benefit from the cooler temperatures – overnight I had been glad to wear my thermal shirt, yet by 8am we already had the windows open for ventilation, by 9am it was getting hot, by 10am the sun was beating down. What a contrast in temperatures! Easy to understand why the desert rocks were fractured and broken into the dust which constantly surrounded us. We followed a busy unpaved road, running straight across arid plains cut by occasional dramatic canyons or dry watercourses, with a brief stop as we crossed the Tropic of Capricorn. Again Malvin halted occasionally to show us the native flora and fauna: a highly poisonous scorpion hiding under a stone; the silk-lined home of a White Lady spider beneath a mound of sand; a prickly cactus known as the Namib Hoodia, so full of moisture that, when we broke off a piece, it poured with water. At Kuiseb Pass we crossed through the mountains to Namibia's coastal plain and Walvis Bay, such a rich fishing port that South Africa had tried to hang on to it when the rest of the country was given independence (it was finally handed over in 1994 under the auspices of President Mandela):

"The tidal flats are thick with flamingos feeding close to the town's promenade (and some pelicans too, fast asleep on a sandbank like a line of white duvets). The flamingos perform as if in a ballet, surging forward to thrust their beaks into the water, then rushing back en masse when a passing pedestrian causes panic. Their grunting call resounds over the mudflats, while gulls scream raucously above them."

A short drive along the smooth coastal highway brought us to Swakopmund, its main street boasting a few typically German baroque-style buildings, and cafes with German names still offering tempting German-style cakes – no doubt here about who founded the town! And what a contrast from the desert landscapes to which we had become accustomed – the air in Swakopmund was cool and moist, even requiring a jacket as the wind picked up at the end of the day. In the town's restaurants we sampled steaks from oryx (very lean and tender) and kudu (rather tough). The campsite was lush and green, provided with all the luxuries of civilisation – multiple shower blocks with hot water, electric points to charge camera batteries … even an itinerant masseuse who massaged my aching back with scented oils in the privacy of my own tent!

Next morning I opted for a Dolphin Cruise, swathed in my trusty pac-a-mac against the chilly, damp air. At first it was the birds which were the stars of the show – the crew tossed pilchards into the air to attract gulls, then massive white pelicans which landed on the foredeck and even tried to enter the cabin in their determination to reach the fish. Further out to sea we encountered dolphins, not attracted by the crew's fishy handouts but rather by the vibration of our motors (which we were told gave them a sexual thrill). Then attention swung to the rear of the boat, where several fur seals had hauled themselves out on to the seats:

"One is unknown to the crew and so is potentially dangerous – he is persuaded back into the water. But the other is well-known and (using the judicious temptation of pilchards) is moved into photogenic poses. I can even pose with him, gazing into his huge bulbous eyes while he is fixated on the fish suspended above my head. In his enthusiasm, his powerful body almost pushes me out of the boat."

Before leaving the area, we visited Cape Cross seal colony (though actually Cape Fur Seals are a type of sealion, not a seal) – location of a controversial daily cull: the Ministry of Fishing insisting that their numbers were kept under control to protect fish stocks, while the Ministry of Tourism was trying to develop the colony as a tourist attraction:

"The noise is the first thing we are aware of, a cacophony of deep braying and bleating, mixed with some throaty barks. As we step from the bus, the smell hits us – a musty, acrid odour, powerful but not too unpleasant. The main herd is constantly on the move – heads swaying, flippers scratching, occasional panicky surges as a group takes flight before our approach, forcing its way deeper into the already densely packed colony. On shore,

hungry animals prepare to go to sea, swaying from flipper to flipper as they wait for the right wave to lift them off the rocks. Out at sea, a carpet of heads coats the surface of the water, indistinguishable from fields of kelp, while the surf is alive with seals on their way in or out of the water."

After just 20 minutes of driving inland, we left behind the chilly coastal climate and returned to arid golden grasslands baked by the African sun, climbing steadily towards the imposing massif of the Brandberg (highest in Namibia, 2600m). We stopped to walk (in the burning midday sun) into the deep gorge which bisects the mountain, meeting a guide from the local Demara tribe who gave us a demonstration of her language, which uses explosive clicks as consonants. She escorted us as far as a deep crack between two huge boulders (the remnants of a collapsed cave) to see rock paintings thought to be thousands of years old. Next day we continued (in cooler morning temperatures) to Twyfelfontein to see a more impressive group of Bushman etchings, declared a World Heritage Site by UNESCO in 2007, including images of many animals once hunted in the area, and the 'Lion Man' which has become a symbol of Namibia.

However our campsite near the Brandberg was the real highlight of this area, for me! We had been warned that it would be a 'wild camp' with few facilities, and that animals might wander through in the night – exactly what I had been waiting for! To enhance the evening, a group of local people arrived in camp to dance and sing for us: not a formal tourist performance, but just the way they might have entertained themselves – singing with intricate harmonies, and dancing with much wiggling of hips:

"I chose to camp so I could hear the sounds of the African night – and wow, were there noises last night! The constant background grating of crickets, punctuated by birds which whistled and fluted ... the sniffing and rummaging of jackals around my tent ... the rumble of elephants' voices and the smashing of branches as they grazed on the trees. Most dramatic were the loud shrieks as another group leader drove off an elephant which had chosen to snack on the acacia tree above his cluster of tents. Next morning, we realise that the elephants have also smashed our open-air showers, seeking water."

The next few days were spent in Namibia's most popular National Park: Etosha. It has been protected as a Game Reserve since 1907, when artificial water holes were sunk into the desert to attract animals (especially in the dry season). From the moment we passed through an imposing stone gateway into the Park, there was wildlife all around us, so well-accustomed to passing vehicles that they did not flee or hide. For the first time, Malvin joined us in the upper cab of our vehicle, impressively spotting and identifying animals and birds with his naked eyes which we could barely see with our binoculars! There were large herds of springbok and impala; kudu with huge spiral horns; ungainly wildebeest; zebras grazing peacefully on the thin grass; giraffes browsing on the branches of trees; birds of every size and colour. We had frequent 'game drives' into different areas of the Park, moving from one waterhole to the next to see what wildlife was approaching to drink. Sometimes we were drawn down a particular track by the sight of a cluster of tourist vehicles, a sure sign that there was something interesting to see there:

"A knot of vehicles on the road – what is it this time? It's lions! 2 or 3 females with at least 4 cubs are resting in the bushes, while a young male lies flat on his back, completely flaked out. At first, we can only see a set of legs as a lioness rolls on her back, and nearby the swishing tails of her cubs – but then another lioness emerges from the bush with a cub nuzzling at her teats."

At many waterholes we saw families of smallish desert elephants, usually with babies, sometimes just drinking, sometimes squirting themselves with water or cool mud. We became almost blasé about elephants, zebra and antelopes of many varieties, but were always on the lookout for something different:

"Another knot of vehicles means something good to see – yes, a young leopard is crossing the road ahead of us. Jabo throws the bus into reverse, following him as he pads along beside the track. He is always alert, learning to hunt for himself – twice we watch him pounce towards a bird, but both times he is unlucky."

We stayed at two different campsites within the Park, both enclosed within fences and gates (firmly closed at night) to protect us from the dangers of hunting animals. All the campsites were located alongside waterholes, partially illuminated by night, so I was able to spend hours sitting on benches on the protected side of the water, watching the parade of animals coming in to drink – a magical experience and an enduring memory. I was up and down to the waterholes all night, watching animals arrive silently and move off with ponderous stealth – there was none of the prey animals' skittishness about these creatures of the night. Life for them seemed to involve a lot of silence and a lot of standing around – sometimes listening and watching, but mostly just standing:

"Featuring currently is a large herd of giraffes, legs splayed wide to be able to drop their heads to drink. The last of the sunlight is behind them, reflecting their gangly posture in water which glows with the dusky pink of the setting sun ... My eyelids are growing heavy, but I hear a single splash of water so open my eyes – and there's a rhino! He has slipped up to the pool in total silence, just as the elephants do (despite their size), and now stands reflected in the water, taking a silent drink with none of the slurping sounds that giraffes make ... Now in come 3 lionesses, lapping loudly at the water, crouching down with no fear of enemies. Then, off-scene, comes the sound I have been waiting for – the roar of a male lion, like strangled coughing repeated over and over again, until it fades away."

Leaving Etosha, we headed north towards the Angolan border, finally encountering a more densely populated part of Namibia (on average, the country only has 8 people per square mile) with villages of thatched huts built in family communities with communal stock pens. Many villages possessed a neat four-square church building, and there was frequently a large shade tree in the heart of the community – in one place we saw a formal group arranged beneath the tree (perhaps a village council?). Men were often working away from the villages, so it was mainly women who were visible: sitting on the ground weaving a new reed fence; standing to pound grain; sweeping floors and paths, often carrying a baby strapped to their backs. We spent our last night in Namibia beside the River Kavango, looking across at busy waterside life in Angola: people washing themselves and their clothes; working their fields and irrigating them laboriously with a watering can; fishing with nets thrown from simple boats; lighting fires to roast wild fowl caught in a trap. Sadly, throughout the tour, Malvin tried hard to avoid us coming into contact with local people – he had memories of tourists offending local sensibilities, resulting in the bus being stoned, and preferred to keep us at arm's length, despite the friendly smiles I saw projected in our direction.

Following the river, we stopped for a brief visit to one more Namibian wildlife park – Mahango NP, though I felt sated with sightings in Etosha and had few expectations here:

"It looks so small on the map – what can it possibly hold? At first there's nothing, but then a flash of iridescent blue announces Namibia's national bird: the Lilac-breasted Roller. It's non-stop from now on – jewel-coloured birds (bee-eaters and rollers) flitting in the bushes; a Snake Eagle perched in the branches of a massive Baobab tree (probably 1000 years old); tiny Blue Waxbills ferreting in the sand; herds of impala and rhebok; hippo and crocodile lurking in the water ... then finally, the sighting Malvin has been seeking: Cape Buffalo, virtually invisible in the thick bush – but that completes our 'Big Five' and he can rest easy now!"

We continued into Botswana following the river, now beginning to break up into the complex of channels which makes up the Okavango Delta – though we camped only at the start of the Delta, in the so-called Panhandle. The campsite felt almost like a 'wild camp', our pitches hidden away amid thick thorny scrub with beds of papyrus between us and the river, where half-submerged crocodiles floated. Vervet monkeys were swinging through the trees all around our tents (tightly fastened so that nothing could get inside), and narrow footpaths wound through the woods to the toilets and camp bar. Wildlife spotting here was a totally different experience from the deserts of Namibia, with few large animals but hundreds of different types of bird. We were woken by a dawn chorus of mysterious rustlings and twitterings from the enchanted forest around us – and by a group of Babblers, who perched above each tent in turn to gabble furiously at each other.

Two cruises (morning and afternoon) took us out on to the river, exclaiming and photographing furiously as we passed egrets and herons; bee-eaters and kingfishers; storks and spoonbills; cormorants and swallows. An African Fish Eagle was persuaded into flight when our boatman tossed a piece of fish into the water, but an ugly Hamerkop (a wading bird with a weight-lifter's head and neck) watched us impassively as we passed. We pushed on into the deeper part of the river to give us a sight of hippos, at first just eyes and ears which rose above the water only to sink again out of sight – but then heads began to pop up all over the water ahead of us. Seeking something new to enliven our afternoon cruise, the boatman crashed his boat into the shore to allow us to disembark in a meadow where an elephant was grazing – though we were reduced to an undignified scramble back aboard when he mock-charged us with flapping ears and a few threatening steps.

Travelling via Namibia's Caprivi Strip (a relic of European political manoeuvring at the end of the 19th century), we re-entered Botswana to visit Chobe NP:

"Our camp is another waterside idyll on the banks of the Chobe River. Settling on to the riverside terrace, my eye is drawn to a group of Reed Warblers which are hopping about, screaming. When I focus my camera on them, I notice a snake is gliding oh so slowly, oh so carefully through the grass, hoping to catch a bird. I take a picture to show Malvin – and he is horrified to see this snake so close to the campsite: it is a Puff Adder, the most deadly snake in Africa (which can kill a human in 30 minutes)!"

Sightseeing in Chobe was highly organised – battalions of special Safari Trucks were loaded with the day's tourists, hurtling around the valleys and marshes of the Park, both on official tracks and 'free-style'. Once again, clusters of vehicles indicated something particularly interesting (though often also a scrum as vehicles tried to push each other out of the way). We were treated to a fine view of an adult leopard reclining on the branch of a dead tree, so relaxed that he even seemed to move around a little to give each truck in turn their photographic moment ... then we jostled into position for a better view of a lioness half-hidden in the grass – only to realise that there was actually a whole pride of lions there, with 3 half-grown cubs. They were undisturbed by us, but instantly vigilant when they spotted a crocodile threatening the cubs from the river. Stars of Chobe's wildlife were its elephants, much bigger and blacker than those in Etosha:

"At the end of the day, the female elephants escort their babies back from an island in the river to the safety of the shore. They choose a spot where they can walk without having to swim, though the babies are out of their depth – the adults encourage them to continue, lifting their tiny trunks as snorkels to breathe when they sink below the surface. Meanwhile, three giraffes are running at top speed across the hillside – clearly something is chasing them. I scour the scene with my binoculars, just in time to see a lioness sink slowly behind a bush with that characteristic 'I wasn't trying anyway' cat shrug."

One more National Park to visit, this time Hwange in Zimbabwe – seeming fairly empty as we cruised up and down its tracks (for hours), seeing mainly elephants and the broken trees which they leave behind them. We visited the

Painted Dog Centre (though there were only two dogs in residence at the time) to learn about efforts to rescue this animal, considered a pest by local farmers and threatened with extinction. One of the conservationists' ideas was to rename the African Wild Dog as the Painted Dog – could a more attractive name actually help to save it? This Park was a disappointment, but the campsite certainly was not! It was located in an unfenced area, accessible to wildlife: we were told to place our tents wide enough apart for elephants to meander through in the night (apparently without any danger of trampling the tents, which they consider to be large boulders and therefore avoid). At a nearby viewing terrace, staff were spreading rock salt specifically to attract elephants – we were almost nose to nose with them at one point, being carefully inspected by their long-lashed, all-knowing eyes. Yet it was not elephants which approached our camp as night fell, but rather the (much more dangerous) Cape Buffalo. A massive herd spent most of the night grunting and crashing in the bush all around our tents, and we were still surrounded at dawn when we got up – unable to leave our tents (even for the toilet) until they had moved on:

"As we finish dinner, crackling and grunting from the bushes around camp tells us that the buffalo are on the move. Gradually they drift closer, making their way again to the salt licks. They are not as bold as the elephants, though a male with a big boss of horns stops to inspect us suspiciously. He stares, nose raised, trying to assess us. Definitely time to retreat to our tents!"

Hwange was our last wildlife centre, but another famous sight awaited us – Victoria Falls, where the mighty River Zambezi (at this point the border between Zimbabwe and Zambia) slips sideways into a deep gorge caused by ancient movements of the earth's crust. On the Zimbabwean side, opposite the river, a well-made path ran the entire length of the Falls with frequent viewing points on the very edge of the cliffs. Across on the Zambian side, I could see tourists wading waist-deep through a (presumably gentle) current to reach a chest-high pool on the very edge of the gorge – not for the faint-hearted! During the wet season when the river is at its fullest, there is apparently so much spray that it is virtually impossible to see the Falls, but when we visited (in the dry season), there were good views – though I was still soaked by spray before I had walked the length of the path:

"The track winds through thick vegetation, sometimes with just a hint of moisture in the air, sometimes a veritable shower. The most impressive

viewpoint is Number 11: here the widest channel of water swirls in a mass of foam over the edge of the cliff, flanked by three other cascades, all engorged with water. Below, the river boils with spray which is blown by the wind to alternately soak or ignore me. This constant spray, catching the evening sun, forms a strong rainbow reaching up from the river to vanish into the blue sky, framing the gorge."

Victoria Falls was certainly an impressive waterfall, making a worthy end to a memorable tour. Now all that remained was to reflect on what I had seen:

"What about Africa? What are my impressions? The landscape is not exceptional – despite impressive desert dunes, much of the land has been dry and arid with mile upon mile of sparse scrub. In places, the animals enliven it – though they are mostly familiar from TV and zoos, it is still a thrill to see them in their native habitat. Most impressive are the amazing birds, gorgeously coloured like jewels. I was told Africa would get under my skin – I don't think it has, but who knows ...?"

Namibia - Sossusvlei Dunes

Bhutan village house

Bhutan - Gangtay monastery

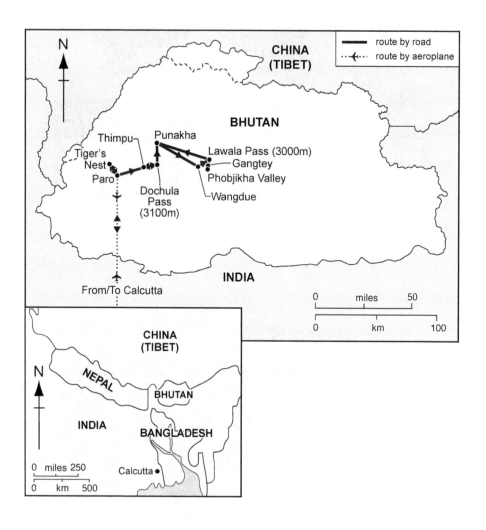

Bhutan (September 2015)

I HAD BEEN FASCINATED BY the Himalayas for many years, but Bhutan had a mysterious allure – virtually closed to outsiders until the 1970s and even after that, remaining a very expensive destination since the government only allowed high quality, all-inclusive tour packages to control the numbers of tourists entering the country. In 1972 the king commented publicly that he preferred to measure the success of his country by Gross National Happiness instead of Gross National Product … so the international press dubbed Bhutan 'the happiest country in the world'.

Start and finish of my tour was in Calcutta (India) – I had never visited before, but did not enjoy the experience:

"A hot and steamy climate makes me stream with sweat; crowds of people jostle each other, living their lives in the street; traffic is snarled up amid a constant cacophony of hooting; broken streets and pavements are polluted with litter and filth everywhere; the River Ganges flows with unappealing, thick grey water … only a few remnants remain of the grand city which was once HQ of the British Raj."

I was glad to leave early in the morning to fly on to Bhutan – less than an hour's flight, yet seemingly a world away. I was excited to see glimpses of sunlit snow-peaks poking through thick cloud cover as we approached Bhutan's only international airport (at Paro), yet those same mountains make it the most dangerous airport in the world – planes must fly almost into the walls of Paro Valley, before swerving at the last minute to line up on the runway! Bhutan sits on the southern slopes of the Himalayas, carved into a series of parallel river valleys running from north to south. As we travelled through the country, our road constantly climbed over thickly forested ridges before descending into the next fertile valley, often clothed in golden-green rice fields almost ready for harvest. Dominating each valley was a massive red-roofed, white-walled dzong (fortress) which, through most of Bhutan's history, had housed independent warring noblemen, each fighting for supremacy over the others: they were only unified under a single king at the start of the 20th century.

We were met at the airport by our bouncy enthusiastic Bhutanese guide (Tashi), wearing his traditional 'Gho' (a long tunic tucked up by a belt, to form a useful pouch above his stomach) together with long socks and well-polished leather shoes. Everyone who worked for the state (including teachers and doctors, as well as tour guides) or was visiting an official venue (offices, schools, dzongs etc) was obliged to wear national dress – a way of reinforcing the sense of national pride which underpinned most of Bhutanese life: in fact, most adult Bhutanese people seemed happy to wear their costumes as part of everyday life. There were rules governing tourists too – we were obliged to clothe ourselves 'formally' when visiting official buildings, not only covering arms and legs but also ensuring that our shirts included a collar. Since I had been unaware of this dress code before arriving in the country, my first priority when official sightseeing ended, was shopping for a man's shirt to wear over my usual garb, to meet this requirement.

These dress rules were just part of the strict discipline which governed the behaviour of every Bhutanese citizen. A formal code (called Driglam Namzha) had been created in 1990, which included: respect for the environment (hunting and fishing were forbidden; tree-felling and even wood-collecting only permitted on licence); an emphasis on national well-being (tobacco was banned from sale since 2004, and the working year was frequently enlivened by national holidays and festivals); a passion for cleanliness. Beside the roads throughout the country, we were entertained by traffic slogans including: 'Mountains are pleasure if you drive with leisure', 'If you are married, divorce speed' and 'Don't litter – it will make your life bitter': part of the government's attempt to mould the population into a unified disciplined community. At the pinnacle of the Driglam Namzha was reverence for the monarchy – Tashi would not tolerate anything less than total respect in all we said about the king and the royal family, who were treated almost as gods.

Official sightseeing began with a visit to Paro Dzong, still in use both for local government offices and a monastery. Tashi took us into the Dzong's central courtyard, overlooked by ornately painted arcades and windows, then on into the temple itself, where he began to instruct us in the intricacies of the Tantric (Tibetan-style) Buddhism which lies at the heart of daily life in Bhutan. It provides different methods of achieving Buddhist nirvana (paradise), gaining 'credits' both from pilgrimage ('kora') around religious sites and from multiple prayers sent up from prayer wheels and flags – and also venerates the spirits of mountains, rivers and other aspects of the natural world. As a thoroughly modern Bhutanese man, Tashi was fervently devout – prostrating himself on the ground in front of the main altar in every temple we visited and bowing discreetly to each 'stupa' (shrine) which we passed.

Later I explored the residential sections of Paro town, greeted on all sides by local people (younger Bhutanese could mostly speak some English, since school classes had been taught in English since the 1980's). Spotting a sign announcing a 'restored farmhouse', I ambled into the courtyard. It was a traditional wooden house, with living quarters sitting on top of stables formerly occupied by livestock, but now (for hygiene reasons) used as a storage area: at the top of the building, a semi-open barn beneath the overhanging roof provided a ventilated area to store grain and other crops. This building was now a guesthouse, but the owner was proud to show me her 'stone-bath' – two wooden tubs side by side, full of water which would be heated by large stones, now being prepared on a massive bonfire outside. Her son then invited me up a steep wooden stairway to view the original kitchen and the living room, its walls glowing with faded paintings.

Next day we left Paro to head eastwards on Bhutan's principal road – in fact, one of the few roads which existed in the country, because of the difficult landscape. Until 2014 (the year before my visit) most of this principal highway was only single-track, but the Indian government (one of Bhutan's main supporters) had sent in engineers and workers to widen the carriageway along its entire length, a task planned to take at least 5 years. There was no possibility of closing the road during the reconstruction, since there was no alternative route, so the traffic (including our coach) simply had to traverse the roadworks as best they could. Between Paro and the capital city Thimpu, the upgrade was complete and we travelled on smooth wide tarmac, achieving the top permitted speed of the country (just 50kph/ 30mph) – but then the road degenerated into a slippery, muddy construction site:

"We are climbing steeply, travelling at just 10 or 20kph on a road turned into a muddy track by the road building work. In places, waterfalls cascade from the rocks above; elsewhere the water is moving rocks to tumble down towards us – our guide and driver both peer nervously upwards as we advance. Fallen trees partially obstruct the route, some hastily pushed aside or smashed through – in one place a gap has been cut through a massive tree-trunk which still lies across the road."

In a country filled with fast-flowing rivers (45% of Bhutan's national income came from the sale of hydro power to India), bridges were vital. Outside Thimpu we stopped to visit a chain bridge supposedly built by Tangtunggelpo (the 'Iron Chain saint') – a 16th century engineer who was sanctified by the population because he built hundreds of bridges suspended from iron chains:

"Tashi launches across without hesitation and, gulping back my nervousness, I hurl myself after him. There are no planks to smooth the way, just strong chicken wire laid across massive chains (supposedly dating from the 16th century) spanning the river. The water roars below us, though that worries me less than my attempt to remain upright, and the fear of tripping on the carpet of uneven wire. But I survive ... and return across the river on a more modern bridge. Both bridges are festooned in prayer flags, entreating the river gods to keep us safe."

We continued past the outskirts of Thimpu to climb towards the next valley, twisting high into the forests, sprinkled with raindrops as we approached cloud-level (this was supposed to be dry season, but we were plagued by low cloud and rain throughout our visit). Finally we reached the top of Dochula Pass (3100m), adorned with 108 stupas built to commemorate a victory won here in battle against Indian militants ... as recently as 2003. At Tashi's instigation we lustily called out 'Hage-Lo' three times to bring us luck, though we had no luck in seeing the view of Bhutan's highest peak (7500m – and still unclimbed, out of respect for its spirits) which we might have seen from here.

The Dochula Pass marked the start of one of Bhutan's favourite stories –

the tale of the Divine Madman, a monk who travelled from Tibet to meet a terrible female demon on this Pass and defeat her with his 'divine thunderbolt' (in other words, his penis). As she fled, he followed her into the neighbouring Punakha Valley to finally destroy her – building a stupa on the site which was later turned into a temple. On arrival at our hotel in the valley, we set off to walk through the rice-fields to visit that tiny temple (Chimi Lhakhang), tended by young monks with masked faces so that their breath did not pollute the images. Throughout the area were numerous walls painted with the Mad Monk's symbol (yes ... a penis!). However my abiding memory of this visit will remain the walk through the rice-fields:

"We return by a narrow track through the paddies, and one mis-step from me has me toppling (on my behind) into the squelchy mud beneath the rice, deep enough that I am unable to get up without help from my fellow travellers (after they have finished laughing, of course). No harm done, except for wounded pride ... and trousers thick with mud."

Overnight the sprinkles of rain and heavy clouds which had characterised our trip so far, turned into torrential rain. We were supposed to be taking a walk in the morning, but a hasty re-juggling of the itinerary saw us heading by coach up the valley to visit Punakha Dzong – far bigger, more decorated and more imposing than any we had seen so far, as was fitting for the winter residence of Bhutan's chief abbot. Inside, local people were prostrating themselves repeatedly in front of the monks and the statue of Buddha, before retreating to squat at the rear of the temple:

"As we approach, the sonorous sound of a horn calls the monks to perform a ceremony. Two blow smaller horns, resting them on the floor, then ranks of monks seated on benches raise large drums in unison, tapping them while others clash cymbals or ring bells. A discordant yet evocative sound with a heavy rhythm, enhanced by the high-pitched wail of bone flutes."

Our tour was built around the grand formal Festival to be held at Thimpu later in the week, but during lunch Tashi heard of a smaller festival taking place at the nearby village of Wangdue and decided to spend the afternoon there. It reminded me of a large country fair, with a vast (muddy) enclave full of tented stalls selling food, toys and clothing, interspersed with booths offering darts, hoopla, airgun shooting and all kinds of gambling games. Though we would see dancing of more religious significance in Thimpu, I loved the relaxed atmosphere of Wangdue Festival, surrounded by crowds of villagers dressed in their very best outfits – entire families clustered around picnic food, babies strapped to their mothers' backs or cuddled on their knees:

"I am drawn by the sound of horns to the dancing ground, where local officials sit underneath the roof of a pavilion while the rest of the crowd sits or squats by the arena – a young girl politely dries off a plastic chair for me. A formal dance is finishing as I arrive, and its place is taken by a comic dance about marital life, which has everyone (children, adults and even the policemen on duty) roaring with laughter at the antics and mock fights of the clowns."

A later start next day gave me the chance for an early morning walk into the pine forest behind our hotel. Life was only waking slowly in the valley below – all was calm and tranquil until I heard the sound of shouting male voices from a side-track. Walking towards them, I discovered an archery ground cut into the hillside, with a match in full swing. Archery is Bhutan's official national sport, originally practised with traditional bamboo bows but more recently using expensive composite weapons. The target was an amazing 500ft from the archer, and team members standing near the target were calling out the result of each shot, either with a derisory hoot when the archer missed his aim or else a celebratory yell when he scored (hence the noise which had attracted me). Whenever he was successful, the archer performed a formalised jig of joy. Yet why were these men not at work? … Later I learned that it was a special Bhutanese holiday, celebrating 'Blessed Rainy Day'. Perhaps we should celebrate the rain at home, too?

Our journey now continued eastwards following the spectacular highway, perched on the side of a cliff with the river far below … and landslips sheering off sections of the road at frequent intervals. In places we could still see the original route, a single track of bumpy tarmac with rocky verges for overtaking manoeuvres (reminiscent of a country lane, though it was the principal highway of the country), but once again our patient driver had to negotiate stretches of chaotic construction work. As we climbed higher through cloud-forest hung with Spanish moss, the houses became ever smaller and simpler, sometimes no more than single-storey huts made of split logs. However, most had the traditional Bhutanese windows with 3 small openings within a single frame (originally only top-ranking citizens were allowed a large window) – in the mountains there was often only glass in one of those 3 windows, with the other openings covered by wooden shutters. Hillside farms were small, usually just a few acres of narrow terraced fields and several cows to support an entire family.

Near the top of the Lawala Pass (3000m) we heard shouting and laughing erupting from a roadside village, so stopped to investigate. We found a darts match in progress (another traditional sport, for those who could not afford archery), though these darts were very different from those used in British pubs. They were nearly a foot long, heavily weighted, and were being hurled along a pitch over 60ft long, using an energetic technique almost like a javelin-thrower:

"We see several successful hits, the dart burying itself satisfyingly into the target board with a resounding thud, whereupon the whole team (at either end of the pitch) gather into a semi-circle for a celebratory stomping and chanting dance."

With another lusty cry of 'Hage Lo!', we crossed the Pass and were immediately rewarded with views over the wide green fields of Gangtey Valley, descending for a visit to Gangtey Monastery, which was heaving with pilgrims for this special festival day. Many were processing (always clockwise) around the main temple, while others were packed inside, telling beads or spinning prayer wheels while they listened to the deep-voiced and monotonous chanting of a cluster of monks. We stopped to join them for a while, but were then summoned by Tashi for what should have been the highlight of the day, a walk along a Nature Trail traversing grassy hillsides, then through pine forest down into the high-altitude meadows of Phobjikha Valley, internationally renowned as an over-wintering spot for the rare Black-necked Crane:

"To start with, we are in high expectation of wildlife, but pine forest never attracts many birds or insects ... and Tashi is continually whooping or whistling to drive off any potentially dangerous boars, so there are no other animals to be seen either. The Trail turns into just a pleasant walk, and then into a miserable trudge as light but steady rain sets in. My last enthusiasm fades as we cross the broad marshy Phobjikha Valley on a cart track deep in mud, with not even a sight of the cranes to make it worthwhile – they don't arrive till later in the year."

My spirits were raised again once we reached our newly-built hotel – I loved my wood-panelled room with a roaring fire in an iron stove (ideal for drying wet clothing), though most of the modern facilities (kettle, hairdryer etc) were rendered useless because, for most of our stay, there was no electricity! Once we had dried out, Tashi took us for a cup of 'yak tea' at a nearby farmhouse, a traditional wooden building (even roofed with wooden shingles secured by heavy stones) surrounded by a tiny garden of flowers and an allotment of turnips and spinach, with sheds piled high with winter supplies of logs. We climbed an exterior stone staircase to the family's living quarters on the upper floor – a single large room festooned with drying spinach leaves, with a clay oven on one side (beside a modern calor gas ring) and an iron stove in the centre, tended throughout the day by an elderly grandmother. To one side was the family altar, kept in a separate room used only for worship or to accommodate any particularly honoured guests. The Bhutanese all squatted on mats on the floor, though we were provided with low benches to sit on, and then tea was served:

"The tea is a dark red concoction containing tea-dust, yak butter, salt and water. I dutifully take a few sips, but it is pungent and strongly flavoured – more like Bovril than tea, and too rich for me. However, to accompany it, there's delicious, cracked corn (like hard popcorn)."

The community of Phobjikha gave me a taste of the way Bhutan used to be, before modern development began to change it. I took an early morning stroll through the village, a mix of elderly single-storey homes (mainly built of wood) with a cattle byre at one end and the house at the other, and more prosperous two-storey homes with storage sheds at ground level and the family's rooms above. Piles of chopped timber were dotted around the village, and narrow plastic pipes led to small concrete tanks or taps – clearly the houses had no running water inside (and a row of long-drop toilets indicated that there was no indoor sanitation either):

"People are just waking up ... cows and horses amble up the main street ... a girl squats by a tap to clean her teeth ... a mother leads her semi-naked toddler toward the toilets. By the time I return to the hotel at 7.30am, there is more activity – the girl who was cleaning her teeth is now washing clothes at the same spot ... children are emerging from houses or crossing roadside fields to hurry in the direction of school, while numerous small

cars (packed to the gills with children) are presumably on the same mission."

I had the impression that modern development was spreading gradually eastwards, stimulated by the activity of the airport at Paro and the rapid growth of the capital city Thimpu (both in the west of the country). If we had had more time, we could have continued east over more ridges into more valleys where we might have seen traditional life continuing as it had for centuries – but sadly we had to retrace our steps from here, negotiating the same highway again. We had been fortunate before, travelling the road on public holidays – now there was more traffic, and more road-building disruption since the navvies were back at work. At one point, we were held up while an excavator high above us hurled rock down to a waiting JCB blocking the route ahead of us ... in many places the newly widened (but not yet sealed) sections of road were collapsing as rainwater flowed over them – for the first time, I could feel our coach slithering and sliding as our driver fought to control it.

Finally we reached Thimpu, this time driving into the city through a forest of new concrete apartment blocks. Looming over them was a massive (50m high) statue of Buddha (hollow so that it could contain a temple), still under construction using Chinese finance and Indian workers (part of the reason for Bhutan's passionate nationalism was in response to the threat of being overwhelmed by these two powerful neighbours). Tashi took us up to the statue next day, intending only to show us the view over the city, but to his surprise we were actually allowed to visit inside (it had been officially consecrated the day before, so construction materials had been temporarily cleared away):

"The lower floor is like a vault, dark and gloomy despite the pure gold-covered pillars and rows of painted Buddha statues, but the next level contains the main temple, gleaming with golden light reflected from pillars and walls covered in gold plate. With shoes removed, our socks crunch over the grain offerings sprinkled liberally yesterday, as we walk up to the huge double abbot's throne and the multi-faced statue of Buddha – adorned with offerings of brightly-coloured baked dough rosettes."

We also visited the large Memorial Stupa (built in 1974 in memory of the 3rd king), surrounded by people circumambulating respectfully, often chanting prayers or telling beads as they walked. Tashi told us that most Thimpu residents came here once a day, often before or after work, and that many elderly residents spent all day here, chanting prayers and ensuring that the large prayer wheels were continuously turning. However, for me, the most interesting visit in Thimpu was to the Takin Reserve, located in the pine forests above the city. This creature is the national animal of Bhutan, so rare that it is only found in Tibet, Sikkim and Bhutan, and such an odd-looking beast! We saw a small herd, each about the size of a cow, with thick shaggy coats and unattractive faces dominated by huge Roman noses. The much-loved 4th king (who abdicated in 2006 but was still alive and greatly revered, when I visited) had decided that it was inappropriate to keep these animals in a zoo, when the country was establishing a code of behaviour which respected all living creatures, so he ordered they should be released. However, the animals were enjoying the attention and fodder given to them by their keepers and refused to leave! So the zoo was transformed into a Reserve where the Takin were protected but could roam at will across wide paddocks – we were lucky to see some close to the fences.

Highlight of the entire tour was to be the 5-day festival held in the courtyard of Thimpu Dzong. The whole city was packed with pilgrims and visitors, and the festival had overflowed to a large, tented area beside the river where I saw again (on a larger scale) the fairground entertainments I had seen at Wangdue, whilst a massive open-air market filled the city's main street, offering toys, trinkets and untidy heaps of clothing. We joined the crowds (all wearing their best outfits) queuing to enter the dzong for Day 3 of the festival, with Tashi pushing us ahead of the line at the security checkpoint to get us inside the courtyard just in time for the start of the dancing. A group of 50 monks dressed in heavy brocade costumes and fearsome masks filed in to sway and swirl in stately fashion for 30 minutes, while crowds continued to pour into the site, filling every corner and cranny, blocking passageways until moved on by police, only for more to fill the newly-created gap – the police had an impossible task. The monks finished their dance with a bow, replaced by a group of professional dancers in yellow skirts and more masks, whirling with skirts flying to the rhythm of cymbals – though I could barely see them through the constant flow of newly arriving spectators.

This pattern was repeated throughout the morning: groups of elaborately costumed dancers prancing or whirling across the courtyard in dances lasting an hour or more. I persevered with the performance for several more hours, watching as 'fools' appeared among the audience and as lines of female dancers moved delicately across the arena, gesticulating gracefully – presumably, these 'acts' were designed to make the serious religious dances of the monks more palatable to the onlookers? Yet my view was always partially obscured by the crowd: in fact, I was finding the audience almost more interesting than the performance:

"Around me the children are getting fractious – they have been fed from their mothers' breasts, then given lollies, then big chunks of cucumber, but it's getting ever hotter and more humid, and the concrete step where we are sitting, is getting hard. A few older people in the crowd are concentrating diligently and telling their prayer beads as the dancers enact religious scenes, but many younger people are chatting and picnicking."

Finally, together with many local people, I left the dzong to spend the afternoon exploring Thimpu's streets. Next day, after official sightseeing in the morning, I decided to return to the festival on my own, finding it far less crowded – in fact, as I entered, I was directed to sit down directly on the performance ground, opposite the 'royal box'. Now that I had a clear view, I could follow the meaning of the dances (with the aid of my programme) far better: first I watched the reverent Tsholing Cham, danced by monks dressed in rich brocade dresses with wide sleeves and skull masks:

"As the monks leave the floor, a deafening cacophony breaks out – drummers move through the crowd and hang out of the dzong windows, while piercing whistles assail our ears. A line of dancers twists and sways across the arena, representing the Tscholing, protectors of Buddhist religion, removing obstacles to faith. Then the Ging dancers appear, dressed minimally in animal skins, moving through the crowd, hitting people on the head with drumsticks to remove impurity while the people whistle to chase away demons."

This dance was far more interesting and exciting than anything I had seen the day before and I was very glad to have returned to see more – but sitting flat on a concrete floor is not comfortable for most western people (and certainly not for me) so after a couple of hours I rose stiffly to my feet, bidding farewell to two little boys who had been chatting with me, and made my way out of the dzong to walk instead in riverside gardens surrounding the Parliament building (since 2008 Bhutan has been a constitutional monarchy).

We had one more destination in Bhutan, driving back towards Paro to visit the Tiger's Nest Monastery – which appears on every poster advertising the country. Legend tells that Guru Rinpoche (founder of Tantric Buddhism) meditated for years in caves located halfway up an inaccessible cliff – brought to the site on the back of a goddess transformed into a flying tiger. Later his disciples built a monastery which clings to the cliff-face surrounding those sacred caves. I had heard tales of the difficulty of the path leading up to the monastery (2500ft of ascent) and was fully expecting not to be able to walk all the way, but I set off hopefully, plodding steeply uphill on a broad path of beaten earth with occasional wooden steps or short cuts up rain-worn gullies, dodging out of the way of horses carrying pilgrims less fit than I:

"A mass of flags and a huge prayer wheel indicate a resting place ... but surprise, surprise! This is already the cafe halfway up – perhaps I WILL manage the climb after all? Sadly the promised 'first view of the monastery' is invisible because of low cloud, but as I sip a cup of tea ... hurray! The cloud is lifting, to reveal a glimpse of a waterfall, then a flash of white walls, then the outlines of buildings decorated with red and gold."

Rejuvenated, I continued up the rocky trail through cloud forest where ferns were bedded in thick banks of moss growing on the tree trunks. For once, the low cloud was a boon, protecting us from the strength of the sun as we climbed. Finally a cluster of camera-toting tourists on a bend of the path, announced that I had arrived on the ridge just above the monastery, looking across a deep ravine to a cluster of buildings apparently attached to the cliff-face by superglue (or, according to legend, by the hairs of the goddess). One last challenge took me down a rough stone stairway, across a waterfall, then up an even steeper stairway to the monastery entrance. Nowhere in Bhutan had we been permitted to photograph inside a temple, and here we were even obliged to deposit all cameras, phones and bags ... plus shoes and my walking poles:

"The first challenge is to climb two flights of very high, steep stone steps (ah well, hands and knees it is!) to reach a chapel set inside a cave, with painted walls and a floor covered with red carpet – though the bumps under my feet confirm that these are not man-made walls or floor, just natural rock.

Now up steep, narrow wooden steps to more tiny chapels squeezed into crevices in the rock-face. One dark stairway leads to a black hole, where primitive wooden ladders descend into a labyrinth of cracks and crevices – the Tiger's Nest itself. Far below, I can hear distressed voices as pilgrims try to negotiate the ladder: I'll give that one a miss!"

The descent was almost more difficult than the ascent, but I was buoyed all the way by the sense of achievement – a dramatic conclusion to a tour which had shown me beautiful landscapes, though none of the high peaks I had hoped for. Instead my impressions of Bhutan were of forested Himalayan foothills, fertile and blessed with abundant rain, yet with less wildlife than I had expected. However, it was good to see a relaxed and fun-loving people whose faith was part of everyday life, and who were still happy to maintain their traditions despite the country's rapid movement into 21st century life.

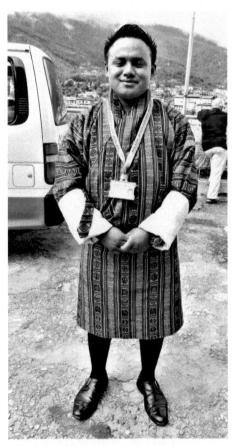

Bhutan - traditional costume

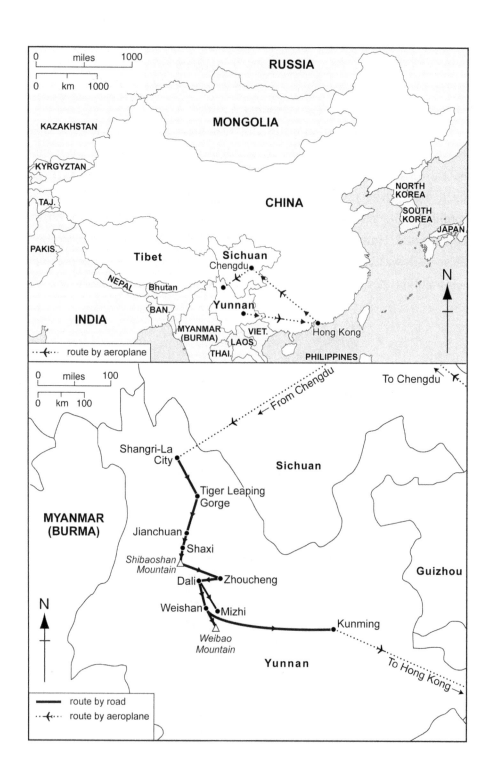

Yunnan – South-west China (February 2016)

I HAD MADE A COMPREHENSIVE classic tour of China in 1986 but was still interested to learn more about the minority peoples of the country (there are 55 minorities, though 92% of China's population belongs to the Han ethnic group) – so I was attracted to a tour in the province of Yunnan, visiting the villages of several different tribes as they celebrated their local festivals. The whole of China was in celebration mode at the time I visited, since it was the period of Chinese New Year (their most important annual holiday).

My flight took me first via Hong Kong into Chengdu, capital of Sichuan province, a thriving modern city which is home to the Panda Breeding Centre – so busy with noisy Chinese crowds wielding selfie-sticks, that I actually preferred exploring a separate reserve of dense bush, where groups of much more active Red Pandas were flitting between the trees in almost total silence. But the Giant Pandas were the undisputed stars of the show:

"First stop is at the enclosure where the 6-month-old cubs are frolicking, watched by a large enthusiastic crowd of excited Chinese visitors. They play-fight, scramble precariously up trees (to the anxious groans of the crowd) and nibble at piles of newly delivered bamboo. In other enclosures, adult pandas sit squarely on fat bottoms, stuffing whole branches of bamboo into their mouths before drifting off to sleep."

Also in Chengdu we visited the New Year Market: a heady mixture of children's fairground rides; food outlets offering everything from candy floss to squid kebabs; stalls selling beads, carved stones and wooden figures – fodder for domestic visitors who were the mainstay of Chengdu's tourist industry. There were few white faces visible here and I caused quite a stir – Chinese people hovered nearby in the hope of a chance to greet me or even to get their children to shake my hand, while they took a 'novelty' photo. We continued to Marijushri Monastery, a rabbit warren of passages linking 5 separate temple courtyards, traditionally visited by pilgrims at New Year to seek luck for the coming year:

"The whole complex is thronged with people, kneeling on big cushions to make obeisance and pray, rocking hands up and down, clutching incense sticks which are lit from massive braziers pouring fragrant smoke into each courtyard. What would Mao make of this apparent outpouring of faith? Or is it just a manifestation of the constant Chinese obsession with good luck?"

Later in the day we flew into Yunnan on a ruthlessly efficient flight which hustled us on board (stewardesses seizing and stowing our hand baggage as we shuffled into the plane), then moved towards take-off even as the last passengers were finding their seats. Our destination was the Diqing Tibetan Autonomous Prefecture, and the picturesquely named city of Shangri-La (originally called Zhongdian but renamed in 2001 in an effort to boost tourism). My ambition was to visit Tibet itself but that seemed like an impossible dream, so I was excited to sample the flavour of Tibetan life in this enclave – a part of Greater Tibet which had been cut off and moved into the administration of Yunnan province (one of the ways in which the Chinese government had sought, over the centuries, to dilute Tibetan nationalism). It was well into the night before we arrived, gasping with breathlessness at the sudden increase in altitude to over 3000m, and shivering in temperatures below freezing – but already I could see tantalising glimpses of Tibetan-style brick homes with carved wooden window frames, their yards enclosed by high walls and gates.

Next morning I was out early to explore the flag-festooned streets of the Old Town, though sadly a lot of the original 17th century settlement burned down in 2014 and had been rebuilt with modern houses superficially dressed in traditional Tibetan style – it was only re-opened to non-residents one month before my visit. In the interim, many of the original Tibetan inhabitants had moved out to the New Town, leaving the reconstruction to become a 'Disney-style' tourist venue:

"I wander through the reconstructed town on smooth concrete roadways,

then enter the rocky alleyways of the surviving original settlement. The old houses are smaller and more rickety, but the solid modern buildings are adorned with facades carved into fantastic designs with dragons on the eaves and decorative fretwork around the windows: no expense spared, but at least traditional carpentry skills are being preserved."

In the heart of the old town, on a hill accessed by a long stairway, stood a Tibetan Buddhist temple filled with the recorded sound of chanting and horns, though only a single monk was present. Alongside the temple was a huge golden prayer wheel, weighing 600 tons (largest in China), which took a concerted effort by eight strong adults to get it moving. Our guide (Neddy) told us that each single revolution represented a million prayers contributed to the worshipper's credit on his route to nirvana.

Even more impressive was the huge Ganden Sumtseling Monastery, located just outside Shangri-La, which was important both for visiting tourists and also for the local Tibetan population since it had been briefly home to the 7th Dalai Lama in the 18th century. Outside it, I saw a young Tibetan couple prostrating themselves progressively in a 'kora' (pilgrimage) around the entire monastery complex, accompanied by their patient toddler. Their hands were protected by thick gloves, their knees by padded aprons, but still what a challenge to complete! There was a challenge for us too – the temples stood at the top of another long staircase which, at this altitude, caused much heart-pounding and breath-gasping:

"We sneak into the main chanting hall where the monks are assembled (except for one young lad who skids in late, at top speed) – all 500 resident monks are sitting cross-legged on their benches, as the chief lama chants in a deep throaty voice. Many of the younger monks are chatting or fidgeting, though a senior lama circulates with a big stick to discipline them. We walk right around the prayer hall, then follow Neddy up two more flights of steps to emerge on the roof amid a maze of imposing golden sculptures and tinkling wind-chimes."

Next day we drove out to explore a Tibetan hamlet, where groups of villagers were performing their brisk morning circumambulation around the local 'stupa' (shrine) whilst others were feeding fragrant pine branches into an incense burner. The people here seemed relatively wealthy with smart new houses (all topped by the customary prayer flags on each corner of the flat roof), and glass-walled porches attached to their homes to enhance winter living. One of the sources of their wealth, Neddy told us, were the black Tibetan pigs which roamed freely around the rough alleys of the hamlet – the Chinese love to eat pork, and this free-range meat commanded an excellent price. Nearby we stopped at Lake Napa to see the large flocks of birds which choose to over-winter there ... including the rare Black-necked Cranes which I had failed to see in Bhutan:

"Snow-capped mountain ranges ring the flat grassland beside the lake; everywhere there are massive racks where hay and beet leaves are drying for winter fodder. On the water we see our first cranes, strolling elegantly at the water's edge, while further out the lake is thick with ducks of many types. Overhead two ospreys are soaring on broad wings, while a herd of yaks is grazing peacefully nearby."

Later we drove on to attend part of a festival taking place at Dejilin Monastery. We arrived too late for the religious ceremonies but were able to join in the afternoon celebrations where families were gathering around large bonfires, cooking up a hot lunch amid laughter and talk, punctuated with screams as firecrackers rattled a loud staccato. One family invited me to join them as they formed a big circle around the fire to perform a slow stamping dance, before scattering more firecrackers:

"Many are in their best costumes – smart tunics decorated with brocade, round pink hats and headscarves for the women, furry hats or broad stetsons for the men. They are delighted to welcome us, photographing us on their smartphones as part of their special day. Finally they hoist on to their backs, panniers containing the remains of the feast, wicker butter baskets and even a wooden butter-tea churner, before plodding off in the direction of their vehicles."

We also returned to our coach, driving away from the lands of the Tibetan people towards villages of the Black Yi (pronounced Ji) tribe. Neddy was a member of the White Yi group, who mainly lived in cities and were reasonably well-off – in contrast, the Black Yi were mountain-dwellers, scratching a living from poor hillsides. We stopped outside the walled compound of a Black Yi family and Neddy went to enquire if we could visit, but they seemed reluctant until he offered a payment. They lived around a cluttered courtyard, with a stable for a single yak and some pigs on one side, a very dark communal living section on another. There was a solar-heated shower within the courtyard, but the toilet hut was situated some distance away. Neddy was pleased to be able to show us the lifestyle of another ethnic group, but I felt embarrassed to be invading their personal space:

"The family pay little attention as we visit (after all, we are not really 'invited' guests), and the children continue with their homework, trying to ignore our distractions. An interesting visit, I suppose, but oh, so awkward and invasive!"

We were now in the heart of the mountains with views across dry fields, still awaiting their springtime planting, to the snow-capped ridges of the Haba Snow Mountain and Jade Dragon Snow Mountain. Between the two ranges was our next destination: Tiger Leaping Gorge – a 3000 metre deep, 17km long gash carved through the rocks by the waters of the upper Yangtze River. Until 1986 this area was uncharted wilderness … till ten years before my visit, there was only a walking trail here … in 2016, we were able to drive along a good road which twisted its way to a parking area where 11 coaches, 12 minibuses and over 50 cars were disgorging the day's hordes of sightseers. (Since my visit, another road and a railway have been built – sometimes I hate the tourist industry which has been integral to my life!) We descended 650 wooden steps to a riverside viewing platform:

"Below me the smooth green river is compressed into a narrow cleft in the rocks, swirling with white foam as it descends a water-chute and smashes against the Tiger Rock itself (supposedly used by a magical tiger as a stepping stone across the river)."

Now Neddy was keen to introduce us to the second most populous tribe of Yunnan (after the Yi) – the Bai people. Once again, their homes were grouped around a walled yard, though often two or three related families would occupy a single courtyard. The Bai people were famous for their artistry and craftsmanship, especially woodcarving, and their villages were easily distinguished by elegant floral designs, and even poetry, painted on to brilliant white exterior walls, while the internal space was filled with potted trees, herbs and flowers. In the town of Jianchuan we were proudly invited into the home of a beaming octogenarian, who lived alone:

"Passing through massive ancient wooden gates, we are first confronted by pieces of bedding airing on a line. Then we turn to the wooden buildings

surrounding us, all with carved fretwork windows which leave their interiors dark and mysterious. In one corner is a huge pile of firewood, in another a rocking chair where our 80-year-old host sits to laugh and joke with us – delighted with this unexpected company."

Back out in the street, we met a couple of ladies returning from shopping, who immediately invited us to visit their home too – a courtyard packed full of plants, and an open-sided living room so full of children's toys and clothes that there was barely room for the table and stools, where grandpa and the children were playing mah-jong as we arrived. They immediately leapt to their feet to offer us peanuts and sweets, delighted to pose for our photographs – what a contrast from the unhappy Black Yi family we had met earlier.

Now we were reaching the towns and villages along the ancient Teahorse Trail, a route once used by traders exchanging Tibetan ponies (historically vital for China's armies) for blocks of Pu'er tea from southern Yunnan – fermented tea packaged into solid blocks for transportation to Tibet, where it formed a vital part of a diet which otherwise comprised only meat and barley. The town of Shaxi was a staging post on the route – its main square lined with traditional guesthouses used by the tea traders, offering stabling and storage areas behind them and open-fronted shops at the front (now transformed into souvenir shops), where Tibetans and Yunnanese once conducted their trade. However, I quickly moved away from the main square, drawn by the sound of cattle bellowing across the river. An ancient high-arched Chinese bridge led me to an open dusty space now in use as an animal market, where cattle were tied to railings or vehicles, and pigs were penned inside portable wire fences. Men were standing around the animals, smoking as they waited for the right beasts to arrive. As I watched, another vehicle drew in, unloading a donkey and a young bullock. Immediately a large crowd gathered, poking and prodding until money changed hands and the donkey was led away.

As the afternoon air cooled, I established myself in a small cafe back in the old town, people-watching as the market stalls in the main square became ever busier. I had hoped to see some of the traditional costumes of the different tribes in the area, but most fascinating were the hats:

"Black Yi ladies are almost invisible beneath huge black sails perched on their heads, while others wear tight black turbans or Mao-style caps, with a

sprinkling of coolie hats worn by both men and women. Most popular of all are elaborate confections of chiffon and ribbon which I would normally call 'wedding hats' – though here they seem to be day-to-day protection against the sun."

Most of the next day was spent exploring the Buddhist mountain of Shibaoshan, climbing long flights of steep stone steps through silent groves of pine, studded with camellias, to visit a series of Buddhist grottoes carved out of the red sandstone rocks over 1000 years ago. There were signs of damage caused by the rampaging Red Army in the Cultural Revolution (1966-76), but fortunately some of the most elaborate carvings in the grottoes were spared because they represented ancient kings rather than religious images. I had expected to find painted caves (as in Dunhuang) but instead, these grottoes comprised complex stone reliefs carved deep into the living rock, protected from the weather by overhanging cliffs. In one grotto, a king was discussing politics with his retinue; in another he was sitting in state, presented almost as if on a stage with carved curtains waiting to drop. Most precious of all was the grotto where a guard escorted us officiously, to ensure we did not take a forbidden photo:

"Here under an overhanging lip of rock, the Buddha figures still show traces of colour – red, green and blue. There is amazing detail in the carvings, especially when you consider how old they are. A female goddess with a peaceful face and a hole in her chest (to show her heart is open to help petitioners) represents the Bai goddess of mercy. The whole cliff-face has been cut away, so that she stands proud, yet still protected within the rock."

One of the highlights of the tour was to be the local festival in the village of Zhoucheng – though my first experience of the village was upsettingly negative. I was not impressed to find a 'village' the size of a small town – noisy, crowded and full of ugly buildings, electric wiring and broken pavements. I found the shopkeepers rude and unhelpful, and Neddy had his difficulties too – we had no breakfast available in our guesthouse and he could not find a cafe willing to open up for us next morning. Eventually he bought some biscuits and bananas in the local market and served them up to us in the guesthouse lobby, together with his own special tea (his normal job was in the tea plantations and he regularly brewed up 'proper' tea for us, during the tour).

However it was impossible to remain disappointed next day, when we emerged to witness the start of the festival. Though no-one really knew what would happen or when, the village was charged with excitement and anticipation. The streets were full of ladies in dark tunics with colourful embroidered sashes and hats, carrying bundles of red incense sticks. We followed them to a small brightly coloured temple on the edge of the village, where a vast smoking urn of incense burned in front of an altar depicting their chief Protector god and his four wives – nearby, smaller statues of the same gods were waiting to be loaded on to biers to be carried through the streets. In the outer courtyard, innumerable ladies were bustling about the task of preparing a feast to follow the procession. Returning to the main temple in the heart of the village, we found the men busy brewing tea for a group of musicians warming up with a few bars of music. At 10.30am, we were invited to join the men at their communal lunch (the ladies were dining separately) eating rice, onion soup and shredded pork at top speed, in Chinese fashion:

"Now things pick up pace. A team of ladies in bright red costumes appears, picking up the poles which will support a traditional 'dancing dragon'. Then they're off – first the dragon, swaying and twirling, then the musicians and the main body of ladies, waving their incense sticks. Finally the men manoeuvre the empty biers, with considerable difficulty, out of the temple gate and under the low-hanging wires in the street. All head for the temple of the Protector gods, where the young men who have been trailing at the rear of the procession, leap into action – lifting the 5 statues in quick succession, draping them in red cloth and carrying them out to the waiting biers, tensely alert in case a statue is dropped. Finally the procession sets off to bless every corner of the village."

I walked with them for a while, past entrance gates where residents had lit tiny fires of pine branches and incense sticks, filling our lungs with smoke. Many had also laid apparently innocuous red ribbons on the ground, which revealed themselves to be firecrackers as the first bier approached, deafening us with explosions and pelting us with bits of detritus. Even the local people broke formation to dodge away, ducking behind each other for shelter! The procession finally returned to the main square, installing the sacred images on a balcony overlooking the heart of the village for the 4-day duration of the festival. I perched on a wall beneath a shady tree to await a promised performance of dancing on the village stage. We waited … and waited…

briefly entertained by the return of the 'dancing dragon' ... then waited some more. Finally, elaborately costumed performers appeared to the sound of pounding drums and clashing cymbals, though their 'dancing' was mainly just striking poses while an official declaimed long speeches, finishing as piles of sweets were hurled out into the audience:

"The day ends with an invitation to dinner with the ladies at the Protector's temple. They make a wonderful picture, their coloured hats sparkling and flashing like peacocks, as they cluster around low tables. Big bowls of rice appear, served by a single volunteer while everyone else chatters companionably, reaching from time to time for mouthfuls of rice and other dishes – no great haste here, unlike the men's meal earlier."

Some days later, we returned to Zhoucheng for a few hours to watch the final procession of their festival. A massive fire was now burning in the main square, both to dispose of the heaps of litter being swept from the streets and to burn incense sticks and wads of 'prayer money' as a final offering to the Protector gods. Once again, the ladies gathered, this time clutching trays of food offerings, lining the route of the sacred images as they were hoisted from their balcony back on to the biers. The whole village then processed back to the Protector's temple, jigging gently in time to the music of horns and drums as they walked.

We spent the intervening days at another village (Mizhi), attending their festival – but what a contrast in style! Mizhi festival was organised by the regional government, instead of being a simple expression of devotion, and took the form of a contest between 15 local villages, attended by hordes of visitors from the entire region. The main street of the village was entirely filled with double rows of stalls cooking up pancakes and kebabs; offering hoopla and gambling games; selling embroidered Bai head-dresses or Chinese medicines including a rare Tibetan worm-fungus (specially for the men!). Balloon sellers wandered through the crowds; sugar-cane vendors stripped canes for customers to suck the sweet juice; children offered cups of tiny super-sweet wild strawberries.

Finally the contest got underway. Each village had brought its own 'dancing dragon', as well as a set of energetic 'lions' and various other dancers, who all performed in a mass spectacle before the contest began, the dragons running around the arena weaving complex patterns, filling the entire space with undulating ribbons of colour. Then pairs of villages were called forward in turn, to present their performances side-by-side on a small stage in front of the judges. Most followed the same pattern – one dragon and one lion each, whirling around their half of the stage before coming together directly before the judges, accompanied by a huge drum (usually on wheels) beating out a complex double rhythm, surrounded by gaggles of costumed girls swaying and waving their fans. Outside the judges' control were a few other entertainers, usually comic characters to keep the audience entertained: especially successful was a man dressed as a water buffalo proving extremely stubborn to the man trying to lead him – that raised a lot of sympathetic laughs (many local farmers would have experienced the same difficulties with their own beasts). The first afternoon saw 8 villages present their performances for judging, and the remainder continued on the next day:

"The dragons whirl; lions and ferocious pecking cranes attack the crowd; water buffalo rear and prance; fans flutter energetically; various hobby-horses, ships and sedan chairs bob up and down to make their sequins sparkle – a feast of colour and movement. Yet one sad little village on the far edge of the stage, can offer only a couple of young boys in yellow paper masks who play-fight with wooden swords – such a contrast to the practised grace and elaborate costumes of most of the teams."

Mizhi festival certainly gave us (and the hordes of Chinese tourists) innumerable photo opportunities, yet I preferred the genuine emotion and open-hearted friendliness of Zhoucheng. Through the past weeks, we had been given a glimpse into the life of some of Yunnan's 25 ethnic groups – though they had clearly taken the path of least resistance (unlike the Uighurs and Tibetans) and had allowed themselves to absorb the values and lifestyle of Han China, retaining their distinctive costumes and festivals for special occasions, but otherwise living in much the same way as the Han Chinese.

A stay in Dali gave us a brief return to western-style civilisation, with a luxurious hotel spread over a complex of courtyards and gardens. Soft golden illuminations bathed the city centre overnight (instead of the dark silent streets in rural communities), with relaxed pedestrians strolling from cafe to bar to ice-cream parlour. The principal tourist attraction was Chongsheng Temple, a vast complex of prayer halls flanked by three ancient pagodas, set in spacious gardens filled with soothing piped music. I dutifully followed the central path and stairways uphill from hall to hall, admiring the massive golden statues of Buddha and other deities, but found no inspiration in any. Poor Neddy had hoped we would be overawed by his local 'attraction' (Dali was his home), but we could raise little enthusiasm, especially as the thick clouds turned to rain – and we retired early back to the city centre.

More inspiring was our visit to Weibao Mountain, an especially holy place for the Yi people – this time dedicated to the Taoist religion, which emphasises care for Nature. In total, there were 6 square kilometres of 'natural scenic area' – acres of fragrant pine forest in which were nestled 14 separate temples, most decorated with magnificent fresco paintings. The tranquillity and lush vegetation encouraged me to clamber up the steep path from temple to temple, with occasional glimpses of Taoist monks in black silk trousers, tunic and cap, with long wispy moustaches or beards:

"An unusual round doorway leads into Wengchang Temple, through an outer hall containing luridly coloured statues of warriors. Behind this lies a fairy-tale courtyard with a fish pool and ornamental bridge leading to a delicate pavilion hung with wooden balconies. Camellias adorn the courtyard; tall weeping willows hang over the pool; moss and lichen colour the stones – it looks like a secret garden. Only birdsong disturbs the utter silence, which even partially absorbs our voices."

We stayed in the nearby town of Weishan, another former staging post on the Teahorse Trail, though little developed for tourism as yet. The main street was again lined with open-fronted shops, as in Shaxi, though they offered the necessities of daily life instead of tourist souvenirs. The area was famous for noodles, and long strands of wheat noodle were hanging in passageways or windows catching the breeze (or even using an electric fan) to dry them. In small cafes, noisy families had gathered to play mah-jong or Chinese chess – otherwise all was quiet. The newer part of town was more lively, remaining active into the night with young people socialising on foot or on scooters. As we walked to a restaurant for dinner, we even passed a line of young women dancing in the main square. Altogether a very interesting town with important historic connections – I was glad to have seen it before mass tourism arrived.

Our last day brought a change of coach and driver: for two weeks we had travelled with Xie, but he had never been to the 'big city' of Kunming and was unwilling to risk any violations of local traffic laws – just two infractions would lead to the loss of his licence, and therefore his living. It was a wise decision, since traffic in Kunming (capital of Yunnan) was impossible! We crawled at slower than walking pace to our hotel, and immediately abandoned any thought of sightseeing by coach, instead simply taking a walk into Green Lake Park (where a massive flock of seagulls swirled above an equally massive crowd of people), and on to the famous Bird Market – though it seemed to sell mainly pet food and bird cages, rather than the actual songbirds which the Chinese like to keep outside their homes.

Once again, I flew home via Hong Kong, deciding to use my 7-hour transit time constructively by taking a trip on the airport express train into the city. As evening crept on, the town became busier and busier with people pouring from buses and taxis, and innumerable buskers set up microphones to entertain the crowds. A total contrast from the village life which had made up the largest part of this trip to South-west China, but a great way to pass the time while waiting for a connecting flight home:

"I had wondered if there was any point in going into the town at night, but it's exactly the right time! The waterfront skyscrapers in Hong Kong are lit up with flashing neon in every colour, all reflected by the surrounding sea. I take the Star Ferry to Kowloon's viewing terrace to watch a fabulous light show – a series of images and coloured patterns projected on to the smooth curved wall of the Cultural Centre. Then there is time to explore the exclusive shopping area around Kowloon's waterfront – so different from the narrow chaotic streets I remember from my visit back in 1986."

Chengdu - baby pandas

Yunnan - Zoucheng festival

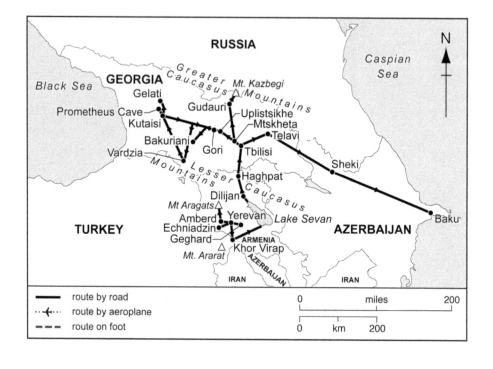

Caucasus region – Armenia, Georgia, Azerbaijan (May/ June 2016)

AS THE YEARS HAVE PROGRESSED, I have found myself inexorably drawn to mountain scenery – so a chance to visit the Lesser and Greater Caucasus Mountains on the furthest eastern boundaries of Europe, was irresistible. However, I had no idea that I would find such complex history in the region, still unfolding today. Each of the three countries which fill this vital strategic bridge between Europe and the Middle East, have expanded into wide-ranging empires at some point in their history, only to shrink again … sometimes to disappear altogether, absorbed by the all-devouring cultures of neighbouring Russia, Turkey or Persia. When I visited, Armenia was in a long-standing dispute with Turkey and had closed that border, while another long-standing war with Azerbaijan had resulted in renewed clashes just a month before my visit – of course, that border was closed too. This war had resulted in the strange (to my eyes) situation that Armenia possessed a region (Karabakh) located in the middle of Azerbaijan, with only a single point of transit into Armenia … while Azerbaijan possessed a region (Naxcivan) on the far side of Armenia, which was totally cut off and accessible only by transiting Iran. Georgia seemed to be doing better, with good relations and open borders with neighbouring Turkey, Armenia and Azerbaijan … but a dangerous dispute with Russia over the provinces of Abkhazia and South Ossetia, resulted in their border with Russia being closed to both Georgians and Russians. What a political mess envelops the beautiful landscapes of the Caucasus region!

My tour started in Armenia, a small nation not much bigger than Britain's West Country. This meant that most of our sightseeing could be accomplished by day trips out of the capital city Yerevan, useful since there was little tourist accommodation elsewhere in the country. The city only became Armenia's capital in 1918 (many of the previous capitals were now located in Turkey after continual re-drawing of borders), and was badly damaged by earthquake in 1931 – so much of it was built in unattractive 20th century Soviet style, best seen by night:

"The avenues are now packed with people strolling and eating ice-cream. Busking musicians play on corners – in one street a full-blown rap concert is underway. There's music in the elegant cafes too, especially near the Opera House where curtained cafe spaces nestle amid beds of roses. In Republic Square the fountains are not just playing, but are also dancing with lights to very loud recorded music, enjoyed by more crowds who sit around the water's edge relaxing in the balmy evening."

Official sightseeing took us uphill to a viewpoint dominated by a massive glowering statue of Mother Armenia, in typical Soviet style. On another hilltop we visited the Genocide Memorial, remembering the ethnic cleansing of Armenians by the Turks (who steadfastly deny any genocide) in the early years of the 20th century – trainloads of young men enlisted into the army in 1915, only to be shot when they thought they were being taken to the front line; women and the elderly marched off towards the Syrian deserts to die. Only half a million (of a total population of 3 million) escaped to countries around the world in a diaspora:

"We walk by a grey wall inscribed with the names of towns and villages 'cleansed' on the orders of Turkey. Ahead lies the memorial, very simple and dignified, in the form of a flower. Within the 'petals', steps descend to an eternal flame, burning fiercely and surrounded by individual stems of roses laid by visitors. The scene is enough to hush us to reflective silence."

Our guide (Laura) told us that numbers of ethnic Armenians living abroad had now reached 9 million (three times the population living inside the country), and that many of them contributed regularly to the 'All Armenian Foundation' which was providing much of the funding needed by the country to rebuild after the collapse of the USSR. An individual donation by an American Armenian had bought the hillside Cascades Centre in Yerevan, an exhibition centre originally intended to commemorate 50 years of Soviet Armenia, converted in 2001 to display modern artworks. Free access via a series of clanking escalators led me up past a series of massive steps, each displaying some of the exhibits – but most impressive was the view from the top of the building, looking across the city to a snow-streaked mountain topped by two perfect volcanic cones: the twin peaks of Mount Ararat, national symbol of Armenia, cut off by Stalin and given to Turkey in 1921 – a very visible reminder of a constant and bitter conflict.

Overlooking Republic Square, in the heart of the city, was the grandiose concrete facade of the History Museum where I spent a few hours trying to understand the complicated history of Armenia. The earliest exhibits dated from thousands of years BC, including two virtually intact wooden carts over 3500 years old (how ever did they survive?), and I was amazed to find bronze armour from an 8th century BC Armenian kingdom based around Lake Van (now in eastern Turkey). After viewing innumerable relics of Christian churches, with photographs of chapels now ruined and abandoned in neighbouring Muslim countries, I came to a disturbing section on the Genocide, with photographs of ragged, barefoot, starving refugees and of the emigrating diaspora sailing to safety. Yet I was surprised to find nothing at all about the Soviet period – perhaps Russia continues to be too good a friend to risk offending them?

Armenia's history seemed to be one long struggle to maintain their identity, with the keystone of that struggle being their Orthodox Christian faith – Laura proudly told us that her country was the very first to convert to Christianity (in 301 AD) and their church was still governed by their own independent Patriarch, the Catholicos. Appropriately, our first excursion outside Yerevan took us to see the mother church of Armenian Orthodoxy at Echmiadzin, so revered by the population that even the Soviet government had been forced to allow it to remain open (though officially as a museum). The original 5th century church sat amid a large complex of later religious buildings, but the hordes of Sunday worshippers had only one goal – to get inside the crowded church:

"Only one small door is open, but I squeeze in, carried on the wave of worshippers past great banks of guttering candles, into the central aisle where priests robed in red and gold are chanting while the choir sings a glorious Amen. Waves of sound rise up into the elaborately painted domed roof, now hazy with incense smoke which drives me outside again. The bells begin to

clang joyously to indicate that the Catholicos is coming: a column of priests and purple-robed bishops stride purposefully towards the church – at the rear is a short, stout, bearded man whose hands move constantly in blessing."

Next day took us further outside the city, into the green hills of the Lesser Caucasus, past villages of small simple homes set amid fields and orchards. As we climbed higher, the road degenerated into a track of broken tarmac, deformed by years of landslips and emergency repairs, until finally we reached the remote medieval Geghard Monastery, built in the 13th century around cave churches in use since the 4th century:

"We pass through the main church into two separate cave chapels, created from earlier monks' cells. They are cool but quite bright, lit from a central skylight filled with sunshine. All around are niches and altars carved from the dark basalt stone and edged by massive pillars. Strains of ethereal music drift down through a hole in the roofline from the hall above, where a group of singers from Yerevan Conservatory are performing songs designed to capture the acoustic properties of the cave."

Further back down the valley we stopped for a completely unexpected sight – the Greek-style temple of Garni rising incongruously from this green mountainous land. Back in the 3rd century BC there had been a fortress here, fortified by a gorge which surrounded it on three sides, later enhanced by a palace and then this pagan temple (built in 77 AD). Everything was destroyed by earthquake in the 17th century and the ruins virtually disappeared until it was decided to rebuild the temple in the 1970s. Despite its antiquity, the site was not particularly interesting – the temple contained only an empty altar and the rest of the structures were nothing more than piles of stone. However, the gorge below the temple was amazing:

"The valley is lined with cliffs of naturally-created octagonal basalt pillars – sometimes eroded so that they form massive bulging overhangs directly above our heads; in other places forced by seismic activity into contorted shapes. Some of the columns are laid on their sides, projecting towards the stream like huge piles of maturing logs; others rise in a graduated swirl, like the skirts of a ballerina's tutu."

Next day's excursion started with a visit to Yerevan's Manuscript Museum ... which I anticipated would be intensely boring, though in fact it was surprisingly interesting. The building itself was unusual, cut deep into a hillside so that the climate could be stabilised to preserve the documents. The exhibits were evidence of another vital strand in the task of maintaining a national Armenian identity: its alphabet – moving from spiky cuneiform shapes into the rounded and elegant style which still characterises Armenian script. Our 'alphabet day' continued when we left the city, stopping at a windy site to admire a newly developed Alphabet Monument where stone-carved letters were scattered across the hillside. On Laura's insistence, we each posed for a photograph alongside the sculpture representing our own first initial – mine resembled the shape of a shepherd's crook. Later in the tour we visited a woodcarving shop producing unusual souvenirs – wooden Armenian letters, each one reinforcing the uniqueness of Armenian culture as it was carried by tourists to destinations around the world.

The main goal of our day's excursion was in the area of Mount Aragats (4090m), Armenia's highest remaining mountain (since Mount Ararat was moved into Turkey). We passed villages of neat houses surrounded by vine-covered terraces and rose beds, with telegraph poles topped by storks' nests … also driving past communities of nomadic Yazidi people who took refuge here from persecution in Iraq and Syria, keeping large flocks of sheep and beehives on the slopes of the Lesser Caucasus. High in the mountains (at 2300m) we reached the ancient fortress of Amberd, built in the 7th century when Armenia was invaded by Arab armies attempting to convert the people to newly-created Islam. Alongside was a tiny church with a door at each end, so that soldiers en route to battle could be given a quick blessing and hustled on through. The fortress itself was ruinous and unstabilised, no more than a jumble of massive rock walls:

"It's an interesting visit, but the glory of Amberd is in its setting – looming over a rushing mountain stream which bounces over the stones through a deep rocky chasm, all the way from snow-flecked mountains behind us. Our path winds through thick vegetation full of wild herbs (thyme, fennel and cardamom) and dotted with yellow buttercups, cream orchids and a host of other flowers. The air is fresh (-10° in the shade), though the sun is warm."

Finally leaving Yerevan behind us, we headed alongside the Turkish border, through the fertile vineyards and fields of the Aras Valley, to visit the tiny, fortified church of Khor Virap perched on a rocky outcrop just across the valley from Mount Ararat – a last bastion of Christianity on the very borders of Muslim Turkey. The story of the church was fascinating: in pre-Christian times criminals were thrown into deep pits and left to starve, which was the fate of St Gregory when he dared to venture into Armenia after his father had killed the king. Thirteen years later (having been fed by local Christians), Gregory was hauled out of the pit to cure the ailing king, who converted to Christianity – so Gregory built a church around his pit:

"I move on ahead of the group into a small chapel, to find that here is the entrance to Gregory's prison, so I decide to attempt to climb down into it. I stretch across the entrance to put my feet on the sturdy steel ladder, then lower myself nervously to the bottom – finding a vaulted chamber (now a chapel), rather than a well. The upward climb is harder, pulling myself vertically upward using the handrails – I'm glad to emerge again safely!"

This part of the country was rich arable land, covered with vineyards and orchards, studded with villages which had been too long under Soviet rule to be pretty, but which were enhanced by vines climbing over their ugly concrete verandahs. However, as we climbed into the Lesser Caucasus mountains again, the orchards and gardens gave way to bare grassy slopes thick with wildflowers (and beehives). For a time we followed the main road to Iran, close to the sensitive border with Azerbaijan's Naxcivan province, amused to see innumerable roadside stalls selling home-made wine in old Coca-Cola bottles, to aid Iranian smugglers hoping to import wine into their strictly teetotal nation. In the heart of the Lesser Caucasus, we turned into a narrow gorge lined with cliffs carved into clusters of caves. Here we stopped for another typical Armenian lunch (once again the feast of salads and wild herbs, which we had enjoyed throughout the country), before visiting the 13th century Noravank Monastery, hidden away in an almost inaccessible valley:

"The location is superb – hemmed in by sheer walls of grey and red cliffs, high above the valley floor. A grand doorway leads into a large porch, then up a steep flight of steps to the main church. Two more chapels flank this one, but most impressive is the fourth building. Unusually it is two storeys high, with magnificent carvings and a terrifyingly narrow double stairway leading to the upper floor, which clings to the outside of the facade."

The road we were following was part of an ancient trading route, once marked with caravanserais every 12km (the distance a loaded camel could travel in a day). Climbing the hairpin bends of the Selim Pass (2400m), we stopped to visit two of them: first the isolated Suleema caravanserai, looking like a Nissan hut from outside but inside a masterpiece of stone vaulting which had survived attack and earthquakes since the 13th century; then the more often-visited Orbelyan caravanserai, built in 1332 almost at the top of the pass, and heavily restored in 1959:

"Inside we duck through a very low entrance to find a long hall with a gully in the centre for rain which might fall through the three roof-lights. The animals would have slept on platforms either side, feeding from troughs cut into the black basalt stone of the walls, whilst merchants would have spread their mattresses and carpets inside two long arcades, set back into the rear of the chamber."

At the top of the Pass a few shepherds grazed their flocks on a grassy plateau, while a group of people wandered across the meadows with heads down and hands clutching bags – Laura told us that they were collecting the fresh herbs served up at most meals in Armenia. Finally we reached a vast stretch of blue water, Lake Sevan (80km x 30km), and the run-down Soviet holiday resort where our hotel was located, picturesquely perched on the lakeside … amid swarms of voracious mosquitoes!

Next day we headed for the border with Georgia, passing former Soviet industrial plants squeezed into narrow gorges amid the mountains, most abandoned when the USSR collapsed (leaving thousands out of work). In Alaverdi, a massive copper factory once employed 6000 of the town's total population of 10,000: many had now left to seek work in Georgia, leaving a ghost-town squatting around the rotting structures of the plant. Nearby, Laura had one last monastery to show us: Haghpat, built as a centre of learning between the 10th and 13th centuries, and again hidden among the narrow, tortuous valleys of the Lesser Caucasus. It was a large complex of black stone chapels and other monastery buildings, including a massive echoing audience hall, intended to be used mainly for political meetings rather than religious ceremonies.

As we reached the Georgian border, we were obliged to walk several hundred metres between the two sets of border control buildings, just as a torrential thundershower struck, leaving us soaked to the skin. We picked our way through a maze of huge puddles and trucks parked up as they completed their paperwork, leaving our Armenian guide and driver behind as we sought out their Georgian counterparts on the far side of the border. This was possibly the most unpleasant border crossing I have made in my life – especially since, in the chaos of trying to tow a suitcase, shelter under an umbrella and keep my passport dry, my camera slipped from its case and was lost, along with all my photos of Armenia. Fortunately, the tour had been so tightly managed that almost everyone had similar photos on their cameras, and I was able to copy them for my own memories. Finally (and rather tearfully on my part) we boarded our new coach for the journey to Tbilisi, capital of Georgia:

"I'm amazed by Tbilisi – it is clearly so much richer than Yerevan! Its site straddling the wide Mtkvari River is dramatic, and some buildings sit atop a high cliff by the river. Many of the historic buildings have been properly restored, and the city is dotted with eye-catching examples of ultra-modern architecture. As evening draws on, much of the city is illuminated and music blares from innumerable cafes and bars – a real night-life community, full of energy and life."

My first experience of Tbilisi was the frustration of trying to find a camera shop … asking any passing citizens who spoke a few words of English … being directed to a shop, to find that it sold only inappropriate professional apparatus. Next day I left the group to start their sightseeing without me, following hints and suggestions of where I might find a tourist-sized handy camera. I successfully negotiated the metro system to reach a huge 4-storey market, wandering through the lines of stalls seeking the recommended store … to discover that it also sold only professional cameras. Finally someone directed me into the market's basement, to a tiny booth selling mobile phones plus a choice of just three small cameras. I had to wait for the battery to be charged, meanwhile seeking out a money-change since they did not take credit cards; then find another tiny booth selling camera cases; another to buy a spare battery; yet another stall supplying memory sticks so that I could copy a fellow-tourist's Armenian photos (all negotiation achieved by gestures and a few simple words of English) – but eventually I was once more a fully equipped tourist!

Now I could focus on city sightseeing in Tbilisi, using my guidebook and its maps to seek out the principal attractions. Of course, to understand historic architecture, it is necessary to understand a bit of national history … but in

Georgia, it seemed much simpler than in Armenia. Their Golden Age lasted for less than 200 years, from the late 11th to 13th centuries, and the star of the period was a king called David the Builder – many of the country's most memorable structures seemed to have been built during his reign. Tbilisi was burned to the ground by invading Persians at the end of the 18th century, but a few years later was annexed by Tsarist Russia and rebuilt. Georgia remained fairly prosperous (though not content) under Soviet Russian rule, but everything went wrong for them after the collapse of the USSR. The 1990s were extremely dark years of intense corruption and unfettered crime, continuing until the Rose Revolution of 2003 which drove out their corrupt President and opened up the country to new investment.

Keen to start exploring the city, I launched across the river into the old town, fascinated by cobbled streets running steeply uphill, lined with traditional houses, their facades adorned with Tbilisi's iconic wooden balconies. In some places these homes were beautifully restored, though in many side streets I saw houses which had not yet been renovated and still sat in crumbling Soviet-era style, draped with electric wires and rusty gas pipes. I approached one impressive church but could not visit since the entire floor inside had been removed in a massive restoration project. Nearby stood the ancient Anchiskhati church, dark and atmospheric with massive stone pillars and thick walls, decorated with colourful murals but blackened by centuries of candle-smoke and now cluttered with innumerable icons. Finally I discovered another large church lying in a sunken plaza below the main street:

"Descending and entering, I realise that I have found the city's most important monument – Sioni Cathedral, the only Tbilisi church allowed to operate in Soviet times. It is large and gaudy, full of icons and with a gleaming silver altar wall. Every inch of ceiling and walls is brightly coloured with frescoes, including an image of the Virgin and Child set against a golden background."

In the old town, I encountered the rest of our group with our guide (Makka), so joined them as they moved on to the newer part of the town to visit the Georgian History Museum – memorable particularly for the displays of gold from ancient Colchis. Now I realised that Georgian history was not quite as simple as I had thought, since the western part of the country (known in ancient times as Colchis) formed a powerful kingdom lasting for over a thousand years until the 1st century BC, and is even thought to have been home to the legendary Golden Fleece:

"The gallery is darkened so that the illuminated showcases of gold or silver jewellery and tableware, sparkle and shine. The exhibit ranges from rings and hairpins dated 3000 BC, up to dishes from 400 AD. Most impressive are the treasures from the 4th century BC tomb of a Colchis lady, including a gold diadem from which two huge pendants dangle – she must have had perfect posture for them to hang correctly!"

Most of the rest of the museum felt predictable and uninteresting (especially in contrast to Yerevan's excellent museum), until I reached the top floor exhibition of Soviet Occupation (only opened in 2009). Where Armenia's museum had diplomatically avoided this period, Georgia was brutally honest:

"All around the walls are black & white photo portraits of those who died between 1921-26 in the 'predetermined extermination of the elite of Georgian society'. Another list names 83 priests who died, including one shot as recently as 1984 – and there is space ready for the next victim. The last exhibit is a map showing the two regions currently disputed, marked with the words 'Occupation Continues'. No wonder relations with Russia are strained!"

Tbilisi offered a vibrant mixture of old and new architecture, from the super-modern, glass and steel Peace Bridge to the historic Nariqala Fortress perched high above the town on a knife-edge of rock. I ascended the hill via a smooth modern cable car, but then had to struggle up a slippery gravel track to reach the battlements. Later in our tour, we returned again to Tbilisi for a few hours extra sightseeing, giving me a chance to walk into the gorge below the fortress, past the slightly unsavoury-smelling Sulphur Baths (though I had no time to sample the hot springs there) and into the cool leafy promenades of the Botanic Gardens, alive with birdsong.

I had enjoyed Tbilisi, but it was time to head off to see what else Georgia could offer. We started with another important church – the 11th century cathedral at Mtskheta with its miraculous shrine to St Sidona. When we visited, the shrine was surrounded by pious women kneeling to kiss it or rub it with hands which they then wiped over their faces for blessing. Every wall and ceiling of the church was coloured with vibrant blue, red and gold frescoes, though it was hard to stop and stare at them because of the huge crowds of worshippers and (mostly domestic) visitors. High on a promontory above the town, we visited the small chapel of the Holy Cross (Jvari), unchanged since it was built in the 6th century, with an amazing dome which soared 22m above the nave – no-one now knew how the early architects managed to build such a structure.

The crowds of domestic tourists accompanied us also to our next visit, the cave town of Uplistsikhe. In the 15th century BC, 700 caves were carved out of limestone cliffs as a pagan religious centre, transformed into a Silk Road trading complex and monastery when Christianity arrived in the 4th century AD. The town was abandoned after attacks by the Mongol leader Tamerlaine in the 14th century, and the caves themselves were badly damaged by a huge earthquake in 1920:

"Ahead is a jumble of rocks, worn into channels and holes. Then suddenly we find ourselves in a series of open-fronted rooms linked by stone doorways. They could be just simple cave rooms, till we look up and see beautifully decorated stone ceilings, carved to look like the embossed wooden ceilings popular in the 2nd century AD. This was no primitive cave dwelling, but a fine city mansion!"

The whole site was a vast warren of caves, stairways and tunnels where I could have spent hours exploring, but sadly we had no time. However, further west we visited another cave town carved into the walls of a gorge in the Lesser Caucasus mountains: Vardzia – this time created as a secret military installation in the 12th century. 100 years later a massive earthquake ripped away the cliffside, destroying all but 500 of the original 3000 caves and crumbling the front walls of those remaining. Since it was no longer a hidden garrison, the soldiers abandoned it, leaving it to be settled by monks until they were driven out by invading Turks in the 16th century. Since Georgian independence in 1991, it was under restoration and a few monks had even returned to re-occupy the caves:

"We do not see even half of this complex – Makka is fearful for our safety since many of the steps and paths are worn and rough, or still under restoration. Metal stairways lead from one level to the next, since the original stone stairways are now almost worn away. We defy Makka to follow a narrow gravel track leading to what looks like a niche set in the rock – it turns out to

be a lovely little frescoed chapel, still in use with candles set on its altar."

Having seen the Colchis gold in Tbilisi's museum, I was excited to drive into the far west of Georgia to Kutaisi, once capital of the Colchis kingdom. We travelled along the country's main highway, following first the valley of the Kura River, then through a tunnel into the valley of the Rioni River – together forming the line dividing the Lesser and Greater Caucasus Mountains. The road itself was constantly busy with trucks from every corner of Europe and the Middle East ... and impatient cars which forced their way past them, whether or not it was safe to overtake! By the roadside were stalls selling locally produced fruit and vegetables; bread and honey; pottery and carved wood; sometimes wickerwork hammocks and chairs (perhaps intended for tourists heading towards the Black Sea resorts?). Finally we reached Kutaisi, but there seemed to have been little investment in this city and most of the structures were poorly maintained and shabby, with stucco facades and ornate wrought iron balconies just crying out for restoration.

Makka had not intended that we spend much time in the city itself, instead visiting various sites nearby – but fate took a hand. On the morning after our arrival, our driver spotted a large stone stuck in his tyre and, after much hacking at it with a screwdriver and then an axe (!), decided he must seek professional help. Meanwhile we set off on foot into the town centre to visit Bagrati Cathedral, burned virtually to the ground by invading Turks in the 16th century and left in ruins until Soviet Georgia decided to rebuild it in the 20th century. The restoration was finally completed in 2011 – accompanied by great controversy because of the modern materials and constructions used. Still killing time, I wandered through the Farmers' Market, packed with women selling cherries and cheese, potatoes and herbs, then discovered the newly-restored Synagogue, beautifully decorated with patterned walls and ceiling – I was only allowed inside after I had bought a cup of tea and a piece of home-made cake in the attached cafe (Jewish business sense?).

With our coach still out of action, we were organised into hastily hired minibuses to visit the Prometheus Caves, only discovered in 1984 and comprising 25km of caverns in total. Just over 1km was opened to the public in 2011, with more planned to be made accessible in future:

"The caves are amazing! We enter through a man-made entrance – a low secret portal leading into a long corridor. Soon the caves open up to reveal

their full glory: immense cathedrals with soaring roofs, weirdly shaped stalagmites, curtains of stalactites. Our path climbs up and down over piles of rock, squeezes through narrow passageways from one vast hall to another, descending into the depths of the complex where an underground river flows, then ascending towards the roof on a stairway which floats over the abyss."

Next day, with our coach finally restored to us, we made our way to the tiny Motsameta monastery, deep in a thickly forested valley, perched above a gorge carved out by a rushing green river. This monastery was recently renovated (in 2013), so worshippers could again walk through a short vaulted tunnel beneath the shrine housing the skull of David the Builder: a sign stated, in English, 'no foreigners' – this particular blessing was reserved for Georgians! Then on to Gelati Monastery – a cluster of medieval structures founded by David the Builder (who is also buried there) and once a major centre of scholarship, located in a remote valley where the scholars could work without disturbance. The whole compound was hidden behind a long wall, almost invisible as we approached:

"The site is idyllic, a haven of peace as we enter through a low arched gateway. Ahead is a complex of old and new buildings, all constructed from golden sandstone which glows in the bright sunlight, the blotchy green tiles of their roofs gleaming with reflected light. The lush grass underfoot is mirrored by rich green forests around us, emphasizing the sense of escape from a hectic world into unhurried tranquillity."

Inevitably, Georgia's twin mountain ranges dictated that we would have to retrace our steps once more along the road running between them – though this time we stopped to visit Gori, birthplace of Stalin. Whereas most of the world remembers him as a brutal tyrant, this little town still had some fond memories of their most famous son, so (in 1957) they created the world's only Stalin Museum – an imposing baroque building with marble stairways, erected around the tiny, very simple home in which he was born. Most of the museum celebrated his life and achievements, but since Georgian independence they had also recognised the brutality of his reign – in the basement was a reconstruction of a cramped prison cell and a darkened room reminiscent of the interrogation rooms of Stalin's secret police, together with the names of some of those sent to Gulag camps in Siberia.

Of course, my main goal was to see the Caucasus Mountains, so I especially enjoyed the nights we spent in mountain resorts. First, we visited the out-of-season ski resort of Bakuriani located at 1800m in the Lesser Caucasus:

"Dumping my suitcase at the hotel, I immediately head off into the hills. An eagle rises out of the trees to inspect me, then soars off easily across the meadows; a cuckoo calls from the trees – the only sound except for the buzz of insects. The path climbs through meadows exquisite with flowers: buttercups, rich purple orchids, pale pink sorrel and tiny mauve violas, then finally peters out in an open alpine pasture, leaving me knee-deep in the foliage of myriad plants I have no hope of identifying."

Later we turned into the Greater Caucasus, following the Georgian Military Road – originally built by Tsarist Russia, then rebuilt by German PoWs during WW2. One of only two roads running through the mountains to the Russian border, it was kept open year-round – but for foreigners only, in a special agreement designed to allow Armenia access to supplies from Russia. We stayed in the ski and climbing centre of Gudauri, surrounded by large flocks of sheep and goats brought up for the summer by nomadic shepherds, but unpleasantly located directly on the busy and noisy main road leading to Jvari Pass (2395m). Next morning we woke to the sound of heavy rain ... just on the day when we were due to make an excursion on foot into the mountains! Our intention was to walk up to the little Gelgeti chapel, from which it might have been possible to see Mount Kazbegi (5033m), second highest in the country:

"I scramble up a rough trail leading through pine forest, then silver birch, until I emerge on an open grassy plain at 2200m, churned into deep mud by 4x4 vehicles. Here the weather makes itself felt – heavy rain is pushed into every gap in my raingear by a strong breeze. I am soaked in no time but plod on towards the squat stone church perched on the far side of the meadow. Briefly some of the cloud roll backs from the snowy peaks around us – what a spectacular location this must be ... on a good day!"

Typically, as we headed east next day, the mountains became ever clearer until finally we were rewarded with magnificent views of snow-capped ranges and peaks: at least we did see the Greater Caucasus, even if not on the day when our walk was planned!

"The cloud rolls back progressively from the entire chain of the Greater

Caucasus, seemingly so close ... just on the other side of the valley. First, green hilltops poke above the cloud, then summits spattered with traces of snow, and finally some of the true snow peaks – gleaming sharp and clear in the evening light. Mountain ranges fill our view as we settle to an al-fresco dinner on the terrace of our guesthouse, the evening sun catching each peak in turn, then releasing it again into hazy gloom."

Now we were travelling into the Khakheti region, stopping at a traditional 'marani' to learn about Georgia's unique method of wine production. After pressing the grapes, the juice (skins included) is poured without any additives into huge, pointed clay jars (quevri) holding up to 75,000 litres, loosely sealed with a glass stopper for the first 3 weeks, then sealed tight with wood and clay for 6 months (for white wine) or a year (for red wine). During this time, the wine filters itself, the skins sinking to the bottom of the jar where they can be harvested to make 'chacha' (schnapps). The fermented and filtered wine is progressively removed, using some and storing the rest in ever-smaller jars (making sure each time that the new jar is totally full, and therefore free of air, before re-sealing). Of course, we were offered samples of this quevri wine – some of the most delicious wine I have ever tasted. How I wish that I had been able to carry more of it back home with me! This fertile region offered lots of good things to eat, too. Our guesthouse provided a luscious breakfast with home-made strawberry jam and creamy yoghurt, before we explored the tempting displays of Telavi market:

"Fruit stalls laden with peaches and apricots, green plums and red or white cherries. Vegetable stalls presenting a riot of colour with massive tomatoes, small yellowish cucumbers, perfectly formed potatoes, onions and peppers. Yellow mushrooms, fresh herbs and shiny purple aubergines complete the show. Then there are displays of nuts – walnuts both in their shells and out, almonds and hazelnuts. Old water or Coke bottles are filled with honey or chacha, fresh round cheeses are piled high. Everywhere the stallholders respond to my smile with the greeting 'Gamar Joba' (good morning)."

One last border saw me towing my suitcase again from one control point to the next (though without rain this time), and I was into Azerbaijan, following the ranges of the Greater Caucasus as they faded from high peaks into thickly forested hills. Azerbaijan had a completely different atmosphere to the other two countries in the Caucasus region – predominantly Muslim instead of passionately Christian; looking south into the Middle East for influences instead of yearning to be recognised as part of Europe; a huge diaspora population (mostly living in Iran) but not dependent on their contributions to support the national economy. In fact, the biggest difference was in national wealth, since Azerbaijan was one of the first countries in the world to exploit reserves of oil: initially from wells close to the city of Baku but, from the 19th century onwards, also taking oil and gas from the Caspian Sea. Surprisingly, my first sight of the country implied a lack of investment in the countryside with simple homes and potholed, broken roads – though our Azerbaijani guide tried to tell us that the central government was ensuring that all parts of the country would benefit from oil wealth.

Nestled among the forests was our first destination: Sheki, once capital of an independent Khanate. The town was an interesting mixture of sanitised and restored ancient monuments (including two caravanserais now transformed into tourist hotels) alongside ruined, abandoned buildings and family homes still strung round with wires and pipes as they were in Soviet times. However, the highlight of our sightseeing was the tiny summer palace of the Khan, just 6 rooms built in 1762:

"Inside the main reception room is a riot of colour: one wall is made of stained glass which glows as sunshine pours through; other walls are painted with busy ornate designs – such a variety that they are overwhelming! Upstairs is the women's accommodation: another highly decorated room with stained glass windows. The floor is plain but would originally have had a mirrored carpet to reflect the floral designs on the ceilings – there would have been no relief to rest your eyes!"

Though I will not forget this gaudy jewel of a building, my memories of Sheki also include the many friendly faces – one man even stopped his car to ask me where I came from, and both adults and children were delighted when I responded to their greetings with the local phrase 'Salaam'. The waiters in my lunchtime restaurant were so helpful, mustering whatever English words they could dig from their memories, to assist me in choosing my food:

"I deliberate over the menu, so picturesque in its English translations (the soups are described as 'watery meals'). Finally I decide on a local speciality: 'Piti', served in a thick pottery mug. I need to enlist the aid of the waiter to

know how to eat it, learning that the richly flavoured lamb broth is drunk first, with bread, then the mug is tipped out into a dish to reveal lean pieces of lamb tail and chickpeas ... and a few massive chunks of pure mutton fat, which should be mushed into the stew. I cannot face that, so put them back into the mug."

As we drove onwards towards Baku, the roads and the quality of the housing improved – clearly the country's wealth was focused on the capital. The landscape was transformed from forested mountains to rolling wheat fields and vineyards (producing wine mainly for export, though Azerbaijan seemed relaxed about the regulations of their Muslim faith), and then to desolate barren wastelands studded with oil derricks. We made a stop to view the sparkling new mosque in Shamaxi, with its massive prayer space and immense mihrab, sparkling with gold and turquoise tiles – an impressive show of wealth (though empty of worshippers).

This profligate spending on architecture continued in Baku – a bus station in the shape of the Titanic; three blue-glass office buildings in the shape of flames (reflecting Azerbaijan's nickname 'Land of Fire'); a shopping mall in the form of a lotus flower; the smooth curves of the Heydar Aliev cultural centre, supposedly representing the waves of the Caspian Sea. There was also an attempt to preserve the city's architectural heritage with heavily restored palaces and mosques, together with the ancient Maiden Tower fortress and 4th century Zoroastrian Fire Temple, all enclosed within 12th century city walls. My biggest disappointment was the Caspian Sea – from the promenade along its shores I looked out over water smeared with the rainbow hues of oil seeping from leaky wells just offshore, and even orange clumps of smelly oil residue. No pleasant beaches or seabirds to watch here! However, Baku was a lively city, especially since it was preparing to host the first Azerbaijan Formula 1 Grand Prix – the streets were being progressively closed down, and the cafes on the promenade were full of team mechanics watching two of the drivers (Button and Hamilton) frolicking in the bucket of a JCB digger.

On my last night, I sat with a beer in a sidewalk cafe watching the passing crowds: what a contrast from the subdued atmosphere of my first evening in Yerevan, just two weeks earlier:

"There is no sign of traditional or even modest Muslim dress here – the

young women wear T-shirts and tight jeans or short skirts, the young men sports shirts and jeans; there are high heels for women, leather casuals or sneakers for men. Teenagers cluster in large groups; little children suck on ice-creams as they wobble across the square on their trikes; a few older boys self-consciously smoke hubble-bubble pipes in the cafes."

Azerbaijan - Baku

Armenia - Geghard Monastery

Tibet - Earth Forest

Tibet - Mt. Kailash

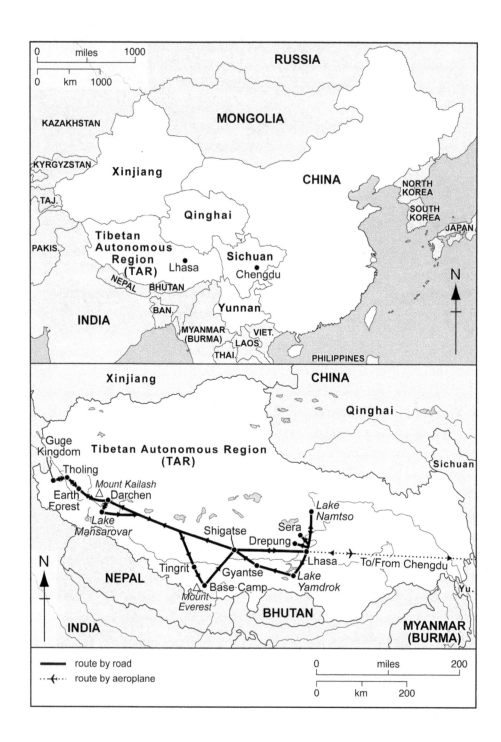

Tibet (October 2016)

AT LAST! FOR SO MANY years I had been tasting Tibetan culture in Nepal, Bhutan, Yunnan ... but Tibet itself had always seemed out of reach – difficult to access and prohibitively expensive. By 2016 I decided to wait no longer – but all the brochures I consulted offered only quick glimpses of the country, usually just a week-long dash from Lhasa to Everest Base Camp. Clearly, I was going to have to organise the trip myself, so I found a guidebook, noting all the sights which caught my interest. Next step was to trawl the internet for a reliable tour operator to organise everything for me – I was seeking a local Tibetan, rather than a Chinese company. I finally started communication with a tour operator in Lhasa, though I did not know until I actually arrived in the country, whether I was really communicating with a genuine business or just an internet scam! Together we worked out a month-long itinerary which took me far beyond the normal tourist routes. I busied myself acquiring a visa for China, while my tour operator handled the extra visa to be allowed to enter Tibet (and all the necessary permits to travel around the region – Tibet is tightly regulated by the Chinese). The Tibet visa could not be posted outside China, so I arranged to spend one night at a hotel in Chengdu (which is in China but outside Tibet) and the visa was sent there. What a relief to arrive after a long flight, to find a battered envelope waiting for me at hotel reception – my precious permit was inside ... next day I was allowed to fly into Lhasa to meet my guide and start my tour!

I had deliberately requested four nights in Lhasa to allow for acclimatisation in one of the lowest parts of Tibet (though at 3656m/ 11,990ft,

Lhasa is one of the highest cities in the world) before touring at altitudes over 5000m. I stayed in a small, family-run hotel in the heart of the old city, built around an indoor courtyard traditionally decorated with painted woodcarvings. Room doors were locked from the outside by massive shiny brass padlocks and from the inside by a wooden bar (just as Tibetan homes are secured). I was delighted with my accommodation, though the first nights at altitude were difficult: hard to sleep with pounding heart and frequent nausea. However, my wonderful young guide Tashi understood my difficulties and was happy to conduct all my Lhasa sightseeing at a gentle unhurried pace (even providing wet wipes when the nausea turned to sickness in a quiet side-street). Already on my first evening, I was determined to explore my surroundings:

"Most streets are totally dark, until I pass through the police X-ray machine into the Barkor – the main street which surrounds Lhasa's most sacred temple: brightly lit with warm yellow lighting and still crowded with pedestrians at 9pm, all walking clockwise around the temple in a 'kora' (pilgrimage). Some walk briskly, muttering prayers with a string of beads or spinning a prayer wheel; others amble and chat. A few are laboriously prostrating themselves, one body-length after another – some still with energy and enthusiasm, others clearly with aching back and sore knees."

The Barkor kora continued day and night, a constant source of fascination whenever I had spare time to watch – young and old walking together, some dressed in western clothing, but most ladies wearing traditional striped aprons and many men in Tibetan tunics with extra-long sleeves. Sometimes I would spot a nomad lady with her hair plaited into thin strips woven together at their ends to make a veil encasing the back of her skull, a heavy amber bead perched on her forehead and an equally heavy silver belt around her hips. It made a peaceful scene of devotion, but clearly one which evoked fear in the Chinese authorities – Tibet's religion has been at the heart of struggles for independence, and their monks have traditionally been the most fervent revolutionaries. Troops of armed police and non-Tibetan army cadres with riot shields regularly patrolled through the crowds, usually striding firmly against the clockwise flow (presumably a deliberate act of defiance?).

Official sightseeing in Lhasa began with a visit to Jokhang Temple, at the heart of the Barkor. Its status as the most important place of worship in the country was evident from the hubbub of pilgrims prostrating themselves at the temple gate. It was good to see such devotion: during the Cultural Revolution (1966-76) worship was forbidden and the army used this temple as a storehouse. Only in the 1980s was it reopened and restored – in the eyes of the Chinese government only as a historic monument, but in the eyes of the Tibetan people as the heart of their faith. We entered the first stone-paved courtyard, its walls painted with well-preserved murals, then the principal temple with its 600-year-old paintings and imposing statues – many representing Bodhisattvas (saints who assist humankind, as Tashi explained). There were many more temples to come during my tour, so I was relieved that Tashi chose to ration his explanations into digestible chunks (especially as my head was still spinning with altitude).

Next morning the sightseeing picked up a little in pace, with a visit to the Potala Palace – originally built in the 7th century by Tibetan kings, but taken as official residence by the 5th Dalai Lama (in the 17th century) when he assumed political as well as religious control of the country. Officially the Chinese considered the Potala to be a museum, but they were nervous that many Tibetans would want to treat it as a temple and spend hours venerating the current (exiled) Dalai Lama there. Consequently there was a strict system of timed tickets – we had to enter at our specified moment and move at a steady pace through the buildings, registering at timed checkpoints along the way to ensure that we did not dally:

"Flight after flight of very steep and dark stairs lead to a courtyard between the white and red palaces. Inside the white palace are beautifully painted chambers with carved wooden doorways – quiet rooms where the Dalai Lama would have reflected on the affairs of the world with his tutor. The red palace contains a warren of passages and terraces with multiple chapels – one actually located in a cave (though with plastered and painted walls). The air is filled with the scent of Tibetan incense ... and everywhere are boxes to collect money from the faithful, used to feed and house the monks."

My ticket allowed plenty of time for a tourist's view of the building, though I would have liked to linger longer in one of the final chapels, housing a line of funeral 'stupas' (shrines) for the Dalai Lamas. Tashi explained that ordinary Tibetans normally used sky burial (exposing the remains on a hillside site, to be taken by the birds), though anyone with a diseased body was 'buried' in running water which would eventually take them to the holy Ganges River. Minor religious leaders (like abbots) were given 'fire burial' (cremation) and their ashes preserved inside a stupa. Only the greatest religious leaders (the Dalai Lamas and Panchen Lamas) were buried intact inside a stupa, their bodies sitting on salt to dry them, encased in preservative herbs, then covered with precious metals studded with jewels – the stupa of the important 5th Dalai Lama included 3700 kilos of gold!

Later in the day we moved on to Sera Monastery, just outside Lhasa – one of the most important centres of Tibetan learning, and also heavily involved in recent Tibetan rebellions. Tibet had a long history of independence, equalling China in terms of power at one time, which came to an end when China annexed the country in 1950. Initial protests peaked in 1959 when the Dalai Lama was forced to flee to India, while Sera Monastery (and many others) were bombed, and many hundreds of monks killed. Protests and revolts continued, until unrest in 2008 (timed to coincide with the Beijing Olympics) brought hundreds of monks from Sera and two other nearby monasteries marching into Lhasa: many Tibetans were killed in the backlash, and many Chinese settlers in Tibet also lost their lives. Tashi was careful not to tell me too much of this saga whilst we were within earshot of police or local authorities (though I heard much more once we had left the major cities behind) – instead, he told me about Sera Monastery's tradition of daily debating sessions:

"We enter an enclosed gravel square shaded by huge trees. A great hubbub is rising from inside, where 30 or 40 pairs of monks are debating noisily. One of each pair sits on a padded cushion ready to answer, whilst the other stands – moving forwards with an energetic clap to announce his question. A few monks answer quietly, but many harangue back furiously. Wandering among the debaters is a tall, heavyset older monk – the master, ensuring that they are answering correctly: one pair who are enjoying themselves too much, are taken to task!"

One more day in Lhasa brought another religious centre: Drepung Monastery (another of those involved in the 2008 revolt) in the hills outside the city. Unfortunately, the only access road was completely blocked by roadworks, so we had to leave our driver behind and walk past deep excavations and massive earthmoving machines to the far side, where we managed to secure places squashed into the back of a communal minibus taxi. Once again, the temples were accessed by precipitously steep stairways (to make the devotion of pilgrims more worthy) and were filled with statues of Bodhisattvas (honoured by offerings of meat, milk and 'chang' barley beer), whilst other statues represented the different aspects of Buddha (with offerings limited to water, butter lamps and incense). At the feet of all the icons were donations of money, usually in small notes – in this monastery I noticed a huge bowl of 'small change' into which the pilgrims were dipping to change their larger notes, so they could distribute their donation evenly between the idols.

By now I was sleeping well and climbing the hotel stairs without too much puffing and panting: I was suitably acclimatised, and we could set off to explore more of Tibet. I had been hearing about Chinese oppression of Tibet, but immediately I could see that the Chinese government was also pouring money into the region: we started out on a smooth tarmac highway (built only in 2006) along the broad valley of Tibet's largest river (Yalung Tsangpo), where the land was covered with fields of barley and hayricks – this lower land was one of the few places in Tibet where crops could be grown. After a time, we turned off to climb in tight hairpins towards Gampa La Pass (4800m), high above the holy Yamdrok Lake, passing scenic laybys where crowds of Chinese tourists were eagerly photographing themselves beside large shaggy Tibetan mastiff dogs (called 'lion dogs' by the Chinese):

"Back and forth we travel in long switchbacks, crawling in a queue of traffic as we weave from side to side. Finally we reach the summit, marked by a jumble of prayer flags strung back and forth across the road. Below us, a long strip of water winds between the hills, muted blue where it lies beneath clouds but vivid turquoise where the sunshine strikes it. It's a spectacular view, marred only by a car-park full of gaudily decorated mastiffs and yaks, mobbed by excited Chinese photographers."

Descending to the lakeshore, we continued through tiny villages and past fields where farmworkers were harvesting the dry, thin grass with hand scythes, and herds of cattle were grazing: this was just about the altitude limit of cattle, which can survive up to 4000m – the higher land was the domain of yaks. I had been watching out for birdlife, seeing little until we reached the marshes at the end of the lake … where a group of Black-necked Cranes were striding elegantly through the grass – so rare in most of the world, yet common in Tibet at this time of year!

Another (higher) pass now awaited us – the Karo La (5045m), where we stopped to admire its glacier, largest in Tibet. Once again people were waiting in the car-park to profit from snap-happy Han Chinese visitors – no dogs or yaks this time, but instead pretty young nomad girls in traditional costume topped by fox-fur hats (their black yak-hair tents were dotted around the nearby hills). Descending back into farmland, we were surrounded by people harvesting barley, turning the mounds of stalks energetically, then tossing forkfuls high into the air to winnow in the wind, collecting the chaff as animal feed and sweeping up the falling grain. In the villages amid the fields, hanks of barley adorned the small towers on each corner of traditional house roofs (more usually topped by prayer-flags) – the first fruits of the harvest, offered to the gods. In one village Tashi took me to see a small water-powered barley mill where the miller was grinding pre-roasted grain brought in by farming families to make Tibet's staple food, tsampa.

Disappointingly, the night was spent in a western-style, Chinese-run hotel in the town of Gyantse, but next day started with a special treat – a visit to the family home of one of Tashi's friends in a nearby village. My hostess was a tiny wrinkled old lady (though questioning revealed that she was actually the same age as me – clearly life is hard for these village women) who pressed me to drink a cup of butter tea (so rich it was more like soup):

"We enter the yard, where pats of animal dung are drying on the walls of outhouses (for fuel) and tethered cattle are munching on hay, then pass through a thick curtain into a dark lobby, ascending a very steep wooden stairway to the family's living quarters. The walls of the 'lounge' are lined with cupboards; a large copper pot is filled with fresh water, fetched each day from a spring by the river. Off to one side is the family chapel, and on another side is a tiny kitchen with a dung-fuelled stove."

Eventually Tashi's friend made an appearance – a monk on holiday from Chalu Monastery nearby. Of course we had to visit this monastery too, once home to up to 7000 monks but now occupied only by 30. Inside Tashi showed me original wall paintings 800 years old, but so blackened from centuries of candle-smoke that they were impossible to interpret. There were no other tourists here at all, just a family prostrating themselves before the statues, and then another family bringing their new baby to be blessed: grandma holding the baby swaddled in a nest of sparkly wrappings while the parents were keeping an eye on their young son (dressed in his best Tibetan costume). Everywhere there were piles of money – not just in front of the statues but on the floor and stuffed into crevices. Tashi told me that the monks checked daily for large notes, but only took the small notes weekly or monthly (and never cleared the entire temple of offerings). The money was used for temple maintenance and also to finance the monastery school, free to students and providing them with three free meals a day. Parents in rural areas would choose whether to send their children to Chinese school, to monastery school (where they would learn only Tibetan language and traditions) or not to send them to school at all – despite a Chinese law which insisted that education is compulsory.

The rest of the day was a challenge to our driver Demshok, with roads now filled with scooters and pedestrians; dogs and cows; tractors towing loads of barley and heavily overloaded trucks – and the occasional supercharged impatient Landcruiser. As he drove on to the city of Shigatse, I could hear him chanting mantras under his breath to help him through! At first, I thought there would be nothing to interest me in Shigatse (Tibet's 2nd city) – I was left to my own devices in a bland Chinese hotel, while Tashi battled with bureaucracy to get the necessary permits for the rest of our journey. However, my guidebook mentioned a 'mini Potala Palace' in the old town, so I set off to trudge through the Chinese districts on pavements choked with parked vehicles; crossing dangerous junctions where vehicles were more concerned with forcing their passage than with avoiding pedestrians. However, it all seemed worthwhile when I entered the Tibetan enclave, where the streets were lined with tiny shops which spilled their wares out on to the street, and mini-cafes which served tea from huge thermos flasks. High above me was the mini-Potala fortress and just a little further on, I glimpsed Tashilhunpo Monastery. Despite my sore feet I decided to walk a little further, following rows of prayer wheels till I emerged on a grand pedestrianised avenue leading up to the monastery gate:

"But what's this? I'm ankle-deep in litter, and a wailing chant interspersed with drumming comes from ahead of me. I make my way through innumerable

picnicking families to a small crowd clustered around a makeshift stage where dancers dressed as animals are waving their arms and swaying in circles around stationary figures clothed in imperial costumes. Tashi later tells me that this is the rarely performed Tibetan Opera dance – how lucky I am to see it!"

I watched the dancing for a while, but eventually realised that the audience was more interesting: weather-beaten country women wearing their hair in decorated plaits wound around their heads, sipping butter tea together ... craggy-faced nomad men drinking beer and debating energetically ... grandmothers left in charge of the youngest children, while gangs of lively, smiling older children chased each other ... clusters of men and women, intent on noisy games of dice, gambling for beads or coins. Good memories of Shigatse after all!

Now we were leaving the usual tourist routes, heading west into a part of Tibet normally visited only by a few Han Chinese travellers. The roads were mainly well-maintained but now almost empty of traffic – though there were frequent checkpoints, both for our permits and my passport to be inspected, and also for speed. At each control, Demshok was given a slip of paper giving the earliest time he was permitted to cross the next control – frequently we ended up stopping just before the checkpoint to kill some time and avoid a fine! We followed meandering rivers through miles of khaki-coloured hills and wide acres of muted green grassland grazed by yaks, sheep and goats, beneath startlingly blue skies. Lunch was in a tiny local restaurant – notable for its very interesting toilet: just two slits over a long-drop, enclosed by a waist-high wall and gate. Why would it need a roof when the view stretched over yak pastures to imposing mountains?

"Suddenly we're climbing. The valley is quickly left behind and the hills close in around us, crumbling loess soil and stones threatening to engulf this intrusive strip of tarmac at any time. Demshok is chanting again! This is the Tsuo La (4160m), a challenging pass with its descent as steep (and as bumpy) as the ascent. Wrecked police cars have been planted at intervals by the roadside, one even with flashing blue lights, to scare the drivers into caution – what a good example of recycling!"

This was one of our longest travelling days, driving past occasional lakes and across more sparse pasture between brown hills dappled with sun and shade, every summit and ridge sharply etched in the crystal-clear air. All chat in the vehicle ceased for a while when Tashi produced some rings of dried cheese made by his mother – tasting pleasantly of curd, but so hard that they clogged our mouths for the 15 minutes or so until they dissolved! We climbed the Bang La (4710m) on another steep ascent of hairpins, once more accompanied by Demshok's Buddhist chant of 'Om Mani Padme Hum' – though less extreme passes warranted only a cheery song under his breath. The landscape grew ever more arid, the horizon now filling with snow-capped mountains as we crossed the Gye La (5089m):

"We creep up on the pass almost unawares from the high plateau where we have been driving, but a sweep of hairpins on the far side drops us into the valley far below. On the hillside I glimpse some elegant animals with ginger backs and cream underbellies – might they be rare Tibetan antelope? A closer look reveals that they are 'kiang' – wild donkeys (also quite rare) ... so much more graceful than our beasts of burden."

Finally we arrived in Saga, a small town existing mainly to service the needs of the nomadic people of the area, with bustling shops, fuel stations, hospital and post office – and a basic hotel for me, their only non-Chinese guest. Continuing westwards at ever higher altitude, the air grew chillier – now taking longer each morning for us to remove padded jackets, hats and gloves as the sun heated the day. The landscape was generally sparse, rolling grassland, with occasional zigzags of road as we climbed over mountain ridges on passes festooned with prayer flags. The meandering rivers transformed themselves first into rushing mountain streams, then into trickles of water which provided little nourishment for vegetation – yet still there were herds of yaks by the roadside, together with the black tents of their nomadic herders.

Our destination was the holy mountain of Kailash (6638m), sacred to both Buddhists and Hindus, as well as Jains and followers of Bon (the ancient Tibetan religion) ... and considered by all to be the 'Navel of the World'. I was keen to see the mountain, though I knew I would be unable to complete the 3 or 4-day kora around it – so instead I had planned a stay in the small town of Darchen, near the foot of the mountain:

"Will Kailash be visible? Yes! Totally clear! A huge block of sunlit, snow-covered rock rising serenely from a stony ridge. As we get nearer, the foothills

fall back to reveal the massive black wall which guards the peak of Kailash. A vertical strip, like a staircase, appears ever more clearly on the mountain's sheer snowy face. What a privilege to see this holy peak on the roof of the world!"

I had been nervous about accommodation in rural Tibet, warned that there would be few facilities and (more important to me) little privacy. In fact the guesthouse in Darchen was a favourable surprise. The rooms actually contained only 3 beds each, and there were so few guests that I had a room to myself, with piles of thick blankets to stack on top of my sleeping bag when the night grew cold, and the promise of electricity provided by generator for a couple of hours in the evening – enough to charge my camera batteries and light me to bed. There was even running water, though only from a cold, constantly-flowing pipe in the courtyard – but I was provided with a thermos of hot water and a plastic bowl from the kitchen, to wash myself. The town itself (located at 4575m) felt like the Wild West – a broad street lined with ramshackle shops which piled their wares outside, including buckets full of walking sticks and umbrellas, plus cooking pots for camping. I set out to explore, following a family setting off for their kora (carrying kettle, thermos, backpacks and a baby), till I reached the checkpoint at the start of the official route. I was stopped there, because I did not have the appropriate permit – there was a strong (though discreetly hidden) Chinese army presence in the area, because of its religious significance to Tibetans:

"As the sun sets, the main street fills with gorgeously dressed nomadic women wearing the striped outer garments I glimpsed earlier, fabulous shell belts and tinkling bells which make them sound like the sheep in their own flocks. Everyone gathers in the warmth of the last sunshine before night-time cold begins to bite."

Next day we set off towards the far south-west of the country, on what turned out to be the most scenically impressive day of the entire tour. Strange patches of colour began to appear in the pale beige rocks – indications of Tibet's rich mineral wealth:

"The scenery becomes ever more spectacular: landscapes made of crumbling conglomerate which have eroded into pinnacles and castles rising out of piles of eroded sand. Flashes of different colours become more dominant, until the entire hillside is an artist's palette of red, green, bluey grey,

bright yellow. We cross a nameless pass, and the colours intensify as we descend, culminating in swathes of white salt crusted on the shores of the tiny river at the foot of the pass."

As we climbed another ridge, an amazing view opened up – the entire horizon filled with a chain of snow-capped peaks: the Himalayas! We were travelling just a couple of valleys away from the mountain wall which had isolated Tibet from the rest of the world for so long. We came closer and closer, till I could see the sun glinting on the glaciers and could clearly make out the shapes of individual peaks (if only I knew which was which!). As if this was not enough, Tashi had been telling me that the highlight of the day would be the Earth Forest – but I had no idea what that might be? My guidebook did not mention it and I had never heard of it, so when we pulled off the road to take a look, I was taken completely by surprise:

"The entire range of brown Himalayan foothills seems to be carved into an ornate palace or hanging garden. I thought perhaps it may be just an eroded earth bank, but this extends for 10km – it's a wonder of the world! Rather like the Grand Canyon, the land is covered in a series of ridges, their flanks eroded by wind and water into vertical gullies, balconies or overhanging pelmets. More erosion has carved the summits into turrets or crenellations like a vast fortress, with features resembling whatever my imagination can conceive: the obvious bosoms and buttocks; Indian chiefs sitting in a row; stupas; dragons; tigers ..."

At the base of the Earth Forest lay our destination – the town of Tholing, just 50 km from the sensitive Indian border (and consequently location of multiple Chinese barracks). After days of hard travelling, my itinerary allowed for two relaxing nights here, in a monastery guesthouse which seemed the height of luxury with 24-hour electricity and two indoor toilets, plus a cosy carpeted bedroom. A basin in the corridor near my room provided only cold water – though again the kitchen provided a thermos of hot water and a plastic bucket for bathing. The town was mostly modern, with a large Han Chinese population, and I had time to indulge in a few western pleasures: fresh fruit (unobtainable in most of Tibet), an indulgent bar of chocolate and a packet of chips (from Tholing's version of the Golden Arches) ... even a trip to the hairdresser. That was quite an experience, since they had never dealt with western hair before – after a thorough massaging shampoo, the hairdresser worked hard with his dryer to remove all traces of my perm to create a smooth flat Chinese style.

It was good to have a chance to eat something different! Tibetan cuisine is not on the list of the world's gourmets, with its highlight being 'momo' dumplings – the steamed ones soft and tasteless (Tibetans accompany all their food with chilli sauce, which provides enough flavour for any dish), though I found fried momos more palatable, crisply cooked in very hot fat. Breakfast for Tibetans was often hot seasoned broth with noodles and tiny pieces of meat, or else the traditional tsampa – portions of barley meal and dried cheese crumbs, mixed with lots of sugar and butter tea (an earthy but pleasant flavour, though very rich). As a concession to me, many of our guesthouses served up an egg for breakfast – though I was equally happy with Chinese-style rice porridge ('congee'). In most places, I was content to take meals wherever Tashi and Demshok chose, eating the same food as them: usually a dish of rice mixed with potato (sometimes with a few slivers of strange pink carrot on top).

The purpose of travelling so far to the west was to visit the so-called Guge Kingdom (better called the Guge Citadel) – a fortress carved in the 9th century from a pillar of soft limestone rock, and home to the Guge kings, rulers of the western part of a divided Tibet until the 17th century. At the base of the rock were four small temples, perched one above the other, and here I finally understood what damage the Cultural Revolution had inflicted on Tibet. Tashi only knew about the events from his grandfather's stories, yet he was clearly still bitter – such irreplaceable damage, and all Mao could say was 'Sorry, I made a mistake'. How many generations will it take to heal these wounds?

"In these temples, the horrible destruction of the Cultural Revolution has not yet been repaired. Most religious buildings across the country have now been restored, but here I am shocked to see precious paintings scratched and defaced. Buddha-shaped outlines on the walls, surrounded by holes for pegs which once supported large statues, demonstrate where the figures were ripped away and smashed – though the faces of the gods have been rescued and are perched incongruously on piles of rubble, covered in money given by the faithful."

I followed Tashi upwards past innumerable small caves (once the homes of soldiers) and the ruined mud-brick shells of houses where the Guge officials had lived. Nearing the top, our path disappeared underground, continuing on steps carved inside the rock and illuminated by small holes from which the soldiers could keep watch in every direction. Finally we emerged into dazzling sunshine on the summit, surrounded by the ruined walls of the royal summer residences. I thought I had seen everything, but Tashi had more to show me:

"We plunge down a very steep staircase through the stony heart of the citadel: at first clutching a chain for support, then with a hand on the roof of the almost vertical passage. It leads to the king's winter palace – a series of rooms carved out of the rock, some totally dark and others lit by windows overlooking the valley. It's like a rabbit warren down here, with chambers of various sizes linked by low tunnels, one so low that I can barely waddle through, with my back scraping the ceiling. Then we have to get back out ... back up those steep stairs, using my hands to pull myself up into the sunshine once more."

There was only one road in this southern part of Tibet, so the next few days saw us inevitably re-tracing our steps across the nomads' pasturelands and the high passes – yet the scenery looked totally different because imminent winter had dusted the hills and even the roadsides with snow. Travelling through these isolated regions, Tashi could give me more information on the Tibetan view of Chinese rule. He told me that, since the 2008 revolt, there had been a conscious effort to preserve Tibetan culture – including the encouragement in schools and offices that their workers should wear traditional dress, eat traditional food and speak pure Tibetan (unmixed with Chinese) every Wednesday. However, I remained aware of the investment the Chinese government were putting into the country, with amazingly engineered roads, whole communities of new housing and, most importantly, hygienic toilet blocks in each village – traditionally Tibetans did not use toilets. I tried to ask Tashi why China was so keen to annexe Tibet, but he could not comprehend my question – he was so proud of his country, that he could not envisage anyone not wanting to seize it. Yet Tibet clearly has strategic importance for China, as well as being the source of a large proportion of Asia's water, and offering vast mineral reserves (including silver, gold and copper).

We reached Kailash once again, but did not return to Darchen – instead, we drove to the holy Lake Mansarovar to scramble up to the tiny but spectacularly located Chiu Temple, perched on a rock high above the lake. We followed a very rough path around the rock to a cave where the founder of the red-hat sect meditated in the 8th century. Clearly this cave was especially significant to Buddhists, since (for the first time) Demshok joined us in our visit, running his hands along the walls of the cave, then wiping the blessing on to his face. Tashi had planned for us to stay in the settlement below the temple: many of the guesthouses were already closed for the winter but finally we found one where we could stay – again in spartan accommodation: a small room with four bedsteads squashed together between peeling walls, with a long-drop toilet 400 yards away and electricity promised only for a couple of hours in the evening ...

"... but who cares, when we are just minutes away from the lakeshore? I pause only to don my woolly hat and thick padded coat (an icy wind is already blowing), then head off to watch the birds. On the water sits a large flock of ducks and several types of geese and gulls, while small birds chirrup in the bushes around me. I wish I could bottle this sense of tranquillity, but I sit on a rock and try to absorb memories which will soothe me to sleep when my busy life at home takes over again."

Back at the guesthouse I found my room dark and cold, so adjourned instead to the warm and cosy 'guest lounge' where a central stove was burning sheep dung (no – it doesn't smell!) and there was hot water to add to my teabags. There were few guests, though several locals dropped in – principally, it seemed, to charge their cell phones when the generator finally kicked in. A group of Chinese travellers arrived, struggling to make themselves understood with a landlady who spoke only Tibetan, but with Tashi's help they were soon settled. In the middle of the night more guests arrived – nomads about to start their kora of the holy lake, who had no money (or inclination) to sleep indoors and instead bedded down on the porch outside my room. When I woke in the night (for a call of nature) I found them snuggled inside their blankets and coated with fresh snow!

In the next days we returned to the main tourist routes as we turned south towards Mount Everest, joining the Nepal-China Friendship Highway – though it was very quiet since the Nepalese border was still closed after the appalling earthquake of 2015. This part of Tibet had also been affected by the quake and we passed several settlements in the area where the population were still living in tents while the Chinese government rebuilt their homes. Stopping for lunch in the village of Old Tingrit, I was so excited when Tashi casually said: 'That's Everest over there!' – a long, impressive snow-capped range, from which an almost triangular, snow-coated rock rose just a little higher than the other peaks.

Rather than take the new (longer) tarmac road to Base Camp, Tashi and Demshok enquired about the condition of the original gravel trail and decided to risk it. Unfortunately, there were major road repairs underway and we had to detour on to field paths, though Demshok seemed to drive with confidence, unerringly selecting a viable route from the choice of tracks. However, I was upset when Tashi began to talk about arriving too late to take the shuttle up to 2nd Base Camp – how could he be more concerned with staying on schedule than with showing me the Tibetan side of the world's highest mountain?

"I allow myself to become distressed that I won't see Everest up close, and my opinion of this track changes from 'an interesting taste of Tibet's old roads' into 'a bad choice of route'. But things become sweeter when we make a brief comfort stop – as I walk to the opposite side of the bus, I find myself in the middle of a colony of 'suslik' (prairie mice) which dart to their holes but then comically poke out their heads to watch me."

Back aboard our minivan, Tashi and I came to an agreement that if we were too late on arrival, we would make time to take the first shuttle in the morning. In fact, it was all a storm in a teacup! We arrived at the huge tourist camp located at 1st Base Camp, asked Demshok to claim bunks for us in one of the communal tents, then ran across the parking lot to board a battered old minibus, just ahead of crowds of other western and Chinese tourists arriving from Lhasa. It hurled itself up the gravel track, climbing a series of hairpins at such a speed that I was left clutching the seat in front to avoid being thrown into the aisle, then finally dropped us off at 2nd Base Camp (5200m/ 17,000ft):

"Tashi and I climb a short hill to the stupa from which I can look along the valley to Everest. The moraine at our feet is dusty and stony, but the mountain is impressive – especially the thickly snow-covered cirque which encloses the glacier. It looks only a short walk over the moraine to the ice, but I'm not trying it! The mountain itself resists such foolish thoughts with a freezing, powerful wind which blasts around me and makes it hard to stand upright."

Back at the vast tourist camp, we found our communal tent with bench-beds on three sides and a sleeping platform on the fourth – I was quick to grab a relatively private bench close to the tent door, then we (and a group of Chinese motorcyclists sharing our tent) settled in for a night snuggled around the central stove, beneath an electric light which burned until midnight when the generator was turned off. Emerging from the tent in the middle of the night, I found the wind had dropped away to leave an enchanting stillness, with Everest lit by a pale pearly glow from the full moon. Next morning I was up before dawn to watch the sunrise over the mountain, joining a cluster of Chinese photographers as the sun gilded first the summit, then the plume of spindrift snow blowing off the peak, then the western ridge and finally the vast snowfields on the mountain's flank – how exhilarating to watch a mountain waking from sleep!

We were among the first to leave next morning, taking with us a local man who needed a lift to the next village and a young Chinese cyclist who had managed to pedal to Base Camp but had now run out of energy and funds – he rode with us all day, silent and grateful on the back seat of our minivan. This time we followed the Friendship Highway all the way back to Shigatse, crossing the Ga'u La (5200m) on a series of wide hairpins encased in shiny new crash barriers (this part of the road was only completed a few months before my visit), stopping at a viewpoint to look out over five of the highest mountains in the world, before continuing back into the barley fields and busy villages of the more populated part of Tibet.

My itinerary included one more highlight, taking us north of Lhasa through areas of volcanic activity including the bubbling hot water streams of Nyemo Marshes, and large geothermal plants which provided power to Lhasa and sent hot water via gleaming insulated pipes to the nearby villages. For a time we followed a busy highway running parallel to the railway line planned to run from Lhasa to Shanghai, still a massive building project at the time – more examples of the money being invested by the Chinese government to reinforce their control of Tibet. My reason for including this area in the itinerary, however, was to visit Namtso Lake, another of the holy lakes of Tibet and one of the highest, at an altitude of 4718m. I walked along the lake shore towards a rocky buttress festooned with prayer flags – every crack and crevice of the rock contained a tiny chapel, each under the protection of nuns living in a simple nunnery nearby:

"A tiny, whitewashed building, hung with a red and gold frieze, is nestled behind a protective stone wall. Entering through two lobbies, I find myself in the heart of the rock – a cave transformed into a temple, its walls plastered with images of Bodhisattva saints and pictures of past Dalai Lamas (images of the current one are banned in China). A huge drum hangs in front of a bench with space for just 2 or 3 nuns to worship, and banks of butter lamps flicker beneath the walls."

Outside again, I walked back to our campsite as the evening sun illuminated the snowfields on the surrounding mountains and a bitterly cold wind grew in strength, ruffling the waters of the lake into large waves. All that remained of my tour was the return journey to Lhasa, its unique atmosphere now seeming commonplace after my weeks in the remote western parts of the country. Tibet had not disappointed me, and the privilege of seeing it with my own individual guide and driver had enhanced the experience into the trip of a lifetime.

Tibetan ladies

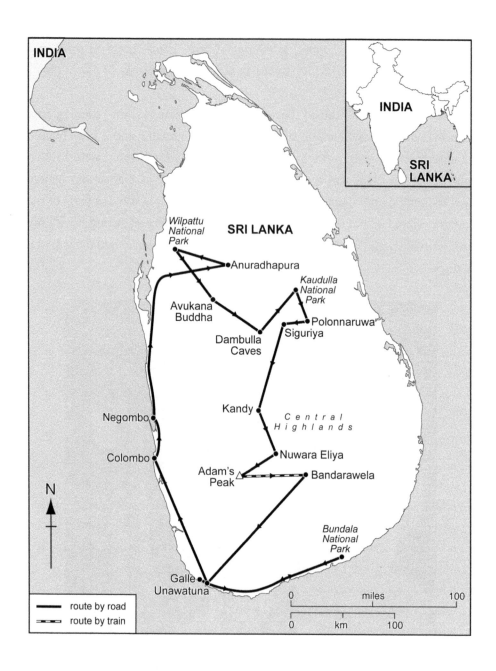

Sri Lanka (January 2017)

DURING MY CAREER AS A tour manager I had escorted several tours to northern India but had not felt comfortable amongst the Indian people I met there and so had never been tempted to explore the sub-continent further. Finally I decided it was time to overcome my prejudices – but perhaps to ease myself into the region with a visit to the island of Sri Lanka instead of India itself. The Sri Lankans proved to be delightfully friendly, their land and wildlife stunningly beautiful ... and I saw none of the abject poverty which plagues their Indian neighbours.

I arrived in the early morning at the seaside town of Negombo, immediately setting off to stroll on the beach beside our hotel, watching the fishermen's small canoes returning to shore. Nearby were piles of fish spread out to dry, thickly salted and netted to prevent the seabirds from stealing them, while in the heart of the town the markets were full of colourful fresh fish and exotic tropical fruits. Heading north along the western coast of Sri Lanka, I was stunned by the lushness of the vegetation – a symphony in every shade of green: vivid young shoots of rice in the paddies; rampant garden shrubs and creepers surrounding every cottage and villa; plantations of stately coconut palms (both the usual brown hairy variety and the smooth golden King Coconuts). In one place our guide, Upali, turned aside to show us a 'toddy plantation':

"We detour to a palm grove beside the beach which bears few fruits because the flowers have been prevented from opening with tight bands – these buds will instead be harvested for their sweet sap, which will be fermented into 'toddy' or used fresh to make sweets. The farmer uses coconut

husk steps to climb the trunk of one tree to reach the buds, then balances precariously across to the next trees on a network of ropes strung high above the ground."

The early part of our tour plunged us into the intricacies of Sri Lankan history. The Sinhalese people came originally from northern India, establishing their capital at Anuradhapura for over 1000 years (4th century BC – 10th century AD) – during which time the Buddhist religion was brought to the island. The kings of Anuradhapura were finally defeated by Hindu invaders from southern India, and after the invasion a new capital was established in Polonnaruwa for 200 years – again defeated by another invasion from southern India. A string of rival kingdoms followed, with 7 different warring rulers on the island by the 16th century when the coastal areas were invaded by the Portuguese. Their place was taken by the Dutch in the 17th and 18th centuries, who occupied the whole island except a small kingdom in the mountains around the city of Kandy. When the British arrived in the 19th century, they conquered the entire island – only giving independence in 1948. This story of repeated conquests left a string of historic sites around the island – which Upali was keen to show us.

First we visited Anuradhapura – a huge 500-acre site which was mostly (and thankfully) seen from the air-conditioned comfort of our coach, with Upali pointing out ruined palaces, ancient 'stupas' (shrines) and a pair of historic bathing pools (now filled with thick green water) as we drove past. However he insisted we must all descend from the coach to view the Samadhi Buddha: a limestone statue sitting serenely under a canopy amid the trees. Later we walked beneath the branches of a huge sacred Bo tree, where one spindly branch was supported by golden poles – supposedly a last vestige of the original tree, 2400 years old and now grafted to a younger tree to preserve it. We also visited the Isurumuniya Temple (oldest in the country), built around a group of massive rocks:

"A short flight of steep rock-cut steps leads to the top of the site – difficult to climb since we have been obliged to leave our shoes and hats at the entrance to the temple, so must now walk barefoot and bare-headed beneath the burning midday sun. We obediently follow the clockwise trail around the various holy sites, but with no reverence and little interest – except in trying to avoid stubbing our toes or twisting our ankles."

Poor Upali – he was so keen to show us everything, yet we were just too hot in this equatorial climate to produce any energy or enthusiasm. Finally he allowed us a rest at our hotel, but as the afternoon cooled there were no more excuses – we were off to Mihintale Mountain:

"This will be a challenge, but the first wide granite steps are shallow and easy to ascend. 100m from the top the problems start – we are now on holy ground and must remove our shoes: no more protection for our delicate western feet. The path is mainly a few scrapings of steps or tiny footholds, too slippery for socks so it has to be barefoot, clinging to the railings. The last steps are so high that I have to climb up on the railings themselves – but the views are fabulous!"

Fortunately, Sri Lanka is not only famous for its historic sites but also for its wildlife. Even as we toured the Buddhist relics of Anuradhapura, my eye was drawn to the fluorescent blue and orange of kingfishers flashing over the sacred pools, and close by the Isurumuniya Temple I was fascinated by a deep cleft in the rock from which issued a cacophony of squeaks and whistles – a colony of fruit bats was nesting inside. We also visited nearby Wilpattu National Park, with ponds where we saw innumerable wading birds (I loved the Woolly-necked Stork, jet black with a thick white neck as if wearing a woolly muffler) and huge crocodiles – I was amazed to learn that the island has no natural lakes: all are man-made 'tanks' created over the centuries since 440 BC, to manage the country's water supply. Upali was desperate to show us one of the 30 leopards which live in the Park, but we were unlucky in this – however, we did spot a rare Sloth Bear rootling around in the leaf litter seeking termites ... one of only 20 in the Park!

We turned southwards now, into the so-called Cultural Triangle in the heart of the island – more temples ... more history. The Avukana Buddha statue was an amazing sight, a huge stone figure standing over 12m high, carved into a cliff in the 5th century:

"The Buddha stands erect, his hair piled high in a topknot, his body sheathed in a flowing pleated robe. Going closer, the apparently free-standing statue is revealed to be actually part of the rock – the feet grow from the pedestal in a welter of tiny chisel marks; the back of the legs are clear, but from thigh to shoulder he is still attached to the cliff-face."

We travelled on through dense forest to the next cultural highlight – the

Dambulla Caves, carved and decorated by monks continuously from the 1st century BC almost until the present day. This time it was a joy to remove our shoes and walk on the cool polished floors of caves hidden away from sunlight by a modern gallery which enclosed their entrances. We started with the oldest temple, entering a narrow doorway leading to a cramped space almost entirely filled by a massive reclining Buddha statue ... then on to the largest cave, its ceiling and walls entirely covered with brightly coloured paintings dating from the 13th century (though often restored), its floor cluttered with multiple seated Buddha statues.

Perhaps Upali had got our measure by now because, after two serious cultural visits, we continued into Kaudulla National Park for more wildlife-spotting. At first all we could see were birds – including a huge Fish Owl and an even larger Fish Eagle (plus a beautifully marked bird unattractively named a 'Thick-knee') ...

"... but all that changes when we emerge from the forest into open grassland. In the distance is our first herd of wild elephants, feasting on lush grass, pulling up big tussocks and swinging them energetically from side to side to clean them before eating. As they move, clouds of insects rise from the disturbed grass – so the land around the herd is thick with egrets and the air above them with martins and bee-eaters, swooping and swirling as they join the feast."

Time for another dose of history as we visited the medieval capital, Polonnaruwa – once more wandering among ruined buildings, trying to find the coolest spots of shade from which to admire them. Though these ruins were much less ancient than Anuradhapura, they seemed to be no better preserved because the invading Hindu armies had smashed them in search of treasure. Upali led us around the Citadel, showing us the colonnaded Council Chamber set on a platform beautifully carved with elephants and lions, then allowed us a short time in the air-conditioned coach, before hustling us on to more temples. Nearby was the Rock Temple, again the work of ancient Sri Lankan artists – four massive Buddhas towering above us, carved out of a single huge boulder. This site should certainly have held our attention, if not for the unbearable increase in humidity as clouds covered the sky – sapping our energy and inducing relentless sweating.

Next day brought us to the iconic Sigiriya Lion Rock, mountain retreat of a prince after he had killed his own father to seize power in the 5th century. He was determined to enjoy all the luxuries of his position, laying out gardens around the base of the rock where hundreds of lovely ladies used to dance for his pleasure – and decorating the sheer cliffs with erotic paintings. On the virtually inaccessible summit of the rock, he built his palaces around a cistern to provide a water supply – and our next goal was to climb the rock to see them:

"Flight after flight of granite steps lead us up through terraced gardens, then up a spiral staircase to a steel walkway clinging to the cliff beside some of the few remaining exotic paintings – topless ladies with heavily made-up faces. Finally, the most difficult part of the ascent: for us, there are metal stairways with railings, but beneath us we can see the original tiny rock-cut steps, hanging above the abyss – the prince was carried up these in a palanquin. How nervous those servants must have been, fearful of dropping their lord and master!"

In miserable drizzling rain, we continued through thick forests into the mountainous heart of the country towards Kandy. It could have been a stunning drive, following a river gorge where houses were built out on stilts from the steep valley sides … but often the roadside was littered with the detritus of woodyards or rusting metal from car workshops. By the time we reached Kandy, the rain was heavier, the roadsides muddier and the traffic totally snarled up – three lines of tuk-tuks and public buses in every lane, pedestrians and scooters squeezing into whatever space was left. No sign of the picturesque World Heritage city I had been expecting. Kandy was the tourist centre of the country, so we were ushered through innumerable craft shops selling traditional woodcarvings, batik, silk and gemstones (Sri Lanka is famous especially for sapphires and rubies), as well as a Folklore Show which culminated in a demonstration of fire-walking (in the rain!). But most interesting was the complex of buildings surrounding the Temple of the Tooth, (supposedly) housing one of Buddha's molars, brought to Sri Lanka in the 4th century and carried from one capital city to another as a symbol of kingship. The complex was badly damaged in 1998 by a bomb set by Tamil Tiger revolutionaries, but the inner temple containing the Tooth was not touched:

"A massive stairway leads into the lobby around the 3-storey temple itself – a beautifully carved and decorated building, roofed with gleaming new

golden tiles. One of the daily ceremonies is underway, with drummers pounding a heart-stopping rhythm and a flute piercing our ears with high-pitched wailing. We climb another stair to find ourselves at the point where, just three times a day, a silver-clad hatch opens to reveal the solid gold casket which encases the Tooth. It is open for just five minutes at a time, so we barely have time to take in the view before the door swings shut again."

Climbing higher into the mountains, we found ourselves surrounded by terraced tea plantations, stopping to visit a tea factory to learn about the different types and grades of tea ranging from Poor (including pieces of stem as well as leaves, artificially dried by massive hot-air blowers) to exclusive White Tea (made from the topmost tips of the shoots and dried only in natural sunshine). Outside in the drizzling rain, ladies were still hard at work picking the daily 35 kilos of leaves required to earn their standard wage of 5 $US per day – tea-picking was one of the worst paid jobs in the country, though accompanied by education and health benefits from the government. Tea was introduced to Sri Lanka by the British in the 19th century, and here in the mountains we discovered the small town of Nuwara Eliya, founded by British settlers in an attempt to find relief from the excessive temperatures in most of the island. The town still boasted grand British-style mansions surrounded by lush gardens, and even the weather was reminiscent of Britain – yet more rain!

Fortunately, the rain eased off in time for our hardest physical challenge – the ascent of Adam's Peak (2243m), a sacred pilgrimage route for Sri Lankan Buddhists, who often try to reach the summit in time for sunrise. Upali left us to decide on our own departure time – I chose to start my climb at 1am, following a good concrete path illuminated all the way up the mountain. Even at this hour the first pilgrims were underway and a few shops selling essential provisions were open beside the path. Buddhist chanting was issuing from small prayer-halls along the way, decorated with flags and flashing fairy-lights. Finally the lines of shops were replaced by continuous flights of steps through the forest, following a rushing stream invisible in the darkness:

"I am alone except for the gurgling and popping of hidden frogs in the undergrowth. My knees are beginning to play up and I am seriously considering giving up as the path arrives at the sharp peak of the mountain, where very high and steep steps strain my body. No-one can tell me how much

more of this there is, but helpful locals suggest 'a short way' so I keep going a little further. One last challenge awaits me: a precipitous stairway which goes on and on. I am reduced to pulling myself up on the metal fence bars, but I've got this far ... to hell with my knees!"

I reached the top, queuing patiently with the pilgrims to enter a plain square hut supposedly enclosing the sacred 'Buddha Footprint' ... only to find it entirely hidden by silk draperies and cash offerings. I found a spot to sit to await the dawn ... but mist rose out of the valleys and swallowed up the view. 13.5km, over 5000 stairs, 4½ hours of exhausting ascent followed by 3½ hours of agonising descent – was it worth it? Of course! How proud I was of my achievement!

We left the mountains on a crowded train through mist-shrouded forest and rain-soaked tea plantations, though at least the waterfalls were in full spate. Finally we reached Bandarawela, where our colonial-style hotel was overrun with wedding parties. Our hotels on this tour had often been the best available, and so were also popular as wedding venues. In Sri Lanka those who could afford to celebrate in style, spent vast sums on full-day festivities on the actual day of the wedding (with bride and groom both wearing white costumes) and then more vast sums on another full day of festivities to celebrate home-coming (from honeymoon), this time with bride and groom wearing red. Frequently I emerged from my hotel room to find a happy couple being directed into pose after pose by professional photographers, often starting at dawn and continuing into the evening.

We were back into the hot, humid lowlands now, driving down a bumpy dirt road to visit another rock-face carved with images of Buddha – though even Upali was unsure how old they were. This stop became one of the highlights of the tour for me, however, because we had managed to get away from other tourists into deep forest filled with the squawks and whistles of invisible birds:

"An enchanted grove ... if only we could stay quietly here for a while! My wish is granted when Upali decides to make a 'comfort stop' beside bushes alive with birds. It turns out that our driver (Mandula) is a keen birdwatcher, and he is able to point out a cheeky Magpie Robin, a Fantail and even an elusive Jerdon's Leafbird – its green plumage matching exactly the bush where he is perched. By now, the entire group is excited by birds and we drive

on, enthusiastically pointing out to each other kingfishers, bee-eaters and woodpeckers. "

We reached the south coast of the island, still showing signs of the horrific tsunami of 2004 which killed 35,000 Sri Lankans and devastated the eastern and southern coastlines. Even after 13 years I still saw badly damaged homes, abandoned by their owners and now being overrun by lush vegetation. We stopped to visit the memorial at Pereliya to the 1270 ticket holders who died when the tsunami washed a packed train from its rails – Upali told us that there were probably many more deaths, since the train would have been carrying on its roof untold numbers of travellers without tickets.

After sticking faithfully with the group for several weeks, I was ready for some independence. Leaving the others to take a cruise in search of whales, I squeezed into the jam-packed local bus to explore Galle, an important Dutch port in the 17th century:

"I don't know what to expect, so am charmed and delighted when I walk inside the massive walls (strong enough still to repel the tsunami and protect the old section) to find a well-preserved colonial town. The streets are narrow and shady, lined with whitewashed arcades and porticoes. Many of the buildings have been turned into small, chic guesthouses – their doors are open to catch the morning breeze, revealing elegant lobbies evoking the comfortable lifestyle of rich Dutch merchants. "

I meandered through the streets, then relaxed for a while in the cool interior of the whitewashed Dutch Reformed Church with its dark wooden pews and stained-glass windows, but the heat and humidity were building up as the morning advanced – time to head back to our resort of Unawatuna … and a delicious Ayurvedic massage. The 'treatment room' was just a tiny hut roofed with palm leaves, containing a single bed where I lay while the masseuse rubbed herbal oils into my skin with rough hands and elbows. She worked right down the back of my body from neck to heels, even rubbing oil into my hair (yuk!) before flipping me over to pummel my front. I emerged feeling energised … but extremely greasy!

Next day was programmed as a day off and most of the group was planning a day on the beach … they were unlucky! We woke to find sheets of rain sluicing down, with flashes of lightning and rumbles of thunder. I had booked a taxi to take me to Bundala National Park (famous for its waterbirds), so we set off at 5am, crawling through crowds of local people walking or cycling under umbrellas to work, swooshing through massive puddles beside tightly laced-up tuk-tuks, minibuses and monster trucks. All the way my driver was telling me that the Park would be closed in this weather and we should turn back, but I insisted on continuing:

"We reach the turn-off to the Park and can go no further in this car – the lagoons are flowing strongly across the road. But the Park's Jeep and its guide/ spotter arrive, and the rain is easing, so my tour begins. There is only one other Jeep in the Park today, so it is just us and the birds – mostly waterbirds, so they're not worried by the rain. The land is so deeply flooded that in places the water comes up to the top of the wheels, but my driver keeps going – he knows where the track lies, though it is currently underwater. We seem to be driving right out among the birds – swallows and bee-eaters flash around us, eagles and kites swoop above us, herons and storks stand beside us to fish; only the peacocks look bedraggled and miserable as they perch on dry branches above the lagoons."

I was in my element – so many different birds that my guide had no time to identify them all for me, though both he and the driver became excited when they noticed a dull-coloured stork near the road: a rare Adjutant Stork, normally keeping well away from visitors. They had never seen one before! Though Upali had diligently shown us the architectural highlights of his country, my abiding memory of Sri Lanka remains these lush green landscapes, rich in birds and other wildlife.

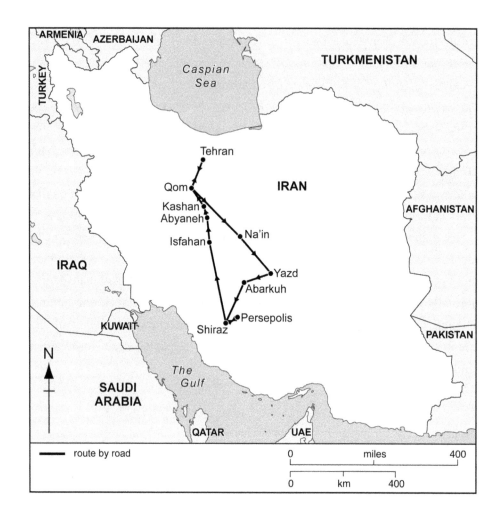

Caspian
Sea

ARMENIA

AZERBAIJAN

TURKMENISTAN

TURKEY

Tehran

Qom

IRAN

Kashan
Abyaneh

AFGHANISTAN

Na'in

Isfahan

IRAQ

Yazd

Abarkuh

Persepolis

KUWAIT

Shiraz

PAKISTAN

N

The
Gulf

SAUDI
ARABIA

QATAR

UAE

—— route by road

| 0 | miles | 400 |

| 0 | km | 400 |

Iran (April 2017)

IRAN … ANCIENT PERSIA … A POWERFUL nation for thousands of years, its wealth displayed in some of the world's most exotic architecture and art … yet for over 30 years, embroiled in political turmoil and violence which made it unwise to attempt to visit. Suddenly I began to see it featured in the pages of tour operators' brochures: the country was opening up to tourism – how could I resist?

It was still not simple to visit: to gain a visa, I had to physically present myself at their London embassy to be fingerprinted and the visa application needed photos depicting me wearing a modest head-covering. The pre-tour information warned that there would be no alcohol available (not a problem for me), but also suggested that it would be difficult for a lone woman to walk the streets: in fact, it quickly became clear that attitudes to women were changing and I often explored alone. It was compulsory to cover my hair at all times and was also recommended that female visitors should wear voluminous clothing which would hide every feminine curve: so I visited multi-cultural Sheffield and bought myself a 'jilbab', a conveniently full-length, sleeved over-dress. More difficult for me was the strictly regimented nature of the tour – tourism was very new to Iran and there was only one established tourist route around the country, so we met the same swarm of visitors (mainly Europeans) at every monument, hotel and restaurant. The newly-trained guides had been taught that especially British and American tourists should be escorted at all times – thankfully, our guide Hadi quickly decided to ignore that aspect of his training and gave us plenty of free time.

My first sight of this mysterious land was on the drive into Tehran (Iran's capital) from the airport – a jumble of new, poorly-constructed concrete apartment blocks and a melee of chaotic traffic which seemed to respect no rights of way nor lane discipline: in other words, a modern city like any other! Within half an hour of arriving at our hotel, Hadi was rushing us out to start sightseeing, hustling us through the Historical Museum where exhibits ranged from 6000-year-old pottery to a mummified head (barely visible amidst a crowd of excited, noisy schoolchildren). Fortunately, Persia's long history could be condensed into a few easily distinguished dynasties, each conveniently based in a different part of the country. In Tehran, a relatively new city (only becoming the capital in 1785), we could focus on just the last two dynasties. In the Golestan complex of palaces, we met the Qajar shahs (kings) who loved multi-coloured tiles and shards of mirror to decorate their walls:

"With plastic bags over our shoes, we climb a staircase plastered with mirror-work into the vast vaulted Coronation Hall, its ceiling of pale blue stucco overwhelmed by mosaics of mirror covering the walls, sparkling in sunlight reinforced by the gleam of five massive chandeliers. The room is stuffed with precious furniture, porcelain and carpets, with European-style paintings depicting the debauched pleasures so popular with these kings."

There was more 'bling' on show when we visited the National Jewels Museum ... where I caused some disruption when I entered. For security reasons, all bags were to be left in lockers at the entrance – but my bumbag was underneath my jilbab, and to remove it would have necessitated showing not only ankles but even my knees! A female attendant took me into a private room for further inspection, but we found the room occupied by a group of men – I lifted my hem anyway, causing the female attendant to gasp in horror, so flustered and embarrassed that she ushered me on into the museum with no further delay:

"I push through the crowds of (mainly Iranian) visitors filling a darkened subterranean room, lit only by the lights in the showcases and by the reflected dazzle of thousands of jewels, set into weapons, brooches, necklaces and tiaras. Here are the three crowns of the last (Pahlavi) shahs, and trays of gold coins and sparkling cut jewels – diamonds, rubies and emeralds, stacked high in an ostentatious display of wealth, still part of Iran's national reserve."

In the northern suburbs of the city, amid the foothills of the snow-capped Alborz Mountains, were the luxurious villas of Iran's wealthiest citizens – and here also were the palaces of the two last Shahs of Iran (the Pahlavi dynasty). The palace of Reza Shah (built in the 1920s) still reflected the Iranian love of 'bling' with more mirror mosaics, especially in the ceremonial hall and in the Shah's bedroom (who could sleep surrounded by all that sparkle?), but the palace of the last Shah (who held power from 1941 until the Revolution in 1979) was deeply unattractive – just a square concrete block which looked like a functional office building, furnished with French rococo chairs in the audience hall and British-style wood panelling in the billiard room. I was puzzled to see this lack of traditional decor, especially since this last Shah had spent a fortune celebrating 2500 years of Persian history with a 4-day party in 1971 (the most expensive party in history and one of the contributing factors to his downfall) – yet his palace seemed to avoid Persian influences? However, the Freedom Tower, built as part of the celebrations and now the symbol of Tehran, was far more impressive:

"It still looks super-modern with exotic, elegant lines: its five planes are considered a mathematical marvel, with flaring skirts which resemble a royal courtesan graciously dropping a curtsey. Inside the arch, lozenges of blue tiling increase in density of colour and design as they rise into the apex. How could the Shah who lived in that monstrosity of a palace, at the same time order this glorious structure?"

Of course, Iran has written a new chapter of history since the time of the Shahs, and we persuaded Hadi to take us to see the crumbling US embassy, abandoned after Ayatollah Khomeini's revolution and the 444-day siege when 52 Americans were held hostage in 1979/80. Its walls were painted with anti-American slogans, though as we toured the country, I noticed few other obvious marks of the ongoing tension between Iran and the West – with a new president taking power just a few years before my visit, those tensions seemed to have eased (though the situation has deteriorated in the ensuing years).

We took the crowded highway south from Tehran, passing military installations, police checkpoints and industrial sites guarded by high walls. Most of the land was arid and seemingly desolate (35% of Iran is officially classified as desert), though wherever there was a well to provide water, the grey stony earth suddenly bloomed into vivid green fields. Most irrigation seemed to be the work of individual families, with little large-scale agriculture (except near Tehran), and we often saw small pumps bringing up ground water for the crops. At one point, Hadi stopped to show us an example of the ancient 'qanat' irrigation system – underground channels, hundreds of kilometres long, bringing cool water from the snows of the mountains into the heart of the deserts. The system was thought to date from 1000 BC and was still functioning – inside this simple domed building we found a stairway leading down to a fast-flowing stream which widened into a pool at the foot of the stairs. Why had it now been abandoned in favour of diesel pumps? Also dotting the landscape were ruined mud-brick structures, which were once caravanserais, providing shelter for merchants travelling the southern Silk Road – many built in the 16th century by one of Persia's greatest rulers, Shah Abbas, who boasted that he had provided 999 caravanserais as he developed vital trade routes across his country.

Our route sped past Qom, the country's holiest city – Iran considers itself the guardian of the Shi'a branch of the Muslim faith. Hadi explained some of the titles they use: the term 'imam' refers only to one of the 11 first descendants of the prophet Muhammad to lead the Shi'as; the term 'mullah' is applied to any religious leader who has studied for at least 4 years, whereas an 'ayatollah' has studied for at least 20 years and published texts relating to the Koran. In the 1980s we tossed the name 'Ayatollah Khomeini' around so easily – it was good to learn what the title really meant!

Later, in the town of Na'in we visited the principal mosque, built in the 12th century by another of the Persian dynasties: this time the Seljuks, whose buildings were distinguished by decorative patterns in brick instead of coloured tiles. The mosque contained two distinct areas of worship – a cosy carpeted hall at ground level, for winter use, and a much cooler subterranean area for summer use: a vital combination in this extreme desert climate. In Na'in we also sampled our first typical Iranian meal: different dishes of coloured rice, dyed saffron yellow or green with broad beans, and so-called 'stews' which had been cooked so long that they were reduced to thick sauces – kidney bean and spinach; sweet lamb with pomegranate and walnut; tangy lamb and green plum. For me, however, Na'in's old town was most fascinating, with narrow cobbled streets winding past high walls pierced by doors leading to private courtyards. Wider openings revealed crumbling arches and gateways … and three 'wind towers': designed to keep the subterranean water cistern cool, by catching the wind through multiple holes at different angles in the tower walls and blowing it down over the water:

"The local people seem to value their historic architecture very little, though there is so much here – 8th century walls and gates, elaborately carved window-frames, remnants of vaulted halls. Is it all too far gone to rescue? Or will the groups of tourists admiring the ruins, convince the townsfolk that it's worth restoring?"

At the end of a very long day we reached Yazd, entering along an avenue lined with pictures of soldiers – one of the many Avenues of Heroes which we saw throughout the country, commemorating the deaths of an entire generation of pitifully young men (many only 15-17 years old) who died in the war with Iraq in the 1980s. Yazd is known as one of the most pious cities in Iran – as we strolled in the alleyways, I saw local ladies swathed in black or grey 'chador' (a voluminous cover-all cape) or modestly dressed in trousers and long black 'manteau' (buttoned coat). Yet there were also female tourists from Tehran wearing much more relaxed fashions, including one young woman loosely draped in a chador with the words 'do you think I'm pretty' embroidered on the back, and others with headscarves perched on the very back of their heads. Again I was fascinated by the old town:

"We twist and turn through a maze of alleys, some shaded by vaults supporting overhead houses, others open to the sun. All are lined with high, blank walls studded with wooden doors, many offering a choice of two knockers – on the left, a long piece of iron for male visitors, on the right a round iron knob for females. Hadi demonstrates that each has a totally different sound, and therefore avoids the social gaffe of the door being opened by a family member of the inappropriate gender."

Yazd was one of the centres of Iran's Zoroastrian faith, the principal religion of the country before the arrival of Islam in the 7th century, and still followed by 25,000 Iranians. We visited their Fire Temple, the building itself less than 100 years old but housing a flame carried from old temple to new for generations and thought to be 1500 years old. The temple seemed small and insignificant beside the magnificent mosques we had already seen in other cities, though Hadi explained that Zoroastrians do not use a building for their regular worship – simply turning to the sun as the embodiment of sacred fire.

On the edge of the city stood the Towers of Silence, a Zoroastrian funeral site in use until 1960, where bodies were exposed inside hilltop walls to be 'recycled' by birds without polluting the earth:

"I walk across a wide compound past small, vaulted brick pavilions where the families of the deceased stayed as they mourned, then climb a flight of wide stone steps to the top of one of the towers. At the summit is just a circular space where the body was laid, surrounded by 10ft walls to hide the action of the vultures from the grieving family. In the centre is a pit where the remaining bones were swept and then dissolved in a sulphur/ lime mixture."

Once back in town, we were taken to see Yazd's historic Friday Mosque, boasting the highest minaret in Iran and originally dating back to the 8th century. The oldest parts were once again adorned with simple patterns laid into the brickwork, but in the 16th century the mosque was rebuilt by the most notable of Iran's dynasties – the Safavids, who loved to cover their structures with blue and turquoise tiles. How clever we felt to be able to look at a mosque and identify its age, simply by the style of its decoration – plain brickwork = 12th century Seljuk dynasty; blue tiling = 16th century Safavid dynasty; multicoloured tiling = 19th century Qajar dynasty … easy!

Later in the day, Hadi told us he was taking us to see traditional 'Zurkhaneh' (whatever was that?) and led us through a mysterious doorway into a sunken arena beneath a large brick dome. The arena was empty as we took seats around it, though piles of differently sized, polished wooden clubs and metal chains gave us a hint of what was coming … a display of 'keep fit', once used to strengthen Persian warriors so that they could wield swords, maces, tightly strung bows or battering rams:

"A single athlete enters and starts spinning as a warm-up, then lifts a shield in each hand to practice whacking the enemy. He is followed by a group of five athletes who leap into the ring to perform some elaborate stretches and very demanding press-ups, all to the insistent chant of a singer/ drummer, then move to the most dramatic exercise: swinging immensely heavy Indian clubs in a steady and majestic rhythm, back and forth over their heads and behind their backs. The demonstration culminates with energetic leaping high into the air."

Back out into the deserts now, climbing through a range of brown, snow-spattered mountains topped by weirdly formed pinnacles – including one imposing rock right beside our road, shaped like a giant eagle squatting on the ground. We passed villages which were almost invisible as their mud-brick homes blended into the colour of the land around – only the eye-catching blue, green or gold of mosque domes indicated their location.

Finally we pulled into the large village of Abarkuh, its historic structures once again in a perilous state of repair, though there was one treasured National Monument which we were to visit here: an ancient cypress tree, 25m tall, 18m girth … and thought to be 4000 years old. There were few visitors apart from us and a local high school teacher, who seized the opportunity to practice his English: everywhere we went in Iran, I found that people (some men but especially women) were delighted to have the chance to talk to me, often in excellent English, always keen to know what I thought of Iran and its values, happy to discuss the role of women or the prospects for peace in the region. In Abarkuh, friendliness moved into hospitality:

"I stop to watch a lady chopping dill in her tiny courtyard, and she invites me inside her home: a series of rooms, all carpeted but with no furniture at all – just a couple of cushions to support your back as you sit on the floor. The kitchen is fully fitted with all the mod cons we would expect, though there is also a wood-fired oven outside in the courtyard – and the tap is there too. She insists I sample her super-tangy pomegranate molasses with a piece of chilled saffron bread."

One more monument awaited us as we drove out of town, this time a 16th century Ice House, surrounded by channels which would have been filled with water from the 'qanat' each winter evening, then left to freeze overnight. In the morning, the ice would be broken up into large pieces and stored inside the Ice House ready for use in the heat of summer:

"This impressive structure rises by the roadside like a layered wedding cake or a beehive. Inside is another soaring masterpiece of brick, rising to a small hole open to the blazing sun. Below the brick, the basement has been largely filled in now – just an earthen pit remains, with the remnants of earth steps descending into the depths."

Our road now cut its way through more arid mountains where nomadic shepherds were driving their sheep and goats in search of grazing – we passed a few mini-trucks laden with the personal possessions of nomads moving up to the high pastures for the summer, each topped off with the rolls of home-made carpet for which these tribes are famous. As we descended towards Shiraz, the land around us was transformed by the presence of water into fields lush with the vivid green of rice shoots or lurid yellow of rapeseed, studded with olive and fig trees. As a wine drinker, I might have expected to see vineyards – though of course, strictly Islamic Iran does not permit the drinking of alcohol. In fact, Hadi told me that there were still vineyards in the area, officially producing only grape juice – though some young Iranians were buying the juice to transform into home-made wine, despite the threat of a prison sentence if caught. Shiraz itself was a large and busy, modern city – famous for hospitals catering to wealthy Arabs coming for cosmetic surgery: I often saw men with large plasters on their faces after operations to reduce the size of their noses!

Sightseeing next day began in Eram Botanical Garden, delightfully fresh and cool in the early morning, the air scented with tangy cypress overlaid with the delicate perfume of orange blossom. A walking tour of central Shiraz took us to Nasir al-Mulk (the Pink Mosque), built in the 19th century as the private mosque of a wealthy merchant and famous for its stained glass and Qajar-style multi-coloured tiles: this time decorative cartouches were set into each panel, some containing pictures representing European villages and even churches – in the 19th century it was fashionable to use images from other cultures. This European influence continued in Qavam House with another demonstration of the 19th century Iranian love of gaudy colour: plastered walls painted with flowers and foliage, idealised Italianate buildings and even females wearing revealingly low-cut clothing. Yet more dramatic was the mirrorwork:

"In the central chamber, glass mosaic sparkles in the sunlight, reflected again and again by banks of mirrors – this is Bling! It continues on the verandah where big mirrors reflect the decorative wall at the far end of the garden. It's almost a relief to move again to the more subdued side rooms, elegant in white plaster with gold tracery, though the ceiling continues to be a riot of gold-enhanced colour."

After resting through the hottest part of the day, sightseeing continued in the gardens surrounding the tomb of Iran's national poet Hafiz – in the cool of the evening, filled with people relaxing, strolling, eating ice-cream and picnicking. There were no mixed gender groups, except if the whole family was together – instead, the men and women gathered separately. However, Shiraz did not seem to be a strictly conservative city: though some women were totally enveloped in chadors, others wore western tight trousers and tight jackets, and the younger women were often plastered with make-up. As female tourists, local people were generally tolerant of our western idea of 'decent' dress (though several ladies thanked me for making the effort to wear my jilbab) ... except when we visited an especially holy shrine in Shiraz. The men entered by the main gate, but the women were ushered through a side door where we were issued with makeshift chadors (mine was just a piece of nylon curtain, so slippery that it was impossible to secure firmly over my head). Yet the illuminated shrine was worth any inconvenience:

"The first courtyard takes my breath away – beautifully illuminated arches and porticoes, reflecting off a polished stone floor. An ethereally lit dome rises from one corner, covering one of the sacred tombs; in the second courtyard is another beautiful dome over the 2ⁿᵈ tomb, encased in sparkling mirrorwork. A heavy curtain bars us from entering the actual shrine, but we can peep through a window to see the gaudy mirrored interior."

We headed back in time as we made an excursion to the ancient cities of Pasargade and Persepolis, capitals of the vast Persian empire in the 6th and 5th centuries BC but destroyed by the armies of Alexander the Great in 330 BC. Pasargade was the oldest, founded by Cyrus the Great as a grand city of palaces and beautiful gardens, yet now reduced just to a vast sun-baked plain with a few scattered remnants of stone walls – Alexander had no mercy on the city and destroyed everything except the tomb of Cyrus himself, buried inside a golden stone sarcophagus raised on a plinth high above us. Nearby were the rock-cut tombs of Cyrus' successors, the builders of Persepolis:

"We turn towards a rock face cut with four great tombs: Xerxes, Darius the Great, Ataxerxes and Darius II. These were the tombs they chose for themselves, cut into towering cliffs with no access for thieves seeking the treasures they were buried with. As in Petra, all the decoration is on the cliff-face outside the tomb; inside is just a tiny room where the body was laid, left open for scavenging birds to enter – following Zoroastrian tradition."

The remains of Persepolis were far more imposing, designed to impress visiting delegations (bringing annual tributes from across the empire) with glorious palaces set high on marble platforms – accessed by very shallow steps so that the delegates could easily carry their loads of treasure or drive their valuable animals upwards to be presented to the emperor. The stairways were carved with magnificent stone reliefs depicting the fashions and hairstyles of representatives from India to Greece, Ethiopia to Russia. I spent several hours wandering among the columns and gateways, past walls adorned with magnificent carvings. So much to see here – even Alexander could not destroy it all!

From Shiraz we turned northwards again, crossing more expanses of arid semi-desert with few settlements. After hours of desert driving, what a shock to enter the sprawling modern suburbs of Isfahan – not the best introduction to this amazing city, but quickly forgotten as I launched out from the hotel to explore. Within minutes I was walking by the river amid crowds of people relaxing in the cool evening air – buying roasted corn from tiny home barbecues alongside the paths, picnicking on the grass or meandering across the water in swan-shaped paddle boats. Dominating the scene was the iconic Si-o-Se bridge – 33 arched spans, topped with a vaulted street, all glowing with soft orange illuminations which reflected in the river below. This became my favourite place to spend any free time whilst in Isfahan, always welcomed by local people who were keen to greet me. Everywhere in Iran I had felt welcome, but especially here in Isfahan – one lady urged me to tell everyone back home how friendly ordinary Iranians are, despite the international image of their politicians:

"Everyone wants to chat today! In the bridge cafe, two young girls invite me to join them in their carpeted window alcove, smiling in sympathy as I explain that I cannot sit cross-legged. A male student is keen to talk, philosophising about the limitations which the Iranian lifestyle brings to his dreams. A family invites me to join their picnic, peeling chunks of cucumber for me, pouring tea with delicious, orange-flavoured fudge – they have little English, but are just delighted that I have agreed to sit with them on their rugs."

Isfahan was the definite highlight of the entire tour, both for the innumerable opportunities to meet local people but also for the magnificence of its architecture and quality of its craftwork. We were taken to see a master renowned for painting exquisite miniature scenes on pieces of camel bone, a group of men using traditional wooden blocks to print designs on calico cloth … and a display of Persian carpets ranging from simple wool rugs made by nomadic tribes to insulate their tents, to magnificent 100% silk carpets tightly woven and knotted by the tiny fingers of young women and children.

At the heart of the city lay Imam Square, laid out in the 17th century by their most glorious ruler – Shah Abbas, star of the Safavid dynasty. He had planned the square as a polo ground, though now it was laid out with gardens and fountains, surrounded by awe-inspiring monuments. At one end were the buildings of the Imam (formerly Shah) Mosque, accessed beneath an imposing tiled gateway leading through splendid silver doors into the heart of the complex – a feast of decoration with both painted tiles and exquisite tile mosaic. Memorable for me, too, was the main portico where a wide gap between the inner and outer domes created a distinctive echo with multiple different strands:

"The 26 echoes are being given a good workout by the shrill voices of innumerable female schoolchildren, though the hubbub is too great to distinguish individual sounds – so Hadi asks me to sing instead. The portico is briefly hushed as I sing the name of Jesus, reverberating in the silence, the echoes creating a choir from my single voice."

On another side of the square stood the Ali Qapu royal palace, where Shah Abbas lived whilst in Isfahan – six floors high, with a delightfully ornate music room on the top floor, and an elegant balcony with panels depicting lovely ladies with diaphanous veils (though in one place the ladies' faces had been erased by zealots after the 1979 revolution, considering them immoral). Most glorious of all was the Blue Mosque, built 1603-19 as the Shah's personal mosque, smaller and more intimate than the Imam Mosque but exquisite in the quality of its tile mosaics:

"The dome is the first part to strike me, glowing above us with golden light from the windows around its base. In the centre is a protruding knob, which reveals itself to be the head of a peacock. The sun shining through the fretwork windows illuminates different sections of the dome, lighting up a 'peacock tail' of gold, constantly moving with the progress of the sun."

Next day we visited the oldest mosque in the city, built in the 10th and 11th centuries so there were no colourful tiles here – just elaborate brickwork patterns, multiple domes, and a labyrinth of arcaded rooms and passageways leading to soaring prayer halls. In total contrast was the Armenian Vank

Cathedral, built by Shah Abbas when he invited Armenian craftsmen to bring their skills to Persia (and still used by a large Armenian population today). From outside it seemed no more than a plain brick church …

"… but as we step inside, there's a communal gasp! Every inch of walls and ceilings is decorated with gaudy illustrations of Bible stories, including a huge painting of the Last Judgement where bodies are rising from the agony of Hell at the behest of the angel Gabriel."

I loved Isfahan! But there was more to see, driving now into the mountains, passing en route an innocuous yellow brick building guarded by anti-aircraft guns under camouflage nets – Hadi urgently told us to put down our cameras and look the other way: it was a nuclear power station and the authorities held him personally responsible for making sure that we did not notice it! We crossed a 2700m pass adorned with more photos of 'heroes' who died in the Iran-Iraq War, then descended into the valley beyond to the village of Abyaneh, where the population still followed the Zoroastrian faith.

It was an interesting village with narrow paved alleys surrounded by tall buildings made of red adobe topped with shiny aluminium roofs, some extending out over the street with wooden balconies. The population wore a traditional costume – baggy trousers and a loose shirt for the men; long black skirt, embroidered blouse and brightly coloured headscarf for the women. All very photogenic, yet this was part of the established 'tourist trail' and, at first, I felt there was little chance of experiencing genuine Iranian village life here. Everywhere I turned, there were visiting Iranian city-dwellers dressing up in local costumes to enhance their walk through the village. I turned off the paved streets to descend to the bottom of the village on muddy tracks through blossoming groves of nut trees, past cave-like stables cut into the hillsides to provide safety for flocks of sheep from the night-time ravages of wolves. This felt more like a genuine working village, and I was delighted to find a tiny shop where a man and his wife were cooking slices of potato on top of an ancient wood stove – they insisted that I sample them, even though I had no intention of buying any of their stock of dried mushrooms or dusty brass pots. As rain set in, I retired to my hotel for one last treat – a splendid rainbow developed opposite my bedroom window, pointing with increasing strength directly into the heart of the village below, fading only as the last golden evening light caressed the convoluted ridges of mountains spreading around us.

We were heading back to Tehran now, with one last historic city to see on the way – Kashan, once a wealthy trading city on the Persian Silk Road. We visited a 19th century merchant's house, almost as grand as the royal palaces we had seen earlier, with fine plastered walls painted with hunting scenes and European-style buildings. We also visited another mosque and theological college, most memorable to me because of the alcove filled with posters and leaflets (in various languages including English) exploring the current situation between Islam and the West. We had already encountered multi-lingual mullahs in Isfahan who spent the day answering tourists' questions and trying to explain that Shi'as were not aggressive like Sunni extremists (*no comment*). In the same alcove were a few quotations from Imam Ali (founder of Shi'ism) – including 'Are women deficient in intelligence?' *(again no comment!)*.

We were caught in a difficult situation en route back to Tehran. Coach and truck drivers in the country were supervised by satellite technology which checked they were respecting speed limits and taking the required rest periods. Unfortunately, the technology had not functioned properly in the mountains, and our driver, Bach'rom, was unable to prove to police at a checkpoint that he had slept overnight in Abyaneh – he was instructed to take a long 'rest' before being allowed to drive on. However, after an hour or so, the problem was solved by sleight of hand. Bach'rom had found an unemployed driver, conveniently offering his services near the checkpoint (clearly this was a common situation), willing to drive the coach onwards – however, he had problems with his feet and could not drive for long. So after a short distance Bach'rom took back the wheel, taking us all the way to the outskirts of Tehran before the spare driver again took the driving seat to cross the final checkpoint:

"What a farce! But it's the only taste we have had of the over-authoritative police force we had been warned about – so we can't really complain."

Time to return home, carrying many memories of a fascinating land. I had anticipated the centuries of history and magnificent architecture, but in the end, it was the open-hearted and hospitable people of Iran who have remained the highlight of my visit. How tragic it will be if international politics once again isolates their country, limiting their prospects and opportunities to take their place in the modern world.

Iran - Abarkuh ice house

Iran - Tehran Freedom Tower

Iranian hospitality

Iran - ancient royal tombs

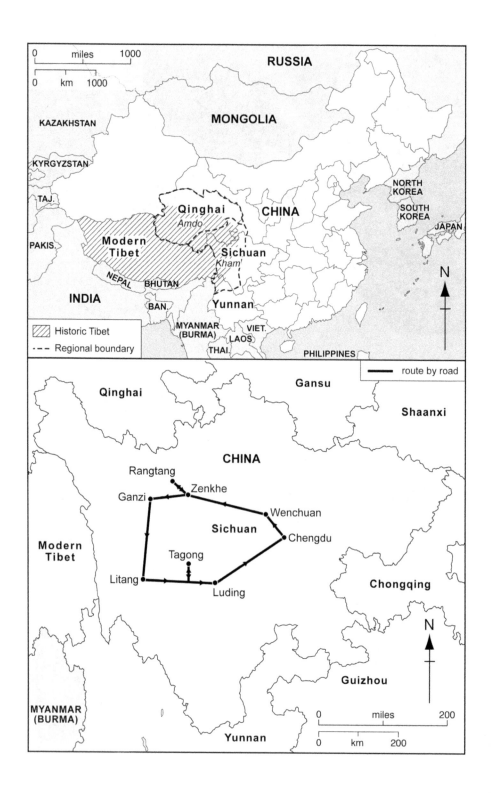

Kham – Eastern Tibet (October 2017)

ARE YOU CONFUSED BY THIS chapter heading? If you've been reading this book chapter by chapter, you may think I have already described Tibet? The answer lies in the history of Tibet – once a powerful country rivalling China itself, much larger than the current boundaries of the Tibetan Autonomous Region of modern China. As Chinese influence grew from the 18th century onwards and especially after re-organisation of provinces in the 1920s and 1950s, the wealthier Tibetan regions of Amdo and Kham (and the smaller Jiarong region between the two) found themselves cut off from the Tibetan AR and assimilated into the current Chinese provinces of Qinghai and Sichuan. This tour was aiming to explore the Tibetan communities in the western part of Sichuan, the ancient regions of Jiarong and Kham.

We started once again in Chengdu with another visit to the adorable panda cubs in the Research Centre, before setting off into the mountains of western Sichuan – on modern roads soaring above deep gorges, cut by fast-flowing rivers originating in the highlands of Tibet. The engineering seemed all the more impressive when our guide, Teddy, told us that the new road was badly damaged by earthquake in 2008 just before it opened – most of the bridges were destroyed. Teddy was actually in one of the valleys when the earthquake struck, stranded on a partially collapsed bridge and eventually rescued by helicopter. The stretch of road to Wenchuan (epicentre of the earthquake) was finally opened in 2011, but the route from that city onwards descended into the gorges once again, twisting and turning beside swirling torrents, through villages squeezed into rare widenings of the valley bottom. Accompanying us most of the way were piles of rubble and towering concrete pillars rising above the rivers – indications that road-building into these remote regions was continuing apace.

Once the road was finished, clearly Jiarong and Kham would be opened up to hordes of domestic tourists – millions of newly wealthy, ethnic Han people from eastern China, now keen to explore the extent of their country. However, when I visited, the region was still quiet and unused to visitors:

"Lunch is in a noodle shop beside the road. They are delighted to see us – both for the income and for the thrill of entertaining foreigners. While one cook prepares our food, the other pulls out her mobile phone to take photographs of us. There is a welcome from everyone in this village: the girls weeding the garden around the community toilet; the neighbours chatting in the street; the sellers of plums and persimmons squatting by the roadside as huge trucks roar past, honking their greetings to us."

The population in this area belonged to the Qiang Tibetan minority (China has 55 ethnic minorities, though 90% of the population belongs to the Han group). Their villages were distinguished by houses decorated beneath the eaves with a geometric frieze in gold or red, and by ladies wearing long black skirts with their hair wrapped around their heads in a single huge plait behind an embroidered headband. As we moved deeper into Jiarong, we began also to see the stone towers which are a feature of their villages. In these narrow valleys there was little space for agriculture and much of the population's income traditionally came from trade. Consequently these had been among the wealthiest of the Tibetan tribes, frequently raided by their cousins from the high plateau to the west – the towers were built up to 1000 years ago to guard against these raiders.

We were travelling more slowly than Teddy had expected – this was the first time this tour had run, and the recce had been conducted in a more swiftly moving car, so we did not reach our first hotel until well after dark. However, this did not prevent me from heading out to explore by torchlight (there is no street lighting in rural Chinese villages), scrambling up paths between solid stone homes hung with drying corncobs and surrounded by vegetable gardens and animal byres. I was especially interested to notice the 'indoor toilets' – a wooden structure attached to the upper walls of the house, with a chute dropping directly into the garden, ready to be spread as fertiliser.

Next day we continued along a narrow, twisting road which followed every curve of the River Dukhe, past frequent obstructions caused by rockfall from the cliffs above. There were less trucks now, but we were left gasping in horror at cars being driven with wild abandon at ridiculous speeds. Teddy told us that, though truck and coach drivers were subject to strict examinations before receiving their licences, car drivers were obliged to undertake only minimal instruction … and it showed!

"There are a few heavy bumps as we hit potholes, then suddenly a huge thud that jerks us to a stop. Have we damaged the coach? Those on the left side of the bus say: 'No, we've hit something' … then 'We've hit a car – badly'. I peer through the windows to see that we've actually turned a car over and it is precariously balanced on the edge of the precipice. Several of our group get out to help – one a Doctor, another a First Aider, others simply strong enough to help move the car to extract the three passengers. All are shocked, of course, and all are bleeding – but fortunately there are no serious injuries."

We could do no more until the police arrived, after an hour's wait. The injured were swiftly taken away by the police to hospital, and Teddy was obliged to go with them – regardless of who was to blame for the accident, we were clearly the richer group and so he was going to have to pay for the casualties' treatment. Other police remained at the scene, diligently completing paperwork and drawing diagrams, ruthlessly questioning our driver (despite his obvious distress) – all under the fascinated gaze of other drivers from the increasingly long queue behind us. No-one seemed stressed or angry at the delay … just part of the normal experience of driving this road? Finally, a tyre lever was found to release the damaged corner of our coach enough for us to drive on, now at a noticeably slower pace – but still without our guide.

Every time we crossed from one district to the next, there were police formalities to be completed – sometimes just handing over a passport list, sometimes stricter. Typically we encountered one of these stricter control posts, just when we were without Teddy to translate for us – a group of four young policemen, clearly bored with their minimal duties on a quiet road, insisted that we descend from the coach to be photographed alongside our passport photos, then to fill in a registration book. All very time-wasting and frustrating for us, though the policemen were smiling and joking throughout, trying out their few words of English and even attempting to communicate with Smartphone translation apps. Finally we were released to continue to our destination at Rangtang, a large modern town. At first sight, it seemed that the town's population were mainly Han people, though once darkness fell, I was delighted to see Tibetans emerging from their homes to perform a traditional Circle Dance in the main square, some clearly more practised than others but all proud to declare their allegiance to Tibetan culture despite the dominance of Han people in their town.

In the middle of the night Teddy re-joined us, telling us that the road we had travelled the previous day was closed to large vehicles soon after we passed, because of landslides – our replacement coach would have to reach us from the opposite direction and would take another day to arrive. So we re-boarded our damaged vehicle for the day's sightseeing, driving up to the Jiu Dao Guai Pass (3920m) to emerge from forested valleys on to wide open grasslands, then descend nine hairpin bends into a high valley. Here we found the village of Rebuka with its two separate monasteries – one belonging to the oldest of Tibet's sects (the Red Hats) and the other to the Jona sect, which believes that everything around us exists only in our minds ... I must admit, that philosophy is beyond me!

Rounding a bend, we saw the Jona sect's Rangtang Temple before us, newly extended and restored with a sparkling golden roof. Throughout the tour we encountered Tibetan monasteries being built and maintained with funds from the Chinese government, unlike the minimal reconstruction I had seen in the Tibetan AR – perhaps a way of keeping the Tibetan population of Sichuan from unrest and rebellion? It was a special holy day in Rangtang, and the monastery was crowded with visitors. Outside the gates were stalls selling snacks and souvenirs to the pilgrims, seemingly just as attractive to them as the monastery itself. The crowds were fascinated by us, too – one man even climbed into our coach to gaze silently at each of us in wonder. At lunchtime we joined the crowd in a sunny square, eating our snacks as we watched churns of butter tea and buckets of rice or noodle soup being doled out to the pilgrims by monastery staff:

"After lunch we join the 'kora' (pilgrim walk) around the temple building, following a narrow path behind a single file of villagers, entering a long concrete corridor filled with prayer wheels. I am almost turned dizzy by their

*whirling and by the plaintive rhythmic chant of the pilgrims, intended to lift us
to another plane of existence."*

We continued along another narrow valley into the heart of the hills,
dodging adult yaks and their calves which wandered freely across both
grassland and roads, till we reached the small picturesque Bangtao Monastery.
Once again it was under renovation and reconstruction, with piles of builders'
rubble littering the site and a group of monks squatting on scaffolding inside
the prayer hall to painstakingly paint the beams with fine brushes. Outside
was a jumble of 'stupas' (shrines), each painted with the all-seeing eyes of
Buddha and surrounded by huge piles of 'mani' stones, carved up to 300 years
ago with the words of the Buddhist 'sutras' (scriptures). Teddy explained that
the tradition of carving stones had died during Mao's Cultural Revolution
(1966-76), only recommencing in 2012 in this region: walking a kora around
the mounds was equivalent to actually reading all those scriptures, purifying
the mind and bringing blessings to the pilgrim.

On the way back from Rangtang we stopped at the monastery of Zenkhe,
also famous for carving mani stones. A hillside village of red-painted log
cabins provided accommodation for the monks and nuns working in this
relatively new temple (built in the 1950s and 1990s) which included four tall
towers (pagodas). At first, I was disappointed to find that the towers were
closed and padlocked, but during our visit we were joined by a group of
pilgrims who had walked for 13 days to get here. One of the towers was
opened for them and I slipped in too. I had been impressed in many countries
by the devotion shown by Tantric Buddhists on their long pilgrimages on foot
or even by prostrating themselves on the ground, but in Zenkhe I encountered
the most perilous kora of all:

*"There's great activity at the Flawless Fearless Pagoda – it has been
opened up for the pilgrims and I follow them, climbing up dark wooden
staircases linking the eight floors, each housing a small room with an altar.
Finally at the top, a low door gives access to a 6-inch slate ledge around the
outside of the pagoda. The kora continues here, though I remain inside to
congratulate the pilgrims as they scramble back from their external circuit of
the tower, 25m above the ground, gasping and trembling with terror."*

Finally we boarded a new undamaged coach to enter the historic Tibetan
region of Kham. Teddy had intended to take us to see Sertar Monastic

School – founded in 1980 and now the largest Tibetan Buddhist school in the world, attended by 40,000 monks and nuns. However, a barrier across the road leading to the settlement confirmed his information that the area was currently closed to visitors, especially to foreign visitors, since there was some unrest amongst the Tibetans there. This was our first indication that Kham was on high alert – there was an important political congress taking place in far-away Beijing, and authorities throughout regions prone to rebellion were nervous. Instead we continued over a high pass, climbing to 4211m to reach an expanse of grassland dotted with the white tents of nomadic herdsmen – in Sichuan most Tibetan nomads were using white canvas tents provided by the government instead of their traditional black yak-hair versions. We turned off on to a brand-new, deliciously smooth road … only to discover an unfinished tunnel a few miles further along, so a precarious 3-point turn brought us back to the old road:

"… broken tarmac beneath a thick layer of mud, winding uphill in a series of hairpins, squeezing past descending trucks with no more than an inch to spare. At the summit we find an area of treeless grassland, crossing it for a time before descending on even tighter hairpins to the valley below, re-joining the highway at a point where the new road flies in via a high bridge."

Another slow-moving checkpoint awaited us – this time a pair of policemen who progressed carefully down the coach photographing each of us together with our passports and visas. The senior policeman was stern and unsmiling, but his younger colleague was clearly excited to be processing a group of westerners, smiling and inviting us to photograph him. Eventually he even took several of us outside the coach for more photos, this time on his own camera-phone. He certainly had a lot to tell his family and friends that night!

Teddy had planned yet another monastery visit this afternoon, to Shouling Monastery which he assured us was one of the most important in the region, but … another monastery? Obediently we followed him past the lines of statues, minds switched off to resist the flow of intricate details about the role of each 'Boddhisattva' (enlightened being), but a boring visit was transformed into a highlight when …

"… a gong sounds, calling the 60 monks for a ceremony. They arrange themselves comfortably on the ground in the temple porch, huddled in thick

felt capes despite the warm sun. At first, they chat and laugh together, then begin to bow their heads to compose themselves, a few telling their prayer-beads or muttering mantras under their breath. Finally the chant-leader arrives, clears his throat and begins a series of droning repetitions, quickly followed by all the others. They are clearly focused on their words, absorbed in their work, some even adding small harmonies to the general deep throaty chanting."

More high passes, this time with glimpses of snow-flecked peaks beyond ... more open grassland grazed by herds of yak and dzo (half yak/ half cow) ... and another strict police checkpoint brought us to the city of Ganzi. Once again there was a distinct difference between the Chinese and the Tibetan parts of town – the two communities kept themselves separate, living very different lives from each other. The Chinese section was modern and featureless, the streets quiet and the businesses shuttered both in the evening and the early morning as our sightseeing commenced. However the Tibetan zone was constantly buzzing with activity: the pavements were crowded with food or clothing stalls, and even fairground-type games set up on street corners, where young men were laughingly trying their hand at hoopla or popping a balloon with an airgun.

Next day the Old Temple was ringed by Tibetans performing their morning kora, as busy as Oxford Street at rush hour. We pushed our way inside the temple, to find two prayer halls cluttered with statues and piles of supplies. In one hall, worshippers were prostrating themselves in front of two thrones draped with silk gowns ready to receive the spirits of the Dalai and Panchen Lamas whenever they chose to 'drop in'. I was interested to see a life-size photo of the current Panchen Lama's face inserted into the robe on his throne – he was selected and approved by the Chinese government. However, there was no picture of the current Dalai Lama, who is officially a non-person according to the Chinese and whose picture is banned. Instead there was a painting of the Bodhisattva whose reincarnation he is considered to be, an image understood by faithful Tibetans but meaningless to the Chinese – a clever way to get around the ban!

A fascinating walk through the narrow streets of the Tibetan town took us past tiny workshops humming with activity – carpenters hammering and planing in a cloud of sawdust; ladies stuffing cotton into duvets; machines grinding barley to make 'tsampa' (traditionally the staple food of Tibet). One household was receiving a delivery of winter fuel – a mound of dried pats of yak dung; others were drying grain on the pavement in front of their homes; several ladies were washing clothing in bowls beneath a communal tap in the street; one lady even had a twin-tub washing machine outside her home – though there was an electricity supply indoors, the only running water was at the standpipe outside. Finally we staggered up a long concrete stairway to the hilltop Ganzi Monastery where, in a cavernous dark chamber, several cooks were already stirring vast, open woks amid clouds of steam and smoke from wood fires, preparing enough food to provide lunch for over 600 monks.

A change in the weather brought heavy rain next day as we left the main highways, following a narrow, forested valley beneath steep slopes crumbling down on to the road in a series of mudslides and falling rocks. At the town of Xinlong we encountered a massive traffic jam of trucks, interwoven by cars squeezing their way forwards through the tiniest of gaps. After 30 minutes, the police appeared to marshal the trucks out of the way so that we could advance to yet another checkpoint, this time a sandbagged entrenchment backed by soldiers with submachine guns:

"Teddy gets off with our passports, then a policeman orders us all to get off the coach. We obey, but meanwhile he has moved on and no-one seems to know why we have disembarked. We mill around for a while, seizing the opportunity to relieve our bladders behind a wall, then get back on board. The chaos of China's police! The policemen are mostly very young and inexperienced – I think they are just terrified of doing the wrong thing, and perhaps losing this lucrative job?"

Our road eventually climbed towards another high pass, following a rushing stream up into the mist-shrouded mountains, a stomach-churning bumpy serpentine route following the twists and turns of the riverbed through the rocks. We stopped briefly in the roadside village of Junba which was a hubbub of activity – a row of houses was being demolished by huge machines, and the stones were being carried away in the arms of an army of local ladies. In addition, a school was registering the arrival of hordes of children who were returning from a weekend at their rural homes, to board here for another week. The whole village seemed to be standing around watching either the demolition or the children and was delighted to turn its attention to the marvel of our arrival, too! After chatting with several ladies, one invited me to see her home – very small and simple with just a single room housing three generations, with kitchen pots at one end and a bedstead at the other. Yet even that seemed luxurious compared to the tents of nomadic people we met camped by the roadside, containing only a few rugs and an iron stove – though the nomads were not poor, since they owned large herds of yak, each worth over £1000 from the butchers who drove up to these high pastures to buy their supplies.

We continued over the Cunge Pass (4482m) where the light, drizzling rain was transformed into a dusting of snow, finally reaching the city of Litang – one of the highest towns in the world at 4000m (13,000ft) and, according to our itinerary, the highlight of the tour. We were supposed to be visiting their world-famous festival with its displays of horsemanship, but there had been a mix-up in the planning of our tour: the horse festival was scheduled for the start of August each year, not October ... and it had actually not taken place for several years before my visit anyway, for security reasons. The festival we were going to visit was just a simple gathering of nomadic peoples for a type of harvest blessing:

"Teddy has some bad news for us. Will he tell us we are not permitted to attend the festival? After all, this is China, a police state, and we are in Tibet, a rebellious province – maybe the authorities want to keep us safe? But we are not banned ... Instead, the whole festival has been postponed because of the 5-yearly Party Congress!"

These disappointments might have spoiled the tour, but in fact Litang became one of our most memorable destinations – offering plenty of time to explore this remote area and meet its people. In the town itself, I visited general stores selling everything a Tibetan household could require, from copper pans and thermos flasks to tsampa (barley flour) and sugar ... and also the early morning markets where pork butchers were using gas-flames to burn off pigs' bristles, and yak butchers were besieged by customers admiring carcases still adorned with long tufted tails. In Litang, we finally found restaurants serving Tibetan food instead of Chinese dishes: tasty yak with roast potatoes, smoked bacon and fried or steamed momos, some of which resembled Cornish pasties. And the people were fascinating: many had the strong features of the nomadic Khampas instead of the rounder, softer faces we had been seeing so far. For once, it was the men who were most interesting – long hair restrained by coloured tassels or stuffed beneath stetson hats, faces burned almost black by the sun. The women were often hidden behind masks topped by wide-brimmed hats, to protect them from the burning rays.

Of course there were temples to visit: a small shrine built around the birthplace of the 7th Dalai Lama in the 18th century, and Litang Monastery – a massive complex of buildings above the town, destroyed in the Cultural Revolution but mostly rebuilt in the 1980s. In one of the smallest temples there, I was amazed to discover a picture of the current Dalai Lama perched on an altar, despite government rules – perhaps this temple was remote enough to be unnoticed by the authorities? Trying to fill the time, Teddy proposed a walk out into the countryside to visit a Sky Burial site – a rare opportunity since normally tourists are not permitted to see these places. Of course, there was no burial taking place at the time but, on an open piece of hillside beneath a network of prayer flags, we saw the altar where the family would lay the body to be cut up by specially trained monks, grinding up the bones and mixing with tsampa before being left for the birds. Even as we approached, a couple of lammergeier vultures circled over our heads, hopeful that we were bringing a burial – Teddy told us that large flocks of lammergeiers would arrive as soon as the incense smoke rose into the air, and the body would be gone within 30 minutes.

Our itinerary gave us three full days to spend in Litang, so we also took excursions out into the nearby countryside. We drove west as far as Haizishai Pass (4685m) where a viewing terrace looked out over a dramatic hairpin descent: here an enterprising salesman was selling smoked pork and yak meat to passing Chinese drivers (including smoked yak penis: Han people love to snack and will eat anything, it seems!). We also checked out the site where the Harvest Festival was due to take place, hoping that some nomads would not have heard about the cancellation – and indeed found one extended family camped beside a small tent where several monks were chanting blessings for them. The families welcomed our visit and we spent time with them:

"They're a very tranquil family: the grandparents sit smiling quietly, urging the children to pose for our cameras. The smallest girl sits on her mother's lap while another young woman busies herself with cooking, rattling

pans inside the tent. In a neighbouring tent sits another grandmother, watching over a tiny baby snuggled into a nest of blankets inside a crate."

On another day we drove south to a monastery at the foot of the holy Zhaga Mountain. We were especially welcomed by the three resident monks to this lonely place, lying at 4000m beneath sheer rock cliffs. There was just one other visitor at the time we were there, an unusually tall pilgrim monk equipped only with a staff, a small backpack and an umbrella – he encouraged us to walk a kora with him around the monastery, before he headed off up the mountain accompanied by the sound of chanting from an I-player in his knapsack. Returning through high pastureland, we were excited to see a man practising his skills at horsemanship, lying flat along the back of his galloping horse in a display of acrobatics – perhaps in the hope that the Chinese government would authorise the Horse Festival to take place next year?

Litang provided me with many special memories, though I will also not forget the extremely visible police and army presence in the town. There had been a history of unrest in this region over many decades and the authorities were ensuring that the population was well aware of the strength of police and army units in the area. From my hotel window I watched the arrival of busloads of armed soldiers from their barracks at precisely 8am each morning, practising baton-charges across the bus station before boarding their armoured cars to parade up and down the streets all day. At the same time, cadres of armed police yomped into place, marching in tight formation through the town at regular intervals. They were joined by police cars patrolling constantly with flashing blue lights, echoing sirens and commands by loudspeaker to clear the roads and pavements. The reaction of the local people? ... They continued with normal life, totally ignoring the activity around them and showing no signs of revolution!

Leaving Litang we returned eastwards, this time following the main road across the Kazilashan Pass (4718m). This area had been easily accessible for only a few months – Teddy told us that, until the middle of the year, the road had climbed a series of difficult switchbacks to the summit of the Gao'ersi Mountain, but now we were gliding back and forth across the valley on a corkscrew of bridges which effectively reduced the gradient as we climbed up to a new 5km tunnel beneath the summit. Chinese road engineers are amazing!

However, the 'scenic viewpoint' was crowded with buses and 4x4s which had disgorged hundreds of Han Chinese tourists to mill around the site, frantically snapping selfies from every angle – now that we were following better roads, we were joined by mass tourism again:

"On this gloriously sunny day, the highest peaks of the Koga Shan range float ethereally against the sky on the furthest horizon, their gleaming snow slopes blending with the brilliance of the sunlit clouds. Another viewpoint is again crowded with vehicles, but we force our way into the melee, disembarking to admire an impressive view down through tall pine trees to some of the 18-hairpin bends which will carry us to the valley far below."

We left the main road, and the tourist hordes, to follow a broad, tree-lined valley dotted with the large, well-built houses of wealthier Tibetans. The road continued into the Valley of Painted Stones, where the rocks lining the valley were carved and painted with religious images and texts: one of the features of the ancient religion of Bon, which was absorbed into Tibetan Buddhism, is its honouring of Nature. At the end of the road lay the small town of Tagong, overlooked by the gleaming snowy peak of the holy Yala Mountain. When I rose next morning, I was amazed to see the town outside my window now covered in a layer of snow, though it did not disrupt the worshippers performing their kora around the town temple, muffled against the cold and striding resolutely onward. Sightseeing started with this temple, the layout now familiar to us though I was impressed by the sense of awe and reverence in the oldest of the buildings:

"In the outer hall a lady is prostrating herself with deep concentration, whilst inside four pilgrims sit cross-legged in an attitude of prayer in front of a small Indian-style Buddha image encrusted with gold, coral and turquoise. To one side of the altar is a short ladder which the worshippers climb to lay silken scarves at Buddha's feet, then reach across to kiss the image."

We walked on through increasingly heavy snow showers to visit the Buddhist College beside the river, at the time being massively increased in size to cope with a surge in interest from young Tibetans. Some of our group elected to return to the hotel to escape the snow, but I followed Teddy to visit another college a little further from town:

"Should I? Will it be worthwhile? ... I'm so glad I decided to continue because, as we enter the courtyard, we hear the hubbub of typical Buddhist

debating – one of their main methods of teaching. In a tiny room at the top of a wooden staircase we find a group of young monks sitting in pairs on the floor, animatedly discussing philosophical tenets under the watchful eye of their masters."

More spectacular scenery accompanied our route back into the Jiarong region as the newly constructed road soared through the snow-capped Mia Guga Mountains, now dusted with fresh snowfall. We joined convoys of trucks twisting back and forth across the hillsides, negotiating hairpin bends with difficulty, until we reached the summit of the Zheduo Shan Pass (4298m) where we stopped to climb slippery snow-covered steps up to a viewpoint whipped by bitterly cold winds, looking down over the traffic-clogged road below and the magnificent mountain peaks all around us. From here it was downhill all the way, not just physically but also in terms of the tour itself: we were back into Han China … farewell to Tibet with its wide-open spaces and passionately spiritual people.

Teddy offered us one more 'highlight' – a visit to Luding Bridge, a chain bridge built in the 18th century to carry the horse caravans bringing tea from Sichuan to Tibet. Yet the bridge's main interest for Chinese tourists is the fact that in May 1935, it was used by the Red Army on their Long March. Their opponents, the KMT, had removed the roadway so 20 Red Army soldiers crossed the river hand-over-hand on the chains to re-open the bridge for their compatriots: a heroic story now commemorated only by rampant commercialisation … or so it seemed to me, as I walked through a forest of stalls selling snacks and Chinese medicines, past booths where tourists could rent Red Army costumes for the duration of their visit, to add interest to their incessant selfies. Then it was back to Chengdu, where Teddy took us to experience the city's nightlife:

"The real old town has been demolished and replaced by a reconstruction with all mod cons, which has become a 'visitor attraction' – in other words a retail park and hub for eateries. Many are offering photo opportunities in a polished-up version of Chinese culture – girls dressed in the exotic costume of the Longhorn Miao, an actor performing a movement of Peking Opera over and over again, a girl pouring tea in a ceremonial way … all to entice the crowds into that shop or restaurant."

This is how modern China seems to me – rushing into the 21st century but with a nostalgic desire to retain a few of the most picturesque aspects of the past; treating their history and culture as a Disneyworld, sanitised and unchallenging. I doubt I will visit the country again, despite the fascination of different peoples and cultures on the edges of its realm. It seems to me that the all-engulfing embrace of Han China will inevitably drown all but the faintest traces of ethnic diversity … and I do not want to see it happen.

Kham - 'kora' around the 'stupa'

Kham - Zheduo Shan Pass

Japanese meiko

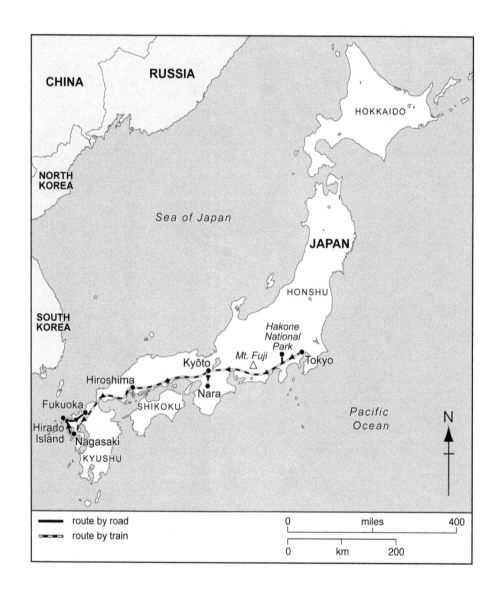

route by road
route by train

CHINA
RUSSIA
HOKKAIDO
NORTH KOREA
Sea of Japan
JAPAN
HONSHU
SOUTH KOREA
Hakone National Park
Mt. Fuji
Kyōto
Tokyo
Hiroshima
Nara
Fukuoka
SHIKOKU
Pacific Ocean
Hirado Island
Nagasaki
KYUSHU

N

0   miles   400
0   km   200

Japan (April 2018)

I'D ALWAYS HAD LOTS OF excuses not to visit Japan. I had been so often to China, yet had never carried on that little bit further ... why? Though travelling friends had often told me that it was a fascinating and beautiful land, my mental image had always been of crowds and huge cities, and I prefer wide-open, sparsely populated spaces. Finally I could not resist the urging of my friends any longer and set off on the 11-hour flight to Tokyo.

At first, all my previous reservations seemed to be realised. Tokyo was a maze of gleaming modern skyscrapers, its streets filled with highly polished cars, lined with well-stocked stores ... and everywhere there were crowds of people walking, eating or being pulled in shiny modern rickshaws. The crowding continued near our hotel, in a pedestrianised area which surrounded the historic Senso-Ji Temple – totally destroyed by fire-bombing in WW2 (as most of the city had been) and rebuilt in the middle of the 20th century with a tall pagoda and multiple smaller halls. However, I soon found myself fascinated by the people, all busy celebrating the Cherry Blossom Festival. Many ladies had rented gorgeously colourful kimonos to wear as they frolicked beneath the cherry trees, while their menfolk wore a more sombre-coloured version – as we toured the country, I discovered that the Japanese love to dress up for any occasion! The temple gave me a first taste of Japanese Buddhism, quite different from the Tibetan version – more like the Chinese obsession with seeking Good Luck, instead of worshipping a deity:

"I am puzzled by a constant clattering as I approach the temple, finally discovering it is the sound of coins being thrown as offerings into metal-

slatted chests. Worshippers then clap loudly to attract the attention of the gods, before folding their hands to make their prayer request. Some go on to shake a wooden spill from a container, reading its number and opening the corresponding drawer from a nearby cabinet, extracting a message like a horoscope."

Sightseeing next day attempted to give us a flavour of the city, though it would be impossible to explore an entire metropolis housing 37 million people in total. We started with a cruise on the waterways – I was surprised to learn that Tokyo is a city of canals, created with the help of Dutch engineers in the 18th and 19th centuries as protection from attack, though now used only by sightseeing boats and water-taxis. We transferred to the metro system, then to the local buses – all comfortable, clean and extremely easy to use. Japan was working hard to prepare to welcome international visitors to the 2020 Olympics and already announcements and signage throughout the public transport systems were in English as well as Japanese. In fact, they were even transforming the public toilets from traditional flat basins to western-style bowls – going one better than any western country I had visited, with toilets which came equipped with a bank of controls to allow for hygienic washing or toilet-seat heating. Japan was determined that their Olympic Games would give a massive boost to their popularity and respect in the rest of the world – what a disappointment it must have been for them when the COVID-19 pandemic caused the postponement of the Games.

Scattered among the skyscraper towers and high-level walkways of Tokyo, we visited several gardens providing an oasis of nature amid the hustle of city life. In

Koishikawa Korakuen garden, stone-paved paths wound in convoluted fashion round a series of low man-made hills, encircling a central lake where carp gaped hungrily at passing visitors. In the midst of a forested park, I visited the shrine commemorating Emperor Meiji, who brought Japan into the modern industrialised world after centuries of self-imposed isolation. Nearby was one of the city's most famous shopping zones, Takeshita Street:

"With the addition of a decorative gateway at its start, and some clever marketing, this street has attracted almost every visitor in the area. It is tightly packed with pedestrians eating every variety of savoury snack or ice-cream – the more weirdly-shaped or oddly-coloured the better. Clearly the

Japanese feel most at home in a crush, since I find I can easily escape the crowds just by walking along the next parallel alleyway."

I did my best to appreciate Tokyo, crossing by metro from one side of the city to the other, following the recommendations of my guidebook – but I found only the crowds and bustle I had feared. The itinerary promised that the next day would be more to my taste – we were to travel into the mountainous terrain of Hakone National Park close to Mount Fuji, highest in the country. However, almost the entire day was spent battling the crowds again: we squeezed on to a 'mountain train' then a 'switchback railway', both offering standing room only, though at least there was still some elbow room. That vanished when we transferred to a funicular train where we queued for 20 minutes then were packed in so tightly that we could not even turn our heads to admire whatever scenery might be visible outside. Finally one more long queue took us aboard the 'ropeway' (cable-car):

"Here at least we have a seat and a respite from the noise, with the whole gondola reserved just for our group. We glide in silence into the mists over thickly forested hills to the highest point of our journey at 1004m, a cool and windy col, pervaded by an offensive aroma rising from steaming vents in a hillside coloured garish yellow by the sulphur spewing from Hakone volcano."

Chilled and miserable we descended via another cable-car, then rode an electric ship disguised as a pirate galleon across Lake Ashi in the volcano's crater, from which we might have had a view of Mount Fuji – but ever-thicker cloud hid it totally from view. I was so disappointed with the day that I could have cried ... until we reached our hotel, a traditional 'ryoken' guesthouse hidden among the hills, boasting two bathing pools fed by natural hot springs. Our hostess instructed us in the etiquette of Japanese bathing (reserve a precise time slot, wash thoroughly at the taps around the bath first) and then I was first to sink into the gloriously hot water, feeling the frustrations of the day melting away. Dressed now in a crisp cotton Yukata robe, attempting in vain to tie the obi belt in the correct manner, I returned to my sparsely furnished room with a futon mattress laid directly on top of wonderfully soft tatami reed mats on the floor. Apart from the difficulty of getting to my feet in the morning (if you are also of a 'certain age', you will know what I mean!), an intensely comfortable night's sleep followed.

Next day an almost empty public bus carried us smoothly to the station to join the 'Shinkansen' – the Japanese 'bullet train' which we used throughout our tour, with reserved seats and no hassle at all. And a few minutes after departure, a shriek of excitement from the right-hand side of the train drew me to the window – there was Mount Fuji, a dramatic snow-capped volcanic cone rising majestically above the car-parks and commercial centres lining the railway tracks. Our destination was Kyoto, for over 1000 years capital of Japan and still the most historic city in the country, spared from bombing by the Allies in WW2 because of its cultural importance. Paradoxically our first sight of the city was the vast 10-storey modern railway station, incorporating a busy shopping centre topped by roof gardens, but soon we were exploring magnificent sights like the Golden Pavilion Temple:

"Wow! A perfectly golden, gleaming, immaculately symmetrical structure, reflected in a surrounding lake and enhanced by the fresh green foliage of trees. As if on command, the sun emerges to add sparkle to the gold leaf."

Once again touring by public bus, we moved on to Kennin-ji Zen Temple, a complex of flimsy rooms with rice-paper walls and exotically curved roofs peeping above precisely pruned trees. Alongside was its formal garden where carefully placed rocks and raked patterns in gravel were designed to assist Zen practitioners to concentrate their meditation and thus transcend the sufferings of life. We also visited Ryoan-ji Zen Temple, though flocks of jabbering Chinese tourists made it difficult to achieve any sense of tranquillity there. While I enjoyed these glimpses into Japan's history, I was surprised to learn how many of the buildings were actually reconstructions: the original Ryoan-ji Temple was wrecked in a civil war in the 15th century which destroyed most of the ancient buildings in the entire country. Only the 13th century Kennin-ji and Golden Temple escaped destruction, though the Golden Temple was burned to the ground in 1950 and had to be rebuilt:

"This place is preserved, but it seems the concept of valuing architectural history is strange to the Japanese – many historic buildings are under threat from the urge for constant modernisation. Perhaps in a country prone to earthquake, fire and war, it just seems pointless to try to preserve anything?"

For me, the most memorable aspect of Kyoto was the continuing tradition of Geishas, here called Geiko. In a country which puts a high priority on apprenticeships for young people, this was the only place where a 5-year apprenticeship in the art of the Geisha was available, teaching young girls how to entertain with conversation, music and dance (but not sexual pleasures). During their training, the girls (at this stage called Meiko) lived with a house mother, wearing precious kimonos (each costing upwards of £10,000) which belonged to the household and contributing all monies earned to their Mama-san. Only after training could they live independent lives, though they remained part of the same household, paying commission to Mama-san in exchange for the use of kimonos and the services of a hairdresser qualified to create their elaborate hairstyles. We visited one of the Geiko districts, walking past rows of small discreet 'tea-houses' where guests could visit the girl of their choice, though we also saw Geiko hurrying along the street dressed in their finery, en route to another venue where their services had been hired. Most interesting of all, we had been invited to an audience with one of the Meiko. It was not possible to visit either Meiko or Geiko unless recommended by a previous customer (as protection for the girls), so this was a rare privilege for a tourist group, possible only because our guide had the right connections ... and the money to pay her fee, of course. Our Meiko was aged 18, in the third year of her apprenticeship. We had precisely one hour of her time, during which she answered our questions frankly (through an interpreter), telling us that she was proud to be helping to preserve this ancient Japanese tradition. Then she played a few simple drinking games with us and performed a dance, observed throughout by her tutor:

"... standing and crouching, swaying, gesturing and nodding – all to the sound of an exotic wailing song. Very slow and stately, but oh so elegant and graceful."

With another day allocated to Kyoto, I decided to take a local train to the nearby community of Nara, famous for its Giant Buddha statue in the Todai-ji Temple – though I was keen only to see the herds of wild deer in the park around the temple. I found the deer, though they were so spoiled by visitors that they were no longer very wild, instead lying around chewing their cud or waiting hopefully by groups of tourists for food. The Buddha was not as impressive as I had expected either, smaller than some I had seen elsewhere (at 20m high) and made of bronze so tarnished that it faded into the dark interior of the temple. I was more impressed when I read the information boards and learned that the statue was 1300 years old – I guess I would be a bit faded if I was that old! However, my visit to Nara came to life when I wandered into the old town:

"The street is lined with traditional wooden merchant homes, their windows obscured from the outside by wooden slats, which paradoxically offer a good view from inside. Each house is long and thin, with minimal frontage – just three residential rooms running one from the next, each carpeted with soft tatami mats and equipped with minimal furniture. A tiny internal garden offers a moment of Zen contemplation and a flight of stairs runs up to an attic – cleverly each step contains a storage drawer."

Next day we boarded another Shinkansen train, travelling beside a grey sea through landscapes where every inch of flat land seemed to be covered in densely packed housing – even the parked cars outside blocks of flats were ingeniously piled vertically on top of each other using hydraulic ramps, to save space. Yet forested hilltops rose untouched from the suburban sprawl – apparently the Japanese venerated their hills and usually avoided developing them.

We left the train at Hiroshima, infamous for the dropping of an atomic bomb on August 6th 1945 – intended to shock the Japanese into surrender. The bomb totally incinerated the entire city centre, which was mainly composed of wooden structures similar to those I had seen in Nara, killing over 100,000 people either immediately or in the ensuing months. The river island which formed the city centre in 1945 was never rebuilt and instead became the Peace Park, where we spent several hours visiting various memorials:

"We enter the Hiroshima Museum, dedicated not to condemnation of the attack but rather to the pursuit of peace. It is crowded but almost silent as everyone takes in the sobering story. A model shows the layout of the city before the bomb dropped, then uses lighting to superimpose images of the attack – a 3 second flash of white light; rolling flames and smoke as it burned; the blackened remains where only a few concrete walls still stood. And there are lots of pictures of the horrific injuries inflicted – massive burns like a crust coating backs or faces, people with the pattern of their clothing burned into their skin ..."

A series of trains took us onwards to Nagasaki, recipient of the second atomic bomb – but this time it fell just outside the city centre, which was protected from the blast by the ranges of hills which enclosed it: as a consequence there were still many historic buildings to see. Nagasaki had been a trading city throughout its history, even when the rest of the country was closed to foreigners – hosting the Portuguese in the 16th century and the Dutch in the 17th century, with the British arriving in the 19th century. I visited Dejima Island, once a foreign enclave where the Portuguese and Dutch merchants were obliged to remain throughout their 3 or 4-month trading visits:

"In the middle of the street an ornate exterior stairway leads up to the factor's residence, a suite of nine rooms packed with furniture and fripperies. After the sparse furnishing I have seen in traditional Japanese homes, it strikes me how claustrophobic Japanese visitors must have found these western-style rooms."

By the time the British arrived, Japan had been forced (by gunboat) to open up to the world, so the splendid mansions of the British traders were located on the hillsides above the old town – with no consideration for the Japanese veneration of hills. Now they were museums set in gardens where Japanese visitors proudly dressed themselves up in 19th century European style. Walking back down into the city centre, I was shocked to see a gaudy red and yellow temple – a Confucian shrine given to Nagasaki by China in 1893: the Chinese were the only foreigners permitted in Japan during the period when the country was closed to other foreigners. The city still had a sizeable community living in a large Chinatown, where old men were sitting outdoors playing board games and snack bars were selling typical Chinese foods.

Throughout my visit I had been amazed by the variety of different cuisines available in Japan. I had expected to be eating 'sushi' (raw fish and vegetables, rolled with rice) most of the time, though discovered that in fact 'sashimi' (raw fish and vegetables but without the rice) was more common. My favourite method of cooking was 'tempura', again fish and vegetables but fried in a light crispy batter. Restaurants rarely offered a range of different styles of cooking – instead, I selected a 'sushi' restaurant or a 'tempura' restaurant and then consulted the menu to see what ingredients they offered in their specialist style. Foreign cuisines were also popular, especially Italian food – I sampled an excellent pizza in a tiny eating house in Nara; in Nagasaki our guide took us to a curry house serving any meat, fish or vegetable accompanied by rice and a thick curry sauce – though it was sweet rather than spicy, and not to my taste at all!

Also in Nagasaki I began to hear stories of the Secret Christians. In the 16th century, Portuguese adventurers offered both trade and also teaching in the secrets of weaponry to the Japanese overlord (the Shogun), but only if he permitted Jesuit missionaries to come to preach. The Shogun ordered some of his Samurai lords to 'convert' in order to satisfy the Portuguese, but later decided that Christianity threatened his power, so the missionaries were expelled. However, there had also been genuine conversions to Christianity – some Japanese priests were martyred but many believers went underground, continuing to practise their faith in secret. Finally, in the middle of the 19th century, freedom of religion was restored and French missionaries were allowed to come to Nagasaki and build a Catholic cathedral. After its inauguration, attended by virtually no Japanese, the French priests were amazed when a few local people appeared, claiming that their families had remained Christian for hundreds of years, continuing to say mass for themselves in a 'secret language' – a bastardisation of Latin. A museum alongside Nagasaki's Ouro Cathedral told their story.

The story continued when we travelled out to Hirado Island, one of over 6000 islands in Japan and an important trading centre between Japan, Korea and China for over 1000 years. Perhaps because they were so accustomed to foreigners and their ideas, a much larger proportion of the island's people became Christian – still 15% of their population. We were shown some of the older houses which contained a secret room equipped with a Christian altar, hidden behind the traditional Shinto and Buddhist altars. Shinto was the oldest of Japan's faiths, blended with Buddhism when it arrived from China and still an important part of 'being Japanese'. In the minds of most Japanese people, Buddhism was concerned mainly with death and the after-life, dictating the ceremonies conducted after death. On the other hand, Shinto represented a way of living: involving orderliness and supreme cleanliness (I even saw someone polishing the escalators in Kyoto station!), purity of spirit and respect for the environment. Shinto was the basis for strict rules about behaviour, including the depth of bow offered to people of different social status, and exaggerated politeness.

Firm rules on behaviour accompanied us when we visited a tea plantation north of Nagasaki, where every terrace across the hillside was filled with very low-clipped bushes (only 1ft high, much lower than those in Sri Lanka). After explaining all the processes and proudly showing us his gleaming new harvesting machines (no hand-picking here), the owner took us to his home for a tea ceremony, conducted by a university-trained 'tea master'. She guided us through the correct procedures, rebuking us when we did not wait to achieve the correct temperature of water before adding it to the tea, or when we added too much hot water. Finally she permitted us to pour the tea into tiny cups to sample, ensuring that each cup received only a small amount on each round of the teapot, so each was of equal strength. Eventually we were permitted to sample it – a fresh green flavour, like newly-cut grass.

Our last nights in Japan were spent on Hirado Island and finally I found a part of the country which I could enjoy. The island was sparsely populated and mountainous, its people living from fishing (including the propagation of pearl oysters) and farming. We visited Neshko Beach, an expanse of deserted white sand beside turquoise water, and drove on to the neighbouring island of Ikitsuki to see the 80m high Shiodawara Cliffs:

"We follow the path up to a lighthouse on the summit, then down the side of the cliffs, high above a crystal-clear, luminously blue sea – like Cornwall on the best of days. Kites and hawks soar overhead, brightly coloured butterflies flit from flower to flower in the sunshine. A viewpoint allows us to look out over the 'Sacks of Salt', basalt pillars formed millions of years ago after a nearby volcano erupted."

Best of all was our accommodation on Hirado, in another traditional 'ryoken' inn. What bliss to sink into the large communal bath reserved for ladies (there was another for the men) … then later, all dressed in our Yukata robes, to recline on floor-cushions for a banquet spread on a low table:

"What an idyll! The ryoken is new and purpose-built so the rooms are spacious, equipped with futon and tatami mats but also a western-style WC and a tiny lounge with easy chairs overlooking the view, where fishing boats chug past and oyster strings bob in sheltered spots out of the current. With the window open, I can hear the birds chirruping and the waves lapping on the shore – later a chorus of frogs sings into the night."

My trip to Japan was over. Perhaps if I had spent longer in the rural communities at the southern end of the island chain, or even visited the much less developed northern island of Hokkaido, I would have enjoyed myself more. It was certainly interesting to learn about the very different Japanese customs and priorities, and we were privileged to have an audience with an apprentice Geisha. Those three delightful nights in 'ryoken' inns remain a highlight. However, my principal memories of Japan are of a natural landscape disciplined by tradition and crushed beneath modern development, plus overwhelming crowds.

Tokyo - Senso Ji temple

Australia - Wave Rock

Purnululu - Cathedral Gorge

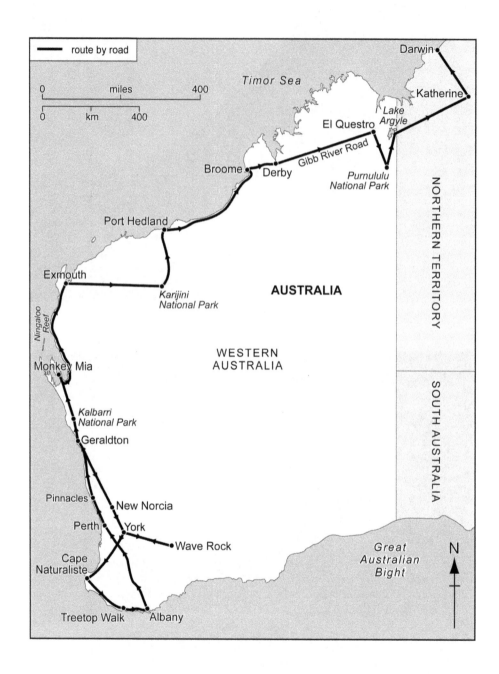

route by road

0   miles   400
0   km   400

Timor Sea

Darwin

Katherine

Lake Argyle

El Questro

Gibb River Road

Broome

Derby

Purnululu
National Park

Port Hedland

Exmouth

Karijini
National Park

AUSTRALIA

Ningaloo
Reef

Monkey Mia

WESTERN
AUSTRALIA

NORTHERN TERRITORY

SOUTH AUSTRALIA

Kalbarri
National Park

Geraldton

Pinnacles

New Norcia

Perth

York

Wave Rock

Cape
Naturaliste

Great
Australian
Bight

N

Treetop Walk

Albany

Western Australia (April/May 2018)

I HAD TRAVELLED ALL THE way to Japan, almost halfway round the world, so why not keep going and complete the circle – visiting some of the more inaccessible regions I had been dreaming of for years? Back in the 1980s I had visited the eastern and central parts of Australia, planning to come back to the west on another occasion, but that occasion had never arrived ... until now! Friends had told me about the Kimberley wilderness, so I was pleased to find a tour exploring that region whilst camping out beneath the stars – but was I still physically able to handle a tour like that? Only one way to find out – the booking was made!

It almost did not happen, since there was a mix-up with my Australian e-visa and the meticulous Japanese ground-staff refused to check me in for the flight to Perth. Fortunately, my flight was due to stop over in Hong Kong, so I persuaded them to allow me to fly that far, thinking to visit an embassy there to sort out the problem. However the Chinese staff proved more flexible, correcting the e-visa error so I could catch my original onward flight, even seeking out and relabelling my baggage themselves – well done Cathay Pacific!

I had a week to spare before joining my tour so I rented a car, first heading northwards from Perth to visit friends living in a rural community outside Geraldton – a wonderful introduction to the relaxed and spontaneous way of life in Western Australia. What a welcome from a delightful family – barbecue in the garden on the first evening, beneath a sky carpeted with stars; a full day sightseeing in and around the grain-port of Geraldton; then a last-minute decision to catch sunset at nearby Lucy's Beach:

"We leap into the car and hurtle down dirt roads through the dunes to the beach. The sun sinks below the horizon just as we arrive, but still we set up chairs on the edge of the sea to drink beer as we watch large waves smash themselves against offshore rocks in huge plumes of spray."

Most of my self-drive week was spent exploring the south-western corner of the state, travelling first inland through vast expanses of silvery stubble left after the wheat harvest – every community was equipped with huge grain silos beside the railway line and dotted with mounds of grain under tarpaulins, just waiting for collection. Frequently there were hints of recent major flooding in the now dried-up streambeds, and blackened tree trunks were reminders of devastating fires – life was clearly not easy in this land of extremes. There were sobering thoughts too, when I visited a huge Catholic college in New Norcia, established in the 19th century by a bishop with the good intentions of teaching local Aborigines to 'protect themselves from the worst aspects of colonial life' (to quote one of the information boards). However from 1901-71 it became a boarding school for Aborigine children forcibly taken from their families to prepare them for living in a white society. Not until a few years prior to my visit had any apology been offered, recognising the immorality of what had taken place there.

I based myself for a couple of nights in the historic town of York, its main street lined with carefully maintained wooden arcades and pediments. My goal was to visit Wave Rock, which I imagined lay in the midst of Australia's desert heart, accessible only by dirt tracks ... in fact a smooth tarmac road led me through more harvested wheat fields directly to the car-park – no cause for worry at all! Wave Rock itself was a surprise too ...

"... relatively short in length, though impressively high – a concave cliff-face decorated with orange and black stripes from the lichen and algae living on the rock. It is simply one edge of a large granite outcrop, though still dramatic."

Having achieved that goal I now headed to the coast, where a string of noisy holiday resorts was punctuated by peaceful reserves intended to protect the dunes and natural scrubland. I stopped to walk to Cape Naturaliste, strolling through waist-high scrub to a viewpoint high above cliffs washed by gentle waves. I was surprised by the amount of vegetation here, though heavy rain showers quickly taught me that this area receives far more rainfall than most of the state. As I continued along the southern part of the coast, the vegetation was transformed into forests of magnificent stately trees, including the Giant Tingle Tree (named for the local Aborigine tribe), over 300 years old and with its heart burned out by forest fire, yet still thriving. Further on I visited the Treetop Walk, a long steel structure sloping upwards to a maximum height of 40m among the treetops ... and terrifyingly bouncy, especially when a family of excited children followed me on the walkway:

"Am I travelling once more along California's Redwood Highway? Tall Karri trees soar up on massive trunks, standing straight as a die and reaching high into the vaulted canopy far above. Standing beneath these giants I feel completely dwarfed – all sound is hushed in this natural cathedral. A few cars pass, scuttling like beetles in the undergrowth, unnoticed by the ancient trees."

Rainfall shrouded my last hours on the coast but faded away as I returned to the arid wheatfields of the interior to head back to Perth and hand in my car. Perth was clearly benefiting from the mining boom in the northern part of Western Australia. The city centre was filled with gleaming glass and steel skyscrapers, though there were still traces of its history – the tiny Old Courthouse from 1837; St George's Anglican cathedral, a heavy brick Gothic construction from the 1880s hemmed in by soaring modern tower blocks; the elegant 1860s Government House hiding discreetly behind high fences and deep lawned gardens. I enjoyed a stroll in King's Park, full of trees and birds (including my first Laughing Kookaburra and some rare Black Cockatoos), but city streets were not what I was seeking. Instead I took a local train to the nearby port of Fremantle, the playground of Perth, with a waterfront lined with fish restaurants and lively bars. Its history as a gateway for European settlers was commemorated in the Maritime Museum with hundreds of 'Welcome Walls' recording the names and arrival dates of over 21,000 migrants.

Now it was time to meet the group I would be travelling with for the next month: a rugged expedition truck containing a mixture of Europeans and Australians, almost all much younger than myself – would they tolerate an 'old woman' in their midst? In fact they were very supportive: encouraging me in every activity, no matter how physically demanding, and helping me along where necessary. Many thanks to all of them! We headed north, on the coast road this time, stopping briefly to view a group of weird fingers of limestone poking up from an expanse of sand – the Pinnacles. Then it was a race against time to reach Kalbarri Cliffs by sunset. Every night our guide Simmo tried to reach a suitably dramatic spot to watch the sunset – a daily highlight to enliven long days of driving from dawn to dusk or beyond:

"The setting sun finds a crack at the base of the cloud to paint a lurid red line along the sea, as if liquid fire has been spread for miles across the water. We stand on the weathered sandstone cliffs, surrounded by eroded and crumbling rock, to watch as the last trace of vivid crimson sun sinks gracefully out of sight, leaving us in soft grey twilight."

The first nights were spent in hostels, with a communal kitchen where we all assisted in preparing and cooking our meals, usually sleeping in rooms with multiple bunks and limited washing facilities – roll on the privacy of a tent! Any discomfort was quickly forgotten however, when we began to encounter the stunning scenery which we had been promised. We drove into Kalbarri National Park, aiming to explore part of the 80km-long Murchison River gorge, hiking all the way down through the cliffs to the river far below. Would I manage to keep up with my youthful fellow travellers? In fact, though I was slower than most, I walked more securely (with the aid of my trusty walking poles) and emerged unscathed from the gorge … while two of the younger ones had to be helped back to the bus with twisted ankles!

"We scramble across huge red sandstone boulders, the most difficult cut into steep stairways, to reach the pools of green water which comprise the river in this season – though patterns of erosion reveal just how violent the churning water can be when there's rain. A few silvery eucalyptus trees cling precariously to cracks in the rock, a splash of contrasting colour amid the deep red of the cliffs."

We continued along a totally straight and featureless road, covering 115km without a single curve – the 2nd longest stretch of straight road on the continent. Simmo was enthusiastically telling us about our next visit: Shark Bay Heritage Site, where we would see extremely rare stromatolites, the most ancient life form on the planet at over 3 billion years old, the first creatures to use oxygen for life:

"Full of enthusiasm to see these rare creatures, we stride out on to a boardwalk built over the shallows of the sea, looking out for dramatic penis-

shaped towers! But on the sand below us are just small black cushions, looking like curved sausages – is that it?"

Far more impressive was our next destination: the bay at Monkey Mia, where for fifty years dolphins had been coming close to shore seeking titbits, initially from local fishermen – now it had been developed into a major tourist destination. The whole experience was strictly regulated by wardens, with spectators only permitted to approach the water when commanded and then only to wade up to calf depth. A few dolphins were already cruising offshore, so the crowd attempted to shuffle forwards as a long description of the lifestyle of dolphins was broadcast over loudspeakers … wardens strictly moved offenders back once more to an acceptable position:

"The dolphins recognise the wardens standing in the water and follow them up and down the length of the beach, bumping their legs and rubbing against them. Finally a few visitors are selected to walk deeper into the water holding small buckets of fish, waiting for the instruction to lay a fish in the water for a dolphin to take. Each receives only five fish, to avoid them becoming dependent on this food source. They know the routine – after their last fish is presented, they immediately turn back out to sea."

Next stop was in the tiny tourist community of Coral Reef, at the southern end of the Ningaloo Reef, 260km long and in much better condition than the more famous Barrier Reef on the other side of the continent: cooler water had produced more resilient hard corals and there was no infestation of destructive Crown of Thorns starfish. I chose to take a snorkelling trip, starting in the so-called Aquarium where the gentlest of currents made the swimming easy. Further out to sea we dropped again into the water, this time seeing a turtle lifting off its bed of coral directly below us – but here the current was stronger, and I was unable to follow as the group swam off behind the turtle. Another snorkelling spot left me fascinated by a deep patch of coral where brilliantly coloured fish popped in and out of a maze of caves and gullies … so absorbed that I failed to notice the boat moving further away from me. It required all my strength to flipper my way back to it:

"The Reef is a delight to snorkel, abounding in creatures of every size and colour: small cheeky black and white tiddlers; pure black fish which can dislocate their jaw to protrude forward in a miniature snout; golden angel fish; parrot fish coloured a vivid combination of turquoise and green. The coral

varies from round 'brains' to massive 'cabbage stalks', and spiky white fingers illuminated by vivid blue 'fairy lights' on their fingertips."

Our journey continued along the length of the Reef to its northern extremity at the town of Exmouth, though we arrived much later than planned at our first tented camp – a mysterious fault had developed in the truck, so we were unable to travel at more than 60kph. As I finally searched out my tent in the darkness, I was accompanied by a large and curious bird later identified by a jealous local 'birder' as a rare Australian Bustard! Because of the vehicle problems, we ended up spending three nights in this rural campsite with lots of time to watch the local wildlife – including common Galah cockatoos and parakeets, plus a lively altercation between a small Euro kangaroo with a joey in her pouch and a randy male: she sent him packing!

Exmouth offered the chance to swim with whale sharks – the world's largest fish, up to 12m in length and with a huge mouth to scoop up plankton as they swim. I was nervous (I had not coped well with the currents INSIDE the reef and for this trip we would be swimming OUTSIDE amid oceanic currents), but I obediently wriggled into the tight wetsuit designed to protect us from 'stingers' (poisonous jellyfish). Then we headed through the reef into the open sea ... worryingly much rougher than the crew usually considered acceptable. Spotters using drones informed the captain where a whale shark had been seen and we powered to the site while the crew organised us into small groups. Once in position, each group dropped into the water in turn when ordered to 'go, go, go':

"I line up alongside our guide, then on command plunge my face into the water ... and there is a whale shark only a couple of feet below me! A massive dark shape speckled with white spots, its huge mouth only partly open as it seeks its food, its gills pulsing as it breathes. It's in no hurry and cruises gently along our row of observers."

The next sighting followed on quickly, but everything began to go wrong for me. The whale shark dived, and my group was held back on the boat's swimming platform, bouncing up and down in the waves and surrounded by nausea-inducing engine fumes – I was sick. However I still joined my group on the platform for the next sighting:

"I'm in position when a sudden swell knocks me upwards to bash my head hard on the upper step. The rest of the group leaps into the water so I also slip

in, looking down and spotting another whale shark in the distance. I try to swim towards it, but other flippers have whipped the water into a cloud of bubbles. Disorientated and semi-conscious, I give up and return to the ship, needing help to be hauled bodily back aboard and to remove my mask and flippers. Then all I can do is perch on a seat, still dazed and sick."

Though I eventually recovered, my confidence was gone, and I did not join any more dives – I was content with the whale sharks I had seen. In the ensuing days we stopped at various white coral beaches where most of the group swam and snorkelled, but I had had enough of the sea for a while and relaxed instead in whatever shade I could find, watching the birds.

With a new vehicle driven up from Perth, 15 hours away, we were finally able to move on into Karijini National Park, leaving the sealed roads to follow dirt tracks into the heart of ranges of heavily eroded mountains – some of the oldest rocks on earth. Over the next three days we explored deep gorges carved out by rivers over millennia – I was amazed by the colours of the rocks in the convoluted strata of the cliffs, ranging from deep purple through rich orange to pink and white. At the bottom of most of the gorges were pools of clear water, so inviting that we plunged in as soon as we reached them:

"It's cool but not cold – a delicious refreshment on a hot day. I paddle my way gently along the gorge, beneath striped and eroded cliffs rising sheer from the water. It's totally silent here except for the gentle lapping of the water against the rock and the distant cries of our group. I float quietly on my back, looking up the cliffs to blue sky and white clouds high above me."

Our first visit was to Hamersley Gorge, relatively easy to reach with just a few rock-cut stairways to negotiate; then came Joffre Gorge where we scrambled down Grade 4 scree slopes to a rocky platform 10m above the river – the ladies stopped briefly there, to build up enough courage to follow the young men over the edge and down a Grade 5 cliff to the river. Most difficult of all was Hancock Gorge:

"First a stretch of broken rock and metal ladders brings us to the stream, where I swap walking boots for watershoes, wading knee deep beneath the cliffs. As we reach some large boulders, it's time to leave my boots and slide down worn and slippery rocks into deeper water, much colder now because the gorge is so narrow that the sun cannot reach it. A short swim, then comes the Spider Walk – a narrow cleft of slippery black rock where we must

straddle the stream with arms and legs wide to emerge into Kermit's Pool, a deep narrow channel beneath vertical cliffs. Wow! I have made it!"

Most of the rest of the group went on to tackle another even more difficult gorge leading to Handrail Pool, where hikers had to hang from a handrail to descend a slippery slope to the water – too much for me, so instead I stopped beside the water in the upper gorge amid beds of reeds. As the group moved off, the water in the pool beside me grew still, transformed into a perfect mirror which reflected exactly the red cliffs, pure white gum trees, blue sky and wispy clouds – a symphony of colour which filled the entire gorge.

Karijini NP was the highlight of the entire trip for me – abiding memories of golden grasses and the convoluted gleaming white branches of Snappy Gum trees; rich red cliffs soaring above refreshing pools; trickling streams where exotic red, blue and yellow dragonflies danced. And Simmo had one last gorge for us before we departed, descending a series of metal walkways and stairs into Dales Gorge to walk through reeds and trees to Fern Pool, a sacred site for local Aborigines where we were asked to maintain silence in respect:

"I am first in, slipping gently into the water and stroking quietly across the calm green waters toward a small waterfall splashing into the pool in a welter of sparkling droplets. I push under the waterfall for a back massage, then float back into the centre of the pool, gazing at the cloudless blue sky and thick banks of reeds waving in a hint of breeze. It's Sunday and this is a sacred spot – a chance to reconnect with my God."

What a contrast as we continued northwards into Western Australia's mining regions, the roads filled with immense 'road trains' – trucks pulling up to 7 trailers, laden with iron ore; difficult to pass (we timed one overtaking manoeuvre as requiring 1.05 minutes to complete). Near the industrial centre of Port Hedland we met a railway line, held up while a train towing 134 ore-carriers crossed the road – we were just pleased that we did not have to wait for a train pulling the record 680 trucks! Finally we pulled into Broome, where the first part of the tour finished – many of the Australians departed for home, and the rest of us had two days to relax before continuing. The group was booked into a hostel in town, but I elected instead to find my own accommodation – a delightful cabin in a nearly empty trailer park, filled with birds and even a few rare Frilled Lizards. Broome was a relaxed (though not particularly scenic) town, with several famous beaches. While we were there, I joined crowds of locals and visitors to watch the 'Staircase to the Moon' on Town Beach – the reflection of the rising moon on rippled mud left behind by the retreating tide. There were only two days each month when that could be seen, but on every night, crowds were gathered at Cable Beach to watch the glowing sunset.

It was time to meet my new guide/ driver (Damien) and his even more rugged expedition truck. Unlike Simmo, he was clearly displeased to find an older person on his tour, preferring the teens and twenties who made up most of the rest of the group. But I am not put off that easily – regardless of his opinions of my capabilities, I was determined to achieve as much as possible! However, I could not fault his expertise in travel through the difficult landscapes ahead of us, nor his huge knowledge of the region, especially the sad tales of the Budaba aboriginal tribe who had been displaced from their traditional lands and way of life by the arrival of sheep and cattle farmers in the 19th century. Damien explained that originally the tribespeople wandered freely, the men making hunting expeditions while the women and children foraged nearer to home. An important part of their lifestyle revolved around socialising, with just 3 or 4 hours a day spent on collecting food, and the rest on building family links and educating the children by chatting and storytelling. As we headed north out of Broome, we saw more and more native people still following that tradition, sitting in groups in shady spots – perhaps a custom interpreted by white Australians as laziness?

Another sign that we were heading into the northern wilderness was the appearance by the roadside of the weird swollen trunks of Baob trees – just outside Derby we stopped to see an especially large, hollow specimen (reputedly 1500 years old) which was once used to confine prisoners en route to the town's courts. At Derby we turned off the smoothly surfaced Route One which runs right around the continent, to bounce along gravel roads through flat landscapes occupied by immense cattle stations, the boundaries of each identified only by a cattlegrid in the road and a few strings of rusty barbed wire. Suddenly the serrated reddish hills of the King Leopold Ranges rose before us, slashed by a dramatic cleft – Windjana Gorge, our first chance to walk in the Kimberley wilderness:

"It's an easy stroll, following a placid river into the depths of the gorge

beneath lurid red and white rocks, beside trees rich in birds. In the river are our first freshwater crocodiles – a group floating immobile in the water while one sits on the bank immediately below us, still as a statue with its mouth open just wide enough to reveal serrated teeth."

Further along the ridge we stopped again to visit Tunnel Creek, picking our way through a jumble of huge boulders to enter a vast dark chamber hung with stalactites, wading through thigh-deep pools of water as the cavern led us right through to the far side of the mountain:

"We turn to retrace our steps and Damien races ahead, leaving a few of us to pick our way more cautiously through the boulders. It's a scary feeling as the other head-torches fade into the distance – clearly this part of the tour will be much harder: maybe here I will have to accept my age and give up on some of the visits? The thought reduces me to frustrated tears."

However a glorious night's camping restored my conviction that I should persevere with my wilderness experience – for the first time we were issued with 'swags' (sleeping bags with a canvas outer covering), laying them out on the sandy ground beneath a sky thick with stars. At first a distant owl hooted and crickets chirped, but as the night progressed and a full moon rose to bathe our campsite in brilliant white light, all sounds faded into deep silence. Next day we continued through eroded sandstone ridges where remnants of the last rains still filled pools and creeks. Clouds of birds swirled above the flooded areas, including elegant white Brolga Cranes and black/white Butcher Birds singing in deliciously liquid tones. Wallabies and dingoes bounded away from us as we rattled along the infamous Gibb River Road into the heart of the Kimberley, stopping to visit some of the remote gorges for which it is famous.

Exploring Bell Gorge involved picking my way from one submerged rock to the next along the riverbed, then down a precipitous path among massive boulders to the edge of a deliciously cool basin fed by a waterfall. A chance for me to swim while the younger group members slid down a water chute to yet lower pools. The afternoon brought us to Galvano Gorge where a rocky path led alongside a tumbling stream to another pool:

"I had decided not to swim again, but this magical, circular pool is just too inviting to ignore – surrounded by broken red cliffs, in places adorned by palm trees. A narrow waterfall tumbles from a stately Baob tree on the highest point, into an invisible pool halfway down the cliff before pouring exuberantly

over a series of stone steps in a powerful stream which provides me with a perfect back massage!"

Another night under the stars followed, this time with a built-in alarm clock at 5am when a huge cloud of Carella cockatoos arrived to celebrate the dawn with raucous shrieks. Our day started with a choice of swimming the river or crossing in a tiny dinghy pulled hand-over-hand across the water – I chose the dinghy! Then a trudge through land blackened by recent fires towards Manning Gorge, with a tricky scramble down rocky cliffs to a large pool fed by a wide waterfall. The rest of the day involved the roughest driving of the entire trip, where our expedition truck came into its own:

"We twist and wind through a sea of golden grasses, climbing over low ridges of tree-covered hills. We cross frequent flooded creeks, watching out for hidden holes or rocks under the water, and bump through poorly maintained sections of road, grabbing wildly for our tumbling possessions. Very little traffic passes us – just occasional 4x4s, some towing reinforced 'outback caravans', all with spare tyres and jerrycans of fuel and water on the roof – this is no place for inexperienced drivers!"

Incongruously this difficult day of driving brought us to the huge tourist complex of El Questro Station, with facilities ranging from luxury cabins to unserviced campsites (where we were allocated space). Despite the large numbers of people accommodated here, I was delighted to discover wildlife all around us – Barking Owls challenging each other in the trees overnight, more noisy Carellas to wake us in the morning, whirring crickets … though I was less enthused by the swarms of poisonous cane toads (a plague newly arrived from the eastern side of the continent) which crawled over every inch of the site by night, making a torchlight trip to the toilets a perilous expedition.

Damien had planned a major expedition for the next morning, taking me to one side to try to discourage me from attempting it – but I was determined, even if I could not manage the entire trek into El Questro Gorge. There was no man-made trail here, just a few markers on the rocks at the bottom of a narrow gorge. We were left to pick our own path among the boulders, criss-crossing the stream frequently in search of the best route – time-consuming, concentration-demanding walking for me, but I refused to stop at the first potential swimming spot: I had decided that I wanted to reach the so-called Halfway Pool, where a massive boulder virtually blocked the valley, forcing the stream into a waterfall. Four of us elected to stop here as the rest of the group scrambled over the boulder, some hauled up bodily by Damien, to continue up the valley. I was delighted to have reached Halfway Pool, but in fact it was too crowded with other tourists for an enjoyable swim, so I chose to return to the first pool instead, stopping briefly to greet a bright green tree snake which slithered across my path:

"The pool ripples in dappled sunshine, silent except for the splash of water against stones and the clatter of wind in the palm leaves. There is no-one else here, so I prepare my own swimming area, moving fallen branches to slip into the water amongst small fish, scooting water-boatmen and dancing butterflies."

The rest of the group were weary with their exertions and spent the afternoon relaxing, but I was exhilarated by my morning's successful achievements and elected to take a boat trip into another, totally flooded valley: Chamberlain Gorge – a gentle method of exploring, but one which gave me a sight of tiny, enchanting Rock Wallabies on the rocky ledges in the cliffs, as well as getting myself soaked by powerful jets of water fired by Archer Fish seeking to knock food pellets out of my hands. Our guide was determined also to show us the famed Barramundi fish:

"He produces a couple of tiddlers to entice the Barramundi to the surface, fighting off the more numerous catfish. Finally a Barramundi rises from the depths to grab the bait ...and the guide's fingers! He offers to draw it out of the water for us to see and there, right under my nose, a huge silver fish rises vertically from the water – what a mighty (and meaty) creature."

Sadly, this was our last night in the Kimberley wilderness, celebrated in grand style by Damien who had spent the afternoon pot-roasting a joint of lamb over the campfire, rounding off the feast with damper bread made in another cast-iron pot encased in hot coals. However, next day one more Kimberley experience awaited me – Emma Gorge. Damien painted a fearsome picture of its difficulty, but by now I was ignoring his advice and making my own choices – and my decision to attempt the walk was well justified. There were a few very large boulders to scramble, slide or crawl over, but nothing as difficult as the day before. I set off ahead of the others, and some had not even caught up with me before I reached the end of the gorge:

"It is amazing! The gorge ends in a huge semi-circular cliff which encloses a beautiful pool of dark green, crystal clear water. I strip off and wade in quickly – I don't have much time to swim before I have to set off back again, if I am to keep to Damien's schedule, but it is good to get one last swim: the Bungle Bungles are dry, and Katherine Gorge is the haunt of huge saltwater crocodiles!"

After the semi-civilisation of El Questro, with washing machines, electric points and flushing toilets, we were moving on to a wild 'bush camp' amid the quaintly named Bungle Bungles. We re-joined the smooth Route One to head southwards towards Purnululu National Park and the Bungle Bungle Mountains – apparently 'the most outstanding example of cone karst in sandstone in the world', a sacred place to the Aborigines, protected from outside eyes by several enclosing ranges of hills. We reached our camping spot just as sunset illuminated those protective mountains in a blaze of red light – we would have to wait for our first sight of Purnululu until next day. Yet what a campsite we had that night!

"We are camped beneath a beautiful white gum tree, eating our dinner in the beam of the truck's headlights. Then the lights are extinguished ... and there is the night sky, packed with stars including the haze of the Milky Way. The only sound is a single cricket whistling plaintively from the nearby bushes, but there are no other campers, no noise, no lights. Just us, a single tap and a bush-toilet!"

Next day we were off before 6am, penetrating the ring of mountains to discover the unique landscape of Purnululu – a cluster of 'beehives', eroded conical hills coloured with stripes of orange, grey and black, looking like an outbreak of pustules on the side of the ridge. The region was unknown to all but the native peoples and a few cattle-hands until the 1980s, when a film-crew was chatting in a bar to some cattle station workers who told them about this place. They filmed it and made it immediately famous, so in no time the land was appropriated by the Australian government and transformed into a National Park. Our explorations started with an easy walk:

"The 'beehives' rise high above us, their sides eroded with caves and open caverns which preserve ancient Aboriginal prints of hands and boomerangs, painted with kangaroo blood to commemorate initiation ceremonies or a first hunt. A dry streambed leads us through a narrow passage into a cavernous

space, the Cathedral, filled with extreme echoes which magnify every voice and cough."

It was impossible to appreciate the scale of Purnululu from the ground, so I elected to take a short sightseeing flight by helicopter over the whole area. From the air it became clear that the Bungle Bungles were actually composed of barren rocky plateaux carved into deep, narrow gorges filled with lush vegetation. The characteristic 'beehives' were simply one heavily eroded side of one of the plateaux. Back on the ground we explored more of those narrow gorges, starting with Echidna Chasm, a tapering canyon cutting deep into the rocks, becoming ever narrower until it finished at a dead end, surrounded by vertical cliffs on every side. Finally to Mini-Palms Gorge, once again accompanied by Damien's dire warnings: this time perhaps fully justified?

"First a rough walk along river stones between high cliffs, then the valley closes into a chasm. The difficulty comes with huge conglomerate boulders which have almost blocked the valley. I have to squeeze through gaps too small even to accommodate my rucksack, scrambling up and down, under and over ... the last boulders are negotiated by steps which finally lead into a dark cave in the rocks – I've made it!"

My triumph was considerably diluted on the return to the bus, however, when I missed a turn in the path and (together with the youngest member of our group) went astray, arriving eventually in the wrong parking place. We returned in the direction from which we had come, not daring to launch away from the trail into the bush, wondering just how we would find the group again. Miraculously, Damien appeared and led us cross-country back to the bus, with no recriminations – I was so thankful for his bushcraft, which had rescued us.

We now crossed into Northern Territory, stopping to take a boat ride on the artificially dammed waters of Lake Argyle. Out in the middle of the lake we were invited to take a swim ... then cruised on to view a large group of freshwater crocodiles nearby! The guide rushed to explain that these Johnson's crocodiles are too small to take live prey and eat only carrion ... but I noticed that we only visited their colony AFTER our swim! We continued to Katherine Gorge, a major tourist attraction which would have been a highlight if I had not seen so many amazing (and uncrowded) Kimberley gorges.

Nearby was a final treat – an easy path led us through groves of flowering eucalyptus trees alongside the Edith River. I walked as far as the Upper Pool, nourished by an abundant cascade of fresh, clear water, for one final 'wild swim' before we continued into the city of Darwin, where our tour ended. My hostel was located in the heart of 'downtown' Mitchell Street, lined by bars and eateries, all blaring with loud music. I retired early to retreat into my memories of camping beneath the stars!

Aboriginal fishing lesson

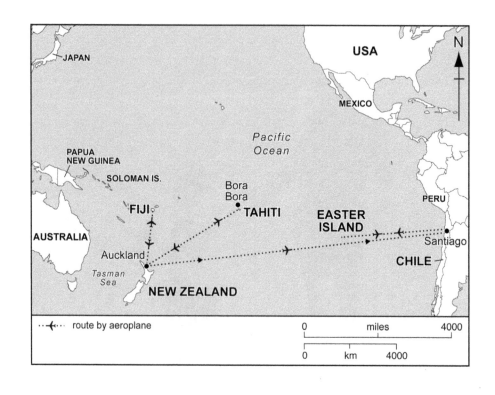

JAPAN

USA

N

MEXICO

Pacific
Ocean

PAPUA
NEW GUINEA

SOLOMAN IS.

Bora
Bora

TAHITI

PERU

FIJI

EASTER
ISLAND

AUSTRALIA

Santiago

Auckland

CHILE

Tasman
Sea

NEW ZEALAND

···✈··· route by aeroplane

0   miles   4000

0   km   4000

Pacific Islands (May/ June 2018)

HAVE YOU EVER BEEN ATTRACTED by pictures of the palm-fringed, white coral beaches of the South Sea islands? I certainly had – and now, on my round-the-world trip, I would finally have the chance to reach these oh-so-distant patches of paradise! Yet there are so many groups of islands … which to choose? Information about their attractions was hard to come by, so eventually I arbitrarily selected one French colony (the Society Islands in French Polynesia) and one former British colony (Fiji). There seemed to be little transportation between the various island groups, so the next weeks involved a lot of time-wasting flights back and forth to New Zealand which acted as the hub for flights to Pacific island nations, and also brought the utter confusion of three crossings of the International Date Line.

First, I gained a day by leaving Auckland airport at 6pm and reaching the island of Tahiti at 1am on the same day – arriving to an airport welcome of Polynesian music and a hula dancer; greeted by my taxi driver with a flower garland; received by my hotel receptionist with a huge smile – all at this ungodly hour of the morning: I was loving the Society Islands already! My first day was spent in Papeete, French Polynesia's capital (and largest town on Tahiti), bustling with shoppers: I was especially fascinated by ladies wearing flowers as jewellery – tucked behind one ear or in the form of a home-made crown (called a 'Hei'). However, I had not come all this way to visit just one island – the only way to get a proper sight of French Polynesia was to join a cruise … and the only one-week cruise I could find was on board the luxurious vessel Paul Gauguin – what a contrast from my weeks in the

Australian outback! The ship was only half full, so our 222 passengers were cosseted by 221 crew members, including some muscular young Polynesian men who normally wore no more than a grass skirt … mmm!

The cruise took me through the Windward group of the Society Islands, calling first at thickly forested Huahine with its villages of spacious bungalow homes set in lush gardens, and wooden churches packed with worshippers (it was Sunday). The guide showed us vines carrying the vanilla pods which were one of the island's main exports, and sacred eels with unusual bulging pale-blue eyes – all the time plying us with information about the islanders' subsistence lifestyle, fishing or growing food in their gardens:

"The heat and humidity are ideal for growing fruits and vegetables, the seas are clean and full of fish: easy living with plenty of time for relaxing and socialising ... BUT the island is also remote and isolated with no hospital and few modern facilities, and virtually no opportunities for salaried employment which means no chance for the population to access higher education and progress in life. These people may live in Paradise, but they are also trapped in Paradise."

We also called at Moorea – a long, forested island with a skyline composed of innumerable sharp peaks and pinnacles like shards of shattered glass. Here I joined a tour by 4x4 vehicle which allowed us to climb the steep slopes of the mountains for spectacular views over the flooded volcanic crater where our ship was anchored, then on into another crater in the heart of the island where the rich red soil was ploughed and planted with acres of pineapples, Moorea's principal agricultural product.

However, the cruise highlight was the island of Bora Bora, immortalised by the film 'South Pacific' – it was fortified by the US navy in 1942, blasting through the coral reef into an unusually large lagoon and installing guns on the surrounding hills. Now it was a hub of luxury tourism with exclusive hotels sprawling around the coastline, most with chains of thatched villas strung out over the water. My tour travelled off-road on rocky tracks into the depths of the island, stopping to visit the remnants of a traditional Polynesian 'marae': a stone platform where the tribe's menfolk absorbed extra strength by walking on the bones of their enemies, buried beneath the stones. While the interior of the island was beautiful, its star attraction lay in the sparkling turquoise seas around its shores which I experienced in a variety of ways. First, I took an Aqua-Safari:

"I slowly descend the ladder from the boat into the sea, stopping when the water reaches my shoulders, for the crew to lower over my head a huge hood (like a bucket) attached to an air-hose. I am now so heavily weighted that I sink straight to an arena of white sand five metres below. A crew member joins me in the arena and attaches a bag of bread to my harness – clouds of tiny fish swarm around my face mask, pecking hard at the crusts."

This was a painless way to see beneath the waves, but I also made the effort to overcome my memories of near-disaster on Australia's Ningaloo Reef, and once again donned a snorkel mask to swim amid Bora Bora's reefs ... this time with sharks! However we were assured that all the sharks in these shallow waters fed exclusively on sick or dead fish, and were no threat to us:

"Clouds of fish are first to surround us, but in no time they are joined by ten small Black-tip Reef Sharks swimming just below the surface, their bodies glistening in the sunlight. Far below them I spot larger, blunt-nosed grey sharks cruising the seabed – these are Blanchette Sharks, each hung with multiple Remora 'cleaner fish'. Though I know I am in no danger, it is still awe-inspiring to be in the direct path of an approaching deep-sea shark."

Another stop in shallow waters brought a large group of stingrays to swim with us, seeking the food which our guides had brought. They twisted and turned around us, happy to be stroked – so soft and velvety! They really seemed to enjoy my touch, snuggling up against me even when they knew I had no food for them. One final stop was the most challenging – we were to swim in the Coral Garden where we were warned we might encounter some stronger currents, but they were nothing compared to the currents I had fought in Western Australia, and I was able to enjoy the sight of a huge sinuous Moray Eel twisting through pathways of purple and blue coral, snapping his formidable mouth:

"The reef is vibrantly alive, with towers and spires tipped with purple, green and deep blue corals adorned with orange and pink anemones and glowing with colourful fish ranging from tiny electric-blue Damsel Fish to large meaty blue-green Parrot Fish. I drift cautiously through the coral 'forest', twisting and winding through the 'valleys'. What a way to finish my visit to Tahiti."

The Society Islands, and especially Bora Bora, fulfilled all my dreams of tropical paradise, but my first impressions of Fiji were very different. I started in the town of Nadi, travelling through heavy rain showers towards the town centre, past poorly maintained houses set in unloved patches of ground (I could not describe them as gardens) littered with rusting cars and motorbikes. My bus was equipped with windows, but in the central bus station I saw many other battered old vehicles with no more than flapping tarpaulins to keep out the rain. The roads were broken and dirty, the river thick with rubbish, the market offering just small piles of cassava or taro root. For the first time on my tour, I even felt threatened by the people in the streets, a mixture of Indian and bushy-haired Fijian men who tried to attach themselves to me as I strolled by. There was also a palpable tension between the efficient Indian tradesmen, descendants of indentured labourers brought in by the British, and the easy-going Polynesian Fijians. Perhaps my short cruise would reveal a more sympathetic picture of Fijian life?

The ship did not impress me on first sight – a small elderly vessel carrying just 130 passengers, which had spent most of its life cruising in Australia's Barrier Reef before retiring to Fiji to spend its last years carrying passengers to the isolated Yasawa Islands. Perhaps relying on the internet to make travel arrangements was not such a good idea after all? What had I let myself in for? However, once aboard the ship, at last I found a warm South Seas welcome from the crew (all native Fijians with the exception of an Australian captain), greeting us with huge smiles and a keen desire that we should enjoy ourselves – overwhelming the practical problems of an elderly ship (ill-fitting doors, damp beds …) with generous hospitality and an abundance of laughter.

The Yasawa Islands (closed to tourism until the 1990s) are located to the west of Fiji's main islands, directly in the line of ferocious typhoons which rake the country on a regular basis: consequently they are sparsely populated, with many of the islands totally uninhabited. The main purpose of our cruise was to visit a range of deserted white sand beaches and to snorkel or dive in clear warm waters – in fact, we were told that we should not stray inland from the beaches, since our cruise permit did not cover access to the interior. However, on Naviti Island we were invited to visit one of the villages … finally I encountered the taste of native culture which I had been seeking:

"We disembark at Gunu village after a strict briefing on the correct

etiquette to observe, including modest dress with covered knees and shoulders but no hats. On our arrival the men of the village greet us with a 'Sevusevu ceremony' where our representatives drink cava with the village leaders. After appropriate words, multiple hand claps and the presentation of a cava root, the rest of our group are permitted to advance and sample the cava drink, still observing strict etiquette: shoes off as I kneel on the official mat ... one clap ... take the bowl ... drain it fully ... three claps ... rise to my feet. It tastes earthy and very watery – I assume it's an especially weak version for us tourists?"

Having been officially welcomed, now we were free to explore the village before a 'lovo' feast of meat, cassava and potatoes – all cooked between hot stones buried into the sandy beach. The evening was rounded off when a group of men and women emerged from the darkness of the village into the floodlit central square to sing and dance for us:

"Much more discreet dancing here than in Tahiti – they are more prudish both in dress and in dance. The ladies move from foot to foot with no excessive hip wiggling, waving fans in a stylised manner whilst the men wave spears instead. One gay man is dancing among the ladies – Fijians seem to accept homosexuality without difficulty."

At the northernmost tip of the Yasawa island chain, we were invited to visit a village primary school where children were taught by newly qualified teachers, obliged to spend three years teaching in these remote parts before being allocated more lucrative jobs on the main islands. The children gathered to sing a medley of hymns to us before enthusiastically grabbing our hands to drag us off to see their classrooms – pitifully poorly equipped with a few desks and simple chalkboards, and home-made teaching aids pinned to the walls. Yet this school was more fortunate than many since our ship regularly called to visit, bringing donations of essential supplies each time. Across the bay from the village was the small rocky islet of Sawa-I-Lau, its limestone cliffs enclosing a hidden jewel – the Blue Lagoon:

"We scramble down steps into a dark crack leading into the heart of the rock – a view opens up of a dark pool beneath looming cliffs. Here we descend a vertical metal ladder into the cool water, swimming on into the main cave – a collapsed cavern lit by sunlight from its former roof far above. The walls are sheer and precipitous, stretching above us like a vast cathedral, resounding with the echoes of our voices."

Returning south again we stopped at Yanggeta Island for a final snorkelling experience, highly vaunted by the crew since we would be swimming in a Marine Protected Area, established just four years earlier. At last I could understand why Fiji is so popular with visitors!

"What a snorkelling experience awaits us! This is a veritable garden of different shapes and colours: hard staghorn, brain and plate corals; delicate white fronds of energetically waving soft corals; bright green, blue, red and rich purple. I drift gently, braking occasionally at a particularly interesting sight: a large bush of purple branches in which fluorescent turquoise Damsel Fish are dancing; a high cliff on the edge of the reef; a deep sandy hole where Parrot Fish bask in rays of sunshine."

My round-the-world trip was almost over, but before returning to Europe I could not miss the opportunity to visit one of the most remote inhabited places on earth: Easter Island. Appropriately my journey there was difficult! I had to fly from Fiji back to New Zealand, then take a flight right past Easter Island to mainland Chile, before flying back to the island. To make things worse, Fiji Air managed such a long delay on my flight to New Zealand (something about birds trapped in the passenger cabin?) that I missed the flight to Chile. Fortunately a very willing and helpful LATAM trainee in Auckland airport spent hours on computer and telephone, re-organising all my arrangements so that I reached Easter Island on the same day as planned (including yet another crossing of the International Date Line), though much later.

The island lies almost 4000km from Chile to the east and over 4000km from Tahiti to the west, the furthest outlier of the South Sea islands, first settled only a thousand years ago by Polynesian people exploring in ocean-going canoes from their homes in the Cook Islands and Tahiti. They developed a very distinctive culture with the usual Polynesian ancestor worship creating stone platforms (Ahu), but here topped by massive stone sculptures (Mo'ai) which embodied the spirits of the ancestors who watched over their descendants' lives. However, in the extreme isolation of this remote island something clearly went wrong within the social structure ... but what? In common with other Polynesian nations, Rapa Nui (as the native population calls their island) had no written language, depending on storytelling to preserve its history – when the population was devastated in the 19th century, their history was lost and all that remained were some native traditions and scientific theories. However, both the island's museum and our local guide suggested that probably there was a civil war caused by the oppression of the working people by the ruling classes, resulting in the toppling of all the Mo'ai (which represented the spirits of former rulers) and the death of almost all the population – by the time it was annexed to Chile in 1888 only 110 islanders remained.

My first sight was Easter Island's only settlement, Hanga Roa, a well-to-do little tourist town with small, neat homes and lush vegetable gardens, walled by black volcanic boulders. After the poverty and disorganisation of Fiji, it looked to be a comfortable place to live – perhaps it is better to remain part of an empire (Chilean in this case) than to attempt independence, as Fiji had done? Outside the town, the landscape was mainly open pasture grazed by horses and beef cattle. The skyline was dotted with distinctive volcanic cones – now all extinct. Strong ocean winds ensured there were few trees, while the coast was lashed by massive waves and surf. Fishing boats plied the waters, though their only customers were the islanders themselves, since any other market was just too far away: the only sources of income from the outside world came from tourism and the Chilean government.

Sightseeing over several days took me to see many of the most imposing Mo'ai statues – my guide proudly informed me that there were 887 statues in total but less than 300 were ever fully finished and 400 still lay in and around the quarries where they were abandoned when war swept the island. By the 1860s all those which had been erected on their Ahu platforms, had been toppled, but from the late 20th century onwards American and Japanese historians had been gradually restoring and re-erecting some of the statues. One of the most impressive sites was at Tongariki:

"A solemn line of fifteen stone figures stands immobile with arms stiffly by their sides, their faces stern and imposing, their eye sockets empty so that their character is hidden. They gaze inland, almost like a line of 'flunkies' with hands behind their backs, their immobility emphasised by the frenetic activity of photographers in front of them."

At Anakena Beach a strip of white coral sand (rare on the island, since most of the coast was covered by black volcanic stone) was guarded by a line of seven Mo'ai, all wearing the red 'topknots' which signified royalty. At Ahu a Kivi, we visited the only Ahu where the statues face the sea instead of facing inland – supposedly because they represent the first seven leaders to settle the island, so were portrayed gazing back towards their Polynesian homeland:

"These Mo'ai are not very well preserved, though they have been re-erected – some have broken heads or noses, their bodies show signs of erosion, yet their eye sockets are deep, and their facial features are well-defined. They have a look of nobility and intelligence, even of interest in their surroundings, unlike the blank stares of other Mo'ai – perhaps appropriate for explorers?"

Easter Island was fascinating for its history, but I also loved its savage beauty and relaxed lifestyle, a delightful finale to my round-the-world trip – as my diary records from my last night on the island, before commencing the long journey home via Santiago and across the Atlantic:

"It's back to the seashore for sunset: below me many young men are surfing the big waves ... more arrive, using short flippers to help them out through the inshore surf, and they continue till the last glow of the sun fades from the sky. Onshore, young and old have gathered to chat and drink beer – some even strum guitars and sing softly. A couple of fishing boats force a passage through the waves out to sea, while others ride the surf back to harbour."

Easter Island - moai statue

Chinstrap penguin

Chile - Maipo valley

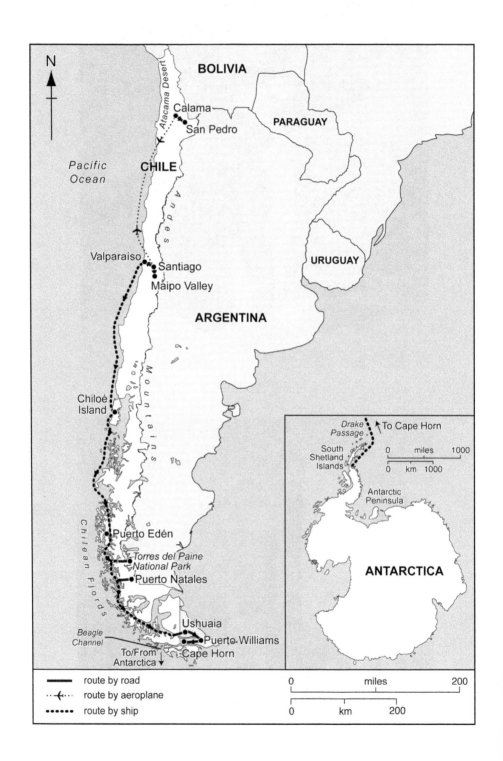

N

Pacific
Ocean

BOLIVIA

Atacama Desert

Calama

San Pedro

PARAGUAY

CHILE

A n d e s

URUGUAY

Valparaíso

Santiago

Maipo Valley

ARGENTINA

M o u n t a i n s

Chiloé
Island

C h i l e a n   F j o r d s

Puerto Edén

*Torres del Paine
National Park*

Puerto Natales

Ushuaia

Puerto Williams

*Beagle
Channel*

To/From
Antarctica

Cape Horn

*Drake
Passage*

To Cape Horn

South
Shetland
Islands

0   miles   1000

0   km   1000

*Antarctic
Peninsula*

ANTARCTICA

——— route by road

···✈··· route by aeroplane

●●●●● route by ship

0   miles   200

0   km   200

Chile and Antarctica (November/ December 2018)

THE LAST DAYS OF MY round-the-world trip were spent in the Chilean capital Santiago, which impressed and interested me so much that I decided to return just five months later – this time planning to explore more of this unusually shaped country: 2700 miles from north to south, yet on average only 110 miles from east to west.

Santiago was an elegant city, with many of its grand classical edifices constructed in the 19th century after Chile finally won its independence from the Spanish empire, creating a country which had never existed as a nation before. Especially I enjoyed the city's central square, Plaza de Armas: a large, paved garden studded with tall palm trees, which seemed to act almost as the city's 'lounge' – in one corner tables were set up for intense games of chess, on another side entertainers posed as human statues or set their audiences rocking with lively music. Both day and night the square was filled with clusters of strolling, chatting people – businessmen, lovers and mothers with babies, mixing easily with beggars and tourists, all watched over by armed guards who were so relaxed that they allowed small children to play with their attack-dogs.

Why were there so many armed guards, however? In the Historical Museum I learned of Chile's violent history: first the subjugation of the native peoples by Spanish settlers from the 16th century onwards, establishing a two-tier society of Elite (of Spanish descent) and Peasant (of native descent); then the battles to win independence from Spain, followed by over a hundred years of political instability and civil war; finally the military coup of 1973 which led to a repressive regime holding the country in an iron grip till 1990. Yet when I visited the atmosphere in Chile seemed relaxed and hopeful of a future filled with progress and justice. Sadly, the mood did not last, since just a year after my visit there were once again violent protests about the unfairness prevalent in Chilean society.

During my two visits to Santiago, I spent time exploring the hills which enfold the city – both the green oasis of Santa Lucia hill rising abruptly from a grid of traffic-choked streets, and also the more extensive parklands of San Cristobal hill, accessed by ancient funicular and modern cable-car. From both, I could see out over the high-rise blocks of the modern city to the peaks of the Andes Mountains which seemed to rise directly out of Santiago's suburbs – how could I resist the chance to travel out into those mountains!

I was making my own arrangements for the first part of this trip, using local Chilean tour operators to organise transfers but finding my own hotels and booking my own sightseeing excursions. With great difficulty I found the only hotel operating in the Maupo Valley, the closest Andean resort to Santiago – just eight guestrooms in a cluster of rustic buildings, set amid rambling gardens on the banks of the river. As I relaxed on my balcony in hot sunshine, the only sound I could hear was the roaring of the river and the rattle of wind in the trees. The hotel staff spoke almost no English, but with my broken Spanish I managed to arrange a guided walk into the Nature Reserve on the opposite side of the valley (accessible only with a local guide):

"A narrow dusty path littered with loose stones, leads me up the steep hillside with views towards snow-spattered peaks as we climb higher. These mountains looked brown from the distance, but I am walking through green shrubs and flowering cactus, studded with beautiful pink Queen's Crown and vivid orange Californian Poppies."

There were few tourists actually staying in the valley (most arrived from Santiago as day-trippers), so I was alone with my walking guide, and also with the Jeep driver on the tour I arranged next day to visit Yeso Dam, higher in the mountains. Sadly, the weather transformed the blue skies into thick grey clouds which hung over Yeso Lake so that it showed little resemblance to the spectacular green waters shown in brochures – what a contrast with the heat of the previous day, when I was seeking shady spots in the garden: now I was glad of my thick coat!

"The tourist buses stop where the road turns to a dirt track, ejecting their chilled passengers to trudge dismally through the mud to the water's edge. But my driver suggests we forge on towards the hint of brightness ahead of us, till we pass right through the clouds to reach the end of the track at 2600m (8000ft). We continue on foot through a wild, windswept landscape to a spot where a fresh water spring spills over to form a marsh. Beyond us the trail continues towards a remote 4000m pass into Argentina, but we turn back as the clouds grow heavy and begin to sprinkle us with snow."

Returning to Santiago, I flew northwards to Calama in the Atacama Desert for the next stage of my Chilean journey. The high plateau of the Atacama was one of the widest points of Chile, home to some of the oldest ridges of the Andes mountain chain as well as some of its newest peaks, created by volcanic activity which still continues today. My taxi crossed a pass at 3600m before descending steeply to the sleepy little town of San Pedro de Atacama, sitting in a broad valley between the snow-capped volcanos and the ancient ridges. The snow melt ran from the volcanos into the valley, but there were no rivers to carry it through the older ridges to the sea: the trapped water lay across the valley in lagoons, slowly evaporating in the hot sun to leave sparkling white salt pans:

"Two hours' flight and I'm in a different world! The sky is unbroken blue, the sun hot, the landscape tawny brown without a trace of green. The road to San Pedro is monotonously straight and featureless, though dotted with frequent shrines to commemorate those who have died, falling asleep at the wheel. We travel through ridges of ancient sedimentary rocks, but my eye is drawn to the dramatic volcanic cones which fill the horizon ahead."

My hotel was mainly used by Brazilian city dwellers seeking a relaxing spa holiday – but I quickly arranged a full programme of sightseeing. I started with a short trip out to view some of the nearby salt lagoons, including the dramatic sinkholes called the Eyes of the Atacama, filled with sparkling fresh green water, then on to several lagoons ringed by thick beds of white salt and inhabited by flocks of flamingos. Next day's tour to Rainbow Valley stopped first to view petroglyphs up to 3000 years old, carved into the rocks by traders resting their caravans of llamas as they travelled from the interior to the coast:

"Now comes a walk through geology – heavy sedimentary mud richly coloured by minerals and flecked with sparkling jewels of gypsum, topped

with a thin layer of white ash from the earliest eruptions of the volcanos. We amble slowly, gasping in awe as one brilliantly coloured slope after another shines in green, turquoise or white, all contrasting with heavily eroded spires of reddish mudstone."

Once the noon-day heat had abated, I set off to explore Moon Valley, a heavily eroded basin surrounded by ridges and pinnacles – most impressive was the Arena: a square-edged amphitheatre filled with sand, seeming man-made though formed naturally. This was probably the most popular local excursion, crowded with tourists, but for me the most impressive excursion started at 5.30am the next day. We drove through vast areas of jumbled rock, open grasslands (where we were lucky enough to see herds of rare wild vicuña) and marshes where huge Giant Coots (up to 2ft long) were nesting on mounds built above the water, till finally a cluster of steaming fumaroles announced that we had arrived at the Tatio Geyser Field, highest thermal region in the world at 4320m (14,000ft):

"We stop beside a large boiling pool, steaming so hard that the water is invisible ... then on to another spring bubbling so violently that we can see spray being hurled from its surface, until the wind changes and we are enveloped in steam. It's a peaceful visit – at this altitude no-one is rushing about or shrieking with excitement. We stroll quietly from geyser to geyser, watching as a few youngsters slip into the bathing pool, turning lobster red from the heat."

Another flight took me back once more to Santiago airport, and into a stressful situation. The transfer company I had organised to meet me both on my first arrival in Santiago and now again when I arrived from Calama, proved to be completely unreliable. There had been no transfer waiting when I first arrived in Chile – which threw me into the clutches of a well-organised taxi scam: seemingly helpful taxi touts offered me the use of their phones to call the transfer company, but then secretly connected me with their own contact who told me my transfer had been cancelled. Still apparently helpful, the tout explained that I had to buy a voucher before arranging my own taxi, took me to a machine and typed in the necessary information. Fortunately, I recognised the machine, just in time, as actually being a cash machine – and was able to grab back the cash which the tout had palmed (saying it was his voucher). With all my experience in travelling, I should have been able to avoid this kind of difficulty – but it is still easy to be caught out by skilled tricksters! When I arrived at the airport from Calama, I found my transfer was again missing – I was approached by the touts, but this time made my phone call from an information desk. The transfer company claimed that I was waiting in the wrong place (not true!) and finally found a driver who happened to be at the airport – he confirmed that their office had forgotten me, but at least (after 2 hours delay) he was able to take me to Valparaiso, a ninety-minute drive away.

Valparaiso is the second city of Chile and was usually their main port, though when I visited, there were many labour problems so that trade was gradually diverting to another smaller port. I was due to join a cruise ship there to visit the southern part of Chile, but first planned a day to explore the city, which climbed the flanks of steep hills rising from a narrow coastal plain. First impressions were not good!

"It's all a bit scruffy – graffiti on the walls and broken glass from smashed windows littering the ground. I set off for one of the funiculars built in the 19th century to ease access to hillside homes, but only find the stairways – stinking of urine and booze. Groups of young men lounge on the steps, still drinking and smoking who knows what – but they are not threatening."

However I did appreciate the bright colours used on the houses to disguise peeling plaster and rusting corrugated iron, and the graffiti in places could actually be classed as 'street art' – the city had been encouraging artists to seek permits to create murals since the 1990s, as part of a plan to boost tourism. It was certainly an interesting city, but after half a day in Valparaiso, I was happy to take the local train to the nearby seaside resort of Viňa del Mar instead:

"I emerge from the station into an exclusive shopping district, clean and well-maintained – a town clustered around an inlet lined with expensive apartment blocks, shaded by palm trees and decorated with hanging baskets of bougainvillea. Such a contrast with nearby Valparaiso!"

Now came another hiccup to my travel plans … a strike closed the port! This was not proving to be the smoothest of my trips! I rang the cruise company's emergency line, to find that they knew nothing about it. Thanks to my phone call, they were able to arrange a berth at another port before the ship arrived at Valparaiso, and (after some confusion) coaches were arranged to take all the joining passengers to meet the ship. However, once aboard the ship I could finally relax: though I enjoy independently planning my trips, it is good to have someone else to sort out any problems which arise – as I said in the Introduction – I am not an adventurer! Yet I can hear you saying: 'Isn't a cruise a bit tame for you?' Well, this was not an average cruise ship, but an expedition ship where serious scientific lectures replaced entertainment shows. Cruising was also the only way to continue my exploration of Chile, since the far south of the country is composed of a jumble of islands and waterways, with no road access.

The first days took us out into the heavy swells of the open Pacific, while I alternated my time between lectures on the geology of the Andes or the formation of icebergs, then on to the outside decks with the wildlife expert to watch the birds – how exciting to learn that the large birds which were our constant companions along the entire coast were actually Black-browed Albatross, the smallest of the albatross family (with a wingspan of 8ft). After two days at sea, we entered the flat calm of the sheltered channels around Chiloé Island, cruising past green pastureland, on water dotted with buoys marking mussel beds. This was to be our first taste of disembarkation by rubber Zodiac dinghy, but the crew were always on hand to offer a firm grip to guide us safely aboard. Chiloé town has been declared a UNESCO World Heritage site because of its unique wooden stilt houses (palafitos) built out over the water, but I decided not to spend all my time in the town. Instead I took a trip out to Chiloé National Park, where wooden boardwalks took us through dense temperate rainforest, thick with bamboo, tree ferns and huge gunnera plants – all indicators of an average rainfall of 2400mm per year (Cornwall gets 900mm, London just 600mm): southern Chile is perpetually wet!

Now we continued through the region known as the Chilean Fjords, though in fact these waterways are not flooded valleys (as in Norway) but rather a complex network of channels between innumerable islands:

"The ship twists and winds its way through narrow passages amid a maze of islands. In places we are so close to the rocky shores that we can observe individual trees in the dense forest which reaches from summit to shore of most islands. Some of the turns we make are very tight, heralded by metallic clanking as stabilisers are drawn in to facilitate the turn, followed by a steady swing of the bows into an initially invisible channel."

In these calm inland waters we watched different varieties of cormorant fishing from rocky beaches, brilliant white terns whirling and screaming above them – then with great excitement we spotted (Magellanic) penguins, at first resembling ducks as they paddled and dived for food. At intervals we had to leave the inner channels to briefly return to the open seas:

"There are more birds here: a carpet of Sooty Shearwaters, sitting on the waves or scooting just above them, using tiny up-currents from each wave to help them conserve energy as they search for food; larger White-chinned Petrels skim a little higher above the waves; big brown bruisers cruising high in the sky are Southern Giant Petrels; and always we are accompanied by elegant Black-browed Albatross soaring effortlessly, revelling in their mastery of the air-currents."

Our next landing was in the isolated fishing village of Puerto Eden, normally accessed only by a twice-weekly ferry. It boasted just 67 permanent residents including a few Kaweskar native people who had once roamed this coastline in their canoes, kept warm and dry by layers of seal grease: well-meaning missionaries in the 19th century insisted they wear recycled clothing (riddled with disease), and the tribe was almost wiped out by the start of the 20th century. This tiny community held the Guinness World Record as the wettest inhabited place on earth, with 5746mm of rain annually – how fortunate we were to visit between showers!

"The whole island is a morass of water, bog and moss – all the structures have to be raised up on stilts, including the boardwalk 'roads' and wooden houses reached by wooden steps. The 'main street' is well-maintained, covered with strong chicken-wire to prevent slipping, but in the depths of the village are pathways of slippery, bouncy wooden planks leading past homes guarded by dogs driven to a frenzy of barking by all these passing strangers."

The scenery was becoming ever more dramatic as we progressed southwards, past ridges of mountain and sheer rocky islands. At one point our Chilean pilot received a round of spontaneous applause as he negotiated the White Narrows through a chain of rocks which seemed almost to block our passage, virtually scraping the rocks to starboard in his efforts to keep in the deep channel despite a ferocious current. The wind increased in strength as we approached the large town of Puerto Natales, located at a spot where a gap in the mountains allows access by road from Argentina (though not from Chile).

As we cruised towards it, the captain informed us that the port was closed because of the wind – but by the time we anchored in the bay, it had opened ... just!

"The journey across the bay by Zodiac is an adventure! Already the sea is rougher than we've known before – lots of spray and a few heavy dousings. Oh dear, we can't even land because the ferry is docking so it's not safe to approach the wharf. Till our ship's captain gives the OK, we bob on the waves or take runs back and forth across the bay ... for half an hour! We are soaked!"

When we could finally land, I took a stroll along the waterfront on the lookout for wildlife – and was delighted to see Black-necked Swans carrying their tiny cygnets safely tucked among the feathers on their backs, to keep them safe from the rough waves. Later there was time to stroll into a town showing signs of newly acquired tourism wealth – the older corrugated iron shacks were being replaced by artistically-designed new homes and hotels, and the artisan market was packed with small shops selling wooden and woollen souvenirs. Puerto Natales is the gateway to Chile's most popular National Park, Torres del Paine, which I had already visited in 2011 – but I remembered such spectacular scenery that I was happy to take another excursion into the Park:

"Our gravel road twists and winds along the hillside above the impossibly turquoise Lake Pehoe, with tantalising views towards Paine Massif's 'horns' – so sharp and clear in today's sunshine, unlike when I visited before. The mountains flirt with puffs of cloud, the glaciers gleam in the sun. We stop to walk across ground crunchy with heather and 'Chaura' shrubs ... but oh, the wind! It is so powerful I can barely stay upright, never mind hold my camera steady."

We sailed on past the southernmost tip of mainland South America (Cape Froward) though it was virtually hidden in thick cloud. Our thoughts were now turning towards Antarctica, with a compulsory ship's briefing outlining the strict rules which govern all tourism on the continent, followed by a busy afternoon as we were issued with heavy-duty 'muckboots' (which could be scrubbed with strong disinfectant before and after each landing) and were then instructed to use vacuum cleaners on each deck to clean out every pocket and seam of the clothing we would be using on Antarctic landings (to remove any stray seeds or other pollutants). We crossed the Strait of Magellan then turned into the Beagle Channel, surrounded by stern black mountains – serrated ridges which lined our channel, many coated with thick layers of snow from which vivid blue glaciers emerged, squeezed into narrow valleys as they strained towards the sea:

"The nights are growing shorter as we travel southwards: it is not dark till 11pm now and is light again by 4.30am. A quick look out of the window when I wake, has me reaching for my camera! Ranges of snow-capped mountains stand out sharp and clear against a cloudless sky of palest pre-dawn blue, the moon tracing a gleaming path across the sea. A large settlement of glowing orange lights is nestled beneath the mountains – it must be Ushuaia, on the Argentinian side of the channel."

We did not call at Ushuaia on this occasion but continued for an unscheduled stop at the Chilean town of Puerto Williams, southernmost town in the world. The ship had been unable to get enough fuel because of the change of departure port from Valparaiso, so needed a few hours in Puerto Williams to fill the tanks before heading off to Antarctica. The main income of the town seemed to come from people replenishing stocks before the same journey – in the most southerly yacht harbour in the world, we saw ocean-going yachts on the same mission. Whilst the oil tenders circled our ship, we were allowed to land for a few hours to explore this peaceful little town at the ends of the earth – home to beautiful birds like the Magellanic Oystercatcher, black and white with vivid red beak and dramatic yellow eye-ring.

With tanks now full, we headed off to the most southerly piece of land in South America – Horn Island and its infamous Cape Horn. Our itinerary did not promise a landing since often the sea was too rough (in fact some of our crew told us that they had passed this way seven times and had not yet managed to land) … yet on this occasion the sea was flat calm, the sun beating down. We cruised to Cape Horn whilst dozing in deckchairs in the sunshine – how blessed we were! We landed on old pallets laid in the water by our crew, who were waiting (up to their waists in water, bless them!) to help us across from the Zodiac to the flight of 175 wooden steps which led to the top of the Cape. Then we walked on special boardwalks (designed to protect the fragile ecosystem) across a landscape of coarse grass and wind-resistant shrubs, to visit the tiny wooden chapel and the lighthouse, where a new keeper had just arrived with his family for his year's stint on duty guarding the light. Finally I crossed the headland to visit the massive rusting albatross monument, commemorating the 10,000 seamen thought to have died trying to 'round the Horn' over the years. As the sun began to sink, bathing the land in a golden evening light, I spotted an Andean Condor (largest flying land bird in the world, with a 10ft wingspan) cruising above me before landing on the highest point of the island. What a magical end to my exploration of Chile!

Ahead of us lay the 2-3 day crossing of Drake Passage, reputedly so rough that I seriously expected to spend most of the journey sick on my bed – yet it proved to be a smooth and tranquil cruise. What a blessing! Now our shipboard lectures were teaching us about the history of Antarctic exploration, with 'heroic' expeditions in the early 20th century culminating in Amundsen's arrival at the South Pole just ahead of Scott, who famously died on his return journey. Soon various countries were claiming parts of the continent, until the Antarctic Treaty of 1959 agreed that no-one could claim ownership … and the Environmental Protocol of 1991 agreed that all 'signs of Man's presence' should be removed unless there was a practical or historical reason for them to remain. We were only planning to see a tiny part of this vast continent, visiting the South Shetland Islands and Antarctic Peninsula … but what a privilege to explore any part of this remote destination!

The thrills began as we traversed the bank of fog which permanently surrounds the continent as sea temperatures drop below 4°C, creating a biological boundary between sub-Antarctica and Antarctica itself. Almost immediately the wildlife became more abundant – huge flocks of magnificent black and white Cape Petrels swirling around the ship, pure white Snow Petrels, imposing blue-eyed Imperial Cormorants, even our first brief sightings of whales:

"I dress warmly and head for my favourite spot on deck to watch the Cape Petrels playing in the air currents behind the ship. OK, better check the view in front, just in case … Wow! A huge square iceberg, bigger than the ship, is sitting off our port side, waves foaming at its base and blue ice gleaming in cracks at its summit. Welcome to Antarctica!"

Soon a low line of rock, snow and ice on the horizon heralded our approach to the South Shetlands, a jumble of larger islands mixed with others which were little more than jagged rocks. Already the winter snows were melting from their peaks and penguins were coming ashore to breed – the smaller penguins of Antarctica need snow-free rock on which to build their nests of piled stones and seize the first possible chance to start the breeding cycle, which must be completed in the short Antarctic summer. The ship anchored for our first shore visit – the initial Zodiac carrying the Expedition Team (always equipped with an emergency kit of tents and enough food for five days, in case the weather changed suddenly and anyone was trapped ashore) who prepared a safe landing place for us. Then we were shipped across in alternating Boat Groups, landing a maximum of 100 people at any one time (part of the Antarctic Protocol). At this first stop my boat group was 4th to land, so we had a long wait aboard before we were called to disembark:

"At last it is our turn – a smooth run to the beach and an easy step into the water to reach land, then I use my sticks to climb the snowslope ... and stop in my tracks! Can I believe it – I am walking in Antarctica! The air is filled with the harsh braying of penguins – both the angry 'Go away!' and the tender 'Hello dear' sound the same to us. All along the ridge Gentoo and Chinstrap penguins are hunkered down on their piles of stones, presumably incubating their eggs."

Next stop was due to be in the caldera of an extinct volcano at Deception Island, but Nature stepped in – a storm was brewing, so our captain decided to run for the better weather which was forecast further south – just the first of many hasty re-arrangements of our itinerary. There were 4 or 5 other ships in the area, all constantly in touch with each other as they organised Plan B, Plan C, Plan D ... re-arranging itineraries between themselves so that we all got to see as much as possible without the risk of arriving at a site together. Well done, Captains!

"We wake to find ourselves cruising alongside the Antarctic Peninsula. Looming out of the cloud come cliffs covered with deep banks of snow; the sea is thick with icebergs, some eroded into artistic sculptures, some gleaming a pure deep turquoise below the water. They grow so dense that we cannot totally avoid them, nudging them to one side with a metallic clang which reverberates throughout the ship. The surface turns greasy with semi-frozen slushy sea-ice – we can go no further: we have arrived in Neko Harbour, surrounded by mountains and glaciers, and by a deep, deep silence."

Once again, our group had to wait to disembark, entertained by the sight of penguins rolling and splashing as they washed themselves before diving for fish, and by the passing of a huge Fin whale (2nd largest whale species, growing up to 88ft/ 27m long). Later a smaller (10m long) Minke whale appeared, curiously cruising round and round our Zodiacs – the water was so clear that we had a perfect view of its entire body just below us. Finally we were allowed to land, plodding through the snow to the penguin colony:

"The birds are still trying to clear the snow with the heat of their own droppings, so currently they are roosting amid a slurry of slush and mud: no wonder they need to wash when they get back out to sea! Yet this is a spectacular site – glaciers, icebergs, mountains all around! Regularly the harsh cawing of the penguins is overlaid with resonating booms from inside the glaciers as ice breaks loose."

We moved on amid heavy snowfall to Orne Harbour, a small bay guarded by massive sentinel rocks, its shores ringed by thick layers of unmarked white snow and glaciers tumbling directly into the sea. Wherever would our crew find a landing spot for us? However the Team landed on a tiny fragment of rock beside the water and immediately began work cutting steps in the snow for us, then trudging laboriously up the mountainside to beat down a manageable zigzag path through the deep snow. The summit of the ridge was our goal, 300m above the sea, where a colony of Chinstrap Penguins had established itself, choosing to make that arduous climb every time they returned from fishing, because the wind had thinned the snow on the mountain-top and therefore it would melt away to bare rock more quickly.

Next stop was due to be at Brown Station, an Argentinian base preserved because of so-called 'historical' associations, though currently unmanned:

"The ship turns and spins repeatedly in the strong cold wind – will we be able to land? The Team tries a test landing, fighting through the waves, drenched in spray – the wind is so strong that I am struggling to stay upright on deck. As expected, the landing is cancelled. From the deck I can see vast glaciers crashing into the sea in cliffs of ice, black volcanic peaks and pinnacles rising into the cloud ... and amid all this grand desolation, the puny foothold that Man has tried to establish here: a cluster of huts huddled in the lee of a cliff."

Nearby was the principal British base in the region, Port Lockroy, established in 1944 as a means of claiming this part of Antarctica and still permitted to remain because it preserved some historic accommodation blocks. It was manned for the summer season and had become a tourist attraction, with a souvenir shop (which accepted only credit cards – what use was cash in Antarctica?). Passengers swarmed ashore to buy postcards with British Antarctic stamps (our own ship carried them back to enter the postal system): I preferred to spend my time watching penguins stealing stones from each other's nests to present to their mates. Nearby was a relatively sheltered valley, where some of the more intrepid cruisers had booked a camping experience in the wilderness:

"Oh, those poor campers! Last night I watched the Team returning at 11pm from helping them to set up in a snowstorm – crawling through thigh-deep snow in exhaustion on hands and knees. Now this morning, the campers are returning – no helpers this time, each hauling their own sled of equipment, many crawling with the sled tied to their waists. I hope it was worth it – I could not have done it!"

Our last sight of Antarctica was the smooth rounded Melchior Islands, bathed in dramatic evening light. All that remained was to cross back over the Drake Passage, though now the weather was transformed. A huge storm was racing towards us from the Pacific and the captain was coaxing every ounce of power from his engines to keep ahead of it – we finally reached our destination port of Ushuaia just as it was being closed by the authorities to prevent shipping from heading out into the storm. But Antarctica had one last treat for me:

"The ship is twisting and rolling, so it's a drunken stagger to the railing to see if there are any birds about. At first there's nothing, but then a bird appears in our wake: white with hints of black on its wings. I hastily open my bird-book ... Could it be? Might it be? Yes! The bird-book identifies it as a Wandering Albatross – the largest flying bird in the world with a 12ft wingspan. Tears come to my eyes – this is the bird I so wanted to see ... and here it is, bidding me farewell to its icy wilderness home!"

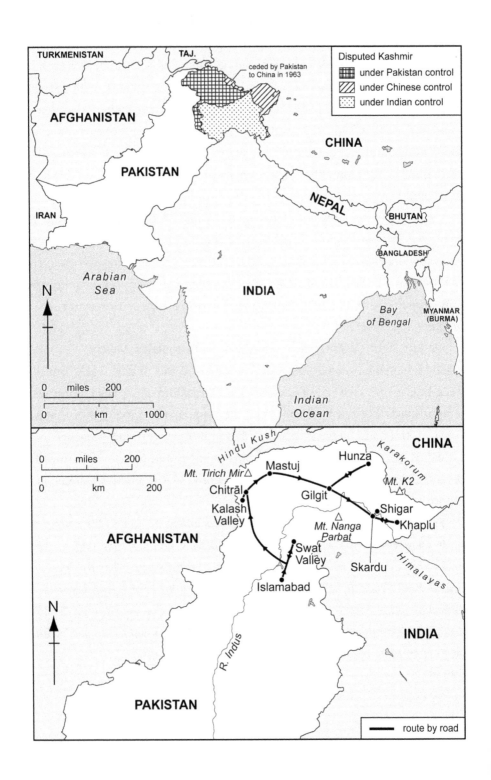

Northern Pakistan (June 2019)

I HAVE ALWAYS LOVED MOUNTAINS, so I decided to return to the most exciting highlands in the world – the complex of mountains at the western end of the Himalayas (incorporating the Karakorum and the Hindu Kush), though it was a region declared by the British Foreign Office as 'inadvisable to visit' and therefore required a special (very expensive) insurance policy. The tour did not start well – unusually heavy traffic on the road to London meant that I missed my flight! However, after a stressful evening on the telephone, I managed to re-arrange my itinerary – even gaining an unexpected half-day in Abu Dhabi for a glimpse of this glistening modern city with its soaring glass and steel skyscrapers and gleaming white Grand Mosque, largest in the world. Finally I reached Islamabad, a day later than planned but still in time to meet up with my travel companions.

We headed north into the mountains, making a brief detour into the Swat Valley – an important centre of Buddhism from the 2nd century BC, devastated by Hun invaders in the 5th century AD and finally destroyed by a disastrous earthquake in the 10th century. There had been some attempt to develop tourism based on this Buddhist history and we visited a museum in Mingora where many fragments of magnificent carvings had been preserved, before continuing to see the remains of Butkara Stupa (shrine) which supposedly contained some of Buddha's cremated ashes. However, the site was little visited – we had to get a local man to climb over a gate to let us in, and inside we found only the weed-ridden bases of a clutter of stupas. Next morning we visited the largest stupa in the Swat Valley at Shingardar:

"It is quite well-preserved with brickwork rising to a rounded top, though the original gleaming white plaster is long gone. Far more interesting to me is the fact that it sits directly in the heart of a village. Children gather round me silently watching as I write my diary, then I am invited to join a group of ladies gathered around a hose, washing out clothing in a bowl."

Our guide Salah was keen to show us the glories of this era – later in my trip he also escorted me around the remains of the ancient city of Taxila, though again it seemed to me just a jumble of ruined walls which had little relevance to the Pakistan I had come to see. My thoughts were already focused on the mountains ahead as we drove towards the Lowari Pass (3000m/ 10,000ft) – once one of the most dangerous roads in the world, but in 2017 tamed by a tunnel beneath its summit. There had been some political unrest in this area, so we were obliged to traverse the tunnel in convoy behind a truck filled with armed police – though we saw no signs of trouble as we travelled into the isolated Chitral Valley, just a few miles from the Afghan border:

"The road is appalling – the surface turns to earth and stone, then degenerates to loose rock and water as we pass miles of roadworks. But the scenery is stunning – a narrow river gorge, still covered on its lower slopes by terraced potato fields and studded with vertiginous homes stuck like swallow nests to the hillsides."

Chitral Valley resembled a Shangri-La paradise: a hidden valley carpeted with golden wheat fields spread beneath snow-flecked mountains, and our hotel was equally magical – a villa set in a magnificent garden and run almost as a house-party by the local Prince who still resided there. At this point we swapped our minibus for Jeeps, allowing us to travel into the valleys where the isolated Kalash people live, following a narrow track cut from the sheer rock face, high above a racing mountain stream. Until the 1970s there was no more than a mule trail leading into these valleys, which had protected the unique Kalash culture: now lines of lowland Pakistanis were trying to coax their city-style cars along the tracks for day trips to celebrate the Eid holiday:

"We launch along the rocky trail cut into the rocks above the river, bouncing and jolting, turning the Jeeps to a 30° incline then back. In places we are stuck behind cars crawling slowly, fearing for their suspension, terrified of the abyss. Salah leaps out frequently to perform his role as

policeman, shouting 'Move over! Climb that slope!', till finally we can roar past in a welter of loose stones."

The Kalash valleys were one of the highlights of my visit to Pakistan – offering the chance to walk into the depths of the Hindu Kush Mountains, almost to the border with Afghanistan, following a riverbed filled with massive boulders rolled along by ferocious spring-melt floods. In the villages, complexes of houses climbed the steep hillsides in tiers of balconies, each resting on the roof of the home below. The Kalash lived mainly from the wheat and barley which they grew in tiny fields scattered through the wider parts of their valleys, and from the meat and milk of their flocks of goats. Many of the people looked very different from typical Pakistanis, with pale skin and blue eyes hinting perhaps at descent from the soldiers of Alexander the Great, and they had preserved their animist religion. However the village headman (who owned the guest house where we stayed) told us of his sadness that gradually his people were being enticed away to Islam because of the advantages which that brought in terms of education and employment (as well as the burden of the hugely expensive funerals demanded by Kalash tradition). The women still wore long black dresses embroidered with colourful designs and topped by elaborate bead headdresses, though families which converted to Islam felt obliged to dress their women in more conventional Islamic dress instead:

"Across from our guest house are successive tiers of verandahs where women dressed in brilliant colours are washing dishes or combing each other's hair, while their drab menfolk (clothed in khaki tunics and trousers) stand in huddles to chat. I stroll into the old village, scrambling from terrace to terrace via elderly wooden ladders or steps cut from lengths of log. Each stairway leads to what seems to be a private verandah, though most spaces here are actually communal. There is no privacy in this village except in the single dark family room, which houses most of the beds and the kitchen."

With the roofs of our Jeeps now open to give unrestricted views towards the soaring heights of the mountains and the awesome depths of the gorges, we set off to follow the Chitral River all the way to its source, passing vivid green patches of unripened barley and villages sparkling with new corrugated iron roofs. The schist rock-face frequently crumbled on to our rough track either as fallen stones or mudslides, and our drivers had to swerve around potholes and cracks. Finally we reached a large green oasis at the town of Mastuj, surrounded by man-made ponds designed to attract Siberian duck on their annual migration ... to be shot by visiting hunters. Though cloud obscured the mountains when we arrived in the village, next morning I woke to unbroken blue sky and sunshine gleaming on a magnificent snow-peak towering over the valley – an elderly man on the road identified it for me: Tirich Mir (7708m), highest peak of the Hindu Kush. We climbed on into ever-cooler air as the altitude increased, towards the Shandur Pass (3700m/ 12,100ft):

"We begin to climb up a precipitous rocky track, zigzagging back and forth across the mountain with spectacular views back over the lush fields of Mastuj, such a contrast from the barren scree slopes and snowy peaks ahead of us. Suddenly a tiny waterfall in a cleft of rock marks the source of the Chitral River, and we emerge into pastureland dotted with grazing yaks, spread around a beautiful lake which reflects the snowy peaks. Incongruously a cluster of luridly coloured buildings beyond the lake announces the world's highest polo ground – used by the local militia for a single match each year."

On the top of the Pass we met the infant Gilgit River, following it for several days as it grew in strength, cutting a dramatic gorge through the last outriders of the Hindu Kush range. Our road clung to the sides of the gorge in a narrow corniche scraped from the cliff-face, while an even more amazingly engineered pathway picked its way from ledge to ledge on the opposite side of the valley, giving access to tiny patches of farmland and isolated homes tucked into cracks in the cliff. Where there was space for more than one house, sometimes a bouncy footbridge made of steel hawsers and planks, led across to the road – but more often the only access (apart from a long walk) was via cables strung across the roaring white water, with a simple trolley to carry goods (or perhaps a single person?).

Finally we descended to the Hunza Valley which divides the mountains of the Hindu Kush from the Karakorum, to enter the bustling city of Gilgit. Here I desperately prowled the shops – the dust on the roads over the Shandur Pass had destroyed my camera ... surely in this commercial centre there must be a camera shop? I could have bought clothing, food, electrical items ... even guns. But no cameras – for the next few days I was reliant on my fellow travellers to take photos for me.

In the Hunza River Valley we joined the KKH (Karakorum Highway), one of the main routes from the Indian subcontinent to China, cutting right through the Karakorum range. We passed the Continent Collision point, where (the sign told us) '55 million years ago the Indian and Eurasian plates collided, buckling the earth's crust to form the Karakorum Mountains – the collision is still happening, causing the mountains to rise at 7mm per year'. At first the landscape was unimpressive with barren mountains covered with scree:

"But soon the scenery turns dramatic again. The highway cuts through a gorge hemmed in by high rocky cliffs with just a hint of snow-peaks peeping through, though their summits are fading into increasingly thick banks of white cloud. The roadsides are lined with tiny vegetable gardens and larger orchards of cherries, walnuts and apricots – all along the KKH are stalls piled high with black and red cherries: just what I expected of the Hunza Valley."

Sadly, the weather was turning for the worse as we climbed up the side of the valley to the Eagle's Nest (2900m) – the light was fading and the peaks were shrouded in cloud, so I could not fully appreciate one of the most famous viewpoints in the world (a 360° view of snow-peaks filling the horizon in every direction). However by the time we left Hunza Valley several days later, the weather had cleared:

"From the hotel terrace I can see a view covering at least 300°. As I spin slowly round, snowy peaks dazzle my eyes where yesterday there was only cloud. In a glacial valley across the river, the conical peak of Diran (7250m), thick with snow, contrasts with the brown ridges enclosing the Hunza. Directly opposite, a great serrated wall of rock soars above the valley side, its flanks thickly dusted with fresh snow. Most imposing of all, peering from behind the shoulder of another lower peak, an elegant, snow-covered mountain stands proud against a patch of pure blue sky – this is Rakaposhi (7788m), one of the 30 highest peaks in the world."

The Hunza Valley has been a vital communication link for many centuries, so sightseeing took us to see some of the fortresses which have guarded it. Most impressive was 11th century Altit Fort, perched dramatically on a huge rock above its village. We entered by a series of dark, narrow passageways and splendidly carved stone doorways, progressing upwards through a series of chambers (one containing a stone column – the tomb of a prince who was walled up here alive). Finally we reached an open balcony from which we could look down a vertical cliff to the river hundreds of feet below – what a fortification! Nestled beneath the fortress was the carefully preserved, historic village of Altit – narrow winding alleyways paved in stone, lined with mysterious wooden doorways giving on to courtyards surrounded by tiny mud-faced homes, some built out over the alleys and accessed by wooden ladders. Though it was clearly a tourist hotspot, the village was still inhabited – a musician practised by an open window, ladies drove their ducks to the village pond or rounded up their toddlers from the streets.

However, in the newer part of town, Karimabad, tourism dominated – the main street was lined with souvenir shops, cafes and hostels geared to climbers and backpackers. Sadly there seemed to be inadequate planning in the development of the town: the smell of sewage hinted at poor building controls; rampant new construction projects made little attempt to preserve the pristine beauty of the mountains; infrastructure was clearly not keeping up with development and most businesses had to run their own generators to provide adequate power – even our apparently luxurious hotel offered hot water only for two hours each morning and evening.

The Hunza region specialises in adventure tourism, which we tasted when we visited the Hoper Glacier where many of the extended treks into the Karakorum begin. We followed a road scraped from the unstable hillside, swerving right and left to dodge piles of fallen stone (the Karakorum is infamous for the instability of its rock – its name means 'black and crumbling'), passing beneath terrifyingly undercut boulders which seemed to be just waiting their turn to fall. As we climbed, we passed villages clustered around miserable fields of potatoes and barley – buildings labelled 'food depot' hinted at necessary efforts to supply villagers when crops failed. Throughout this part of Pakistan we were encountering projects supplied by the Aga Khan's Foundation, providing clinics and hospitals, new roads and bridges, clean water supplies and hundreds of new rural schools: to celebrate 50 years of the current Aga Khan's leadership, his Ismaili followers throughout the world had donated his bodyweight in gold and jewels, to pay for an education programme:

"Finally we emerge in a broad, high valley dotted with glacial moraines. The air is cold up here (why didn't I wear thermals under my trousers?), but

we are just beneath the level of the new snow. Below us the valley is filled with deeply crevassed ice, mainly covered with muddy black dirt, ground from the rocks by the glacier's passage."

Back on the KKH, we turned northwards toward the passes into China, but stopped when we reached the green water of Attabad Lake – so tranquil and picturesque now, but scene of a major tragedy in 2010. A massive landslide (still visible as a vast scree-slope) brought an entire mountainside down into the valley, carrying a village with it. The Hunza River was dammed and quickly rose into a flood 100m deep, drowning other villages and their fields, and blocking all access to the Upper Hunza valley. In order to keep the valley's residents supplied, and to attempt to keep this vital trading route open, trucks had to be transported by boat along the 12 miles of flooded valley for the next five years, until a new road (financed by the Chinese) could be built higher up the mountainside. Now sightseeing boats were plying the waters of the lake, yet it was a sobering reminder of the difficulties of life in this region. As we returned down the KKH to Gilgit, we encountered numerous rock- and mudslides partially blocking the road, brought on by the couple of days of rain we had experienced. In some places the crash barriers or even the edges of the road had been swept away, and in one place we met a couple of motorcyclists cowering inside a road tunnel, fearful to continue on to the next stretch of road where loose rocks were still falling – our two drivers accelerated hard to cross that zone as fast as possible!

What a blessing! In a tiny roadside village I unexpectedly found a shop selling the type of compact camera I like to use. I could take my own photos again... just in time for two of us to leave our group and travel further east into the remote mountains of Baltistan. This province is part of the Kashmir region, disputed since 1957 by Pakistan, India and China and still the scene of hugely expensive military skirmishes high amid the glaciers where the three countries meet. We followed the Gilgit River to the point where it flowed into the mighty Indus, stopping briefly to admire the junction of the Hindu Kush, Karakorum and Himalayan mountain ranges – a dry and dusty spot, yet so inspiring:

"Behind us, a wall of grey rock dusted with snow forms the end of the Hindu Kush ... to the left, landslides of smashed rocks and broken ice mark the western end of the Karakorum ... most impressive of all is a magnificent

mound of rock and thick snow to the right – the Himalayan peak of Nanga
Parbat, 9th highest in the world at over 8000m. And I am standing here,
amongst all this grandeur – can I believe it?"

The rest of this long day was spent following the dramatic gorge of the River Indus, 130km long and up to 4500m deep, forming the geographical boundary between the Karakorum and Himalayan mountain ranges. Our narrow rocky trail was made even more difficult to travel by roadworks being undertaken by the Pakistani army to improve access to this disputed area. At one place we were held up for over an hour while the army shifted a massive landslide: huge diggers were clearing enough space for smaller vehicles like our Landcruiser, but heavily laden trucks had already been brought to a standstill for several days and were anticipating a few more days' delay before they would be able to pass – causing shortages in provisions and fuel further down the road, since this route provided the only access into the valleys of Baltistan. Amazingly, there was no anger among the drivers – clearly this was part of the normal driving experience in the region: drivers were resting in the shade beneath their vehicles, squatting to play cards together or even (in one case) setting up a roadside barbecue to roast an entire sheep to share among themselves.

We continued along a track littered with deep potholes, over mounds of mudslide and through vast puddles which hid the condition of the ground below. Often the road was literally carved out of the cliff-face (how ever did the local lorries with their towering, brightly painted wooden superstructure, manage to squeeze beneath the rock overhangs?). The gorge was so precipitous that there was little room for any human habitation, though wherever there was a break in the cliffs, patches of land were terraced and planted with apricot trees or vegetables around a simple home – accessed by a wire with a trolley attached to it. In one place, our new guide Mr Atta stopped to show us a cluster of khaki tents perched beside the roaring white waters far below us. They belonged to nomadic Mohan tribesmen, who moved between the glacial rivers panning for gold with simple wooden filters – barely making enough income to live, their children having no access to education:

"When we stop, a crowd of young boys materialises around us, followed by
a stately man with a large black beard – a community leader, keen to meet us.
Then a group of young men begins to climb the steep path up to the road, one

carrying on his back an ancient man – over 100 years old, we are told. A rented car is waiting to give him an outing to a nearby cafe: a change from his normal monotonous life – and meeting us is just the icing on the cake!"

The Indus Gorge finally ended as the valley opened up into a broad expanse of sand dunes ringed by snow-capped mountains. Here lay the only city in the region, Skardu, sprawling across the plain, but we continued deeper into the Karakorum along the tributary Shigar River towards a cluster of villages … to find them destroyed. Just three days earlier, the rain which was an inconvenience to us in the Hunza Valley, had here caused a huge slide of mud and rock which had engulfed three villages and all their fields:

"It's been a big slide – the villagers have lost their homes, now filled almost to the roof with mud, and their fields with all this year's crops. Local government has sent some tents, but there is nowhere to pitch them – they really need a digger to shift the boulders and move some of the mud. The people are clearly still shocked, sitting gazing at their village or praying – a few have started to pull some possessions from the buildings, spreading carpets and clothing on the flat roofs of their former homes, to dry in the sun."

Mr Atta found a community leader to accept some donations of money from us, then we drove on in sombre mood to what should have been one of the highlights of our stay in Baltistan – a night in the 450-year-old Shigar Fort, restored by the Aga Khan Foundation and transformed into a comfortable hotel. My room was enchanting – a tiny cell, accessed by a steep narrow stairway and a magnificently carved doorway … but it also evokes miserable memories, since here I woke to an episode of severe vertigo and nausea: the first attack of what has now been diagnosed as Meniere's Disease, an incurable condition which will inevitably place some limits on my travels in the future. Yet my troubles fade into obscurity when compared to the devastation we had seen in the nearby villages.

In Baltistan I had my first sight of magnificent Kashmiri craftsmanship – Shigar's 14th century Amburiq Mosque, a tiny yet perfectly proportioned mosque topped by a typical 'bird-wing' minaret and enhanced by splendid carving on all of its woodwork; and Khaplu Palace (where we stayed in outbuildings transformed into hotel rooms) with its intricately carved and painted ceilings, doors, beams and balconies. Our guide around the palace was a member of the former princely family, though President Bhutto had abolished all princely states in 1974. Whilst in Khaplu we finally had the chance to watch a game of polo, favourite sport of Kashmiri nobility in the past and still popular with local people rich enough to keep their own strings of ponies (though the passion of ordinary Pakistanis was cricket – played by children and men of every age, in roadways or on any patch of available open ground). We were ushered to stone seats opposite the centre of the dusty polo field and I (as the only woman present) was given the honour of throwing in the wooden ball to start the match. It was played with local rules – no changing of horses, only one break halfway through, changing direction of play after each goal. When someone scored a goal, he was allowed an unchallenged gallop the length of the pitch, hitting the ball from mid-way in an attempt to score again. It was fascinating!

"I am quickly aware of the strengths and weaknesses of the players – the Rajah spends most of his time watching the others, though he is virtually permitted to score one free goal of his own; Mr Red Cap is having a whale of a time, scoring lots of goals, though he pauses for a mobile phone conversation part way through the 2nd half; Mr Orange Shirt is young, talented and deadly serious in his play – perhaps looking for promotion to the top team?"

An excursion from Khaplu took us further east, closer to the disputed Indian border, then north into the Hushe Valley. If we had had time to drive further (and the strength for an 8-hour trek), we could have reached a point from which there might have been a view of K2 – 2nd highest mountain in the world at 8611m/ 28,250ft. However we dared not risk driving these rough tracks by night, so contented ourselves with a walk in the little village of Machuco, being developed as a tourism and trekking centre by the Pakistani government. They were also building a road deeper into the mountains so that mass tourism could reach the viewpoint over K2 – a positive development? Or the beginning of the end for a wild and remote region?

We returned to Shigar before flying back to Islamabad from Skardu airport, passing again the devastated villages. The local Commissioner had arrived (after five days delay) with a helicopter and convoys of armed guards, though he did not seem to have brought any useful aid and now crowds of displaced men were squatting by the roadside with banners pleading for help. Walking through Shigar village, I was approached by a young girl speaking good English (she had just qualified from the university of Skardu), who invited me back to her home for a cup of tea … then started making chapattis for me, served with home-made yoghurt – both delicious! While she cooked, her younger sisters took me on a tour of their gardens, filled with apricot, walnut, mulberry and cherry trees as well as lots of vegetables.

Such hospitality offered to a stranger who was just wandering the streets of their village … such a delightful final memory of a dramatically beautiful land, where I met only with warmth and friendliness from the local people, with no sign of the potential dangers which our Foreign Office warned against.

Pakistan - Mohan people

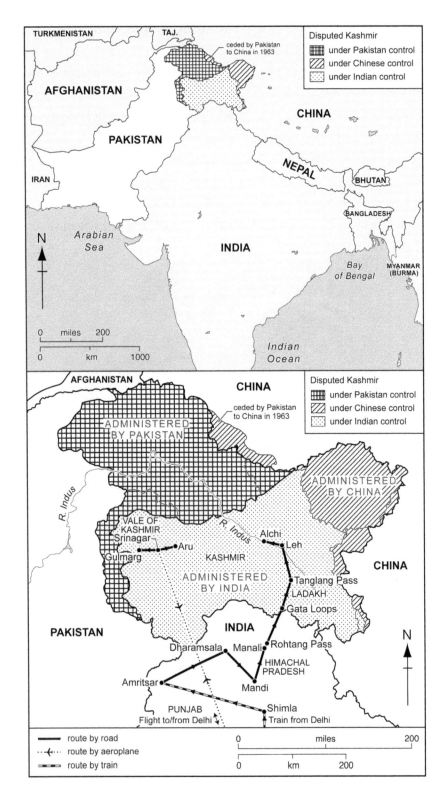

Himalayan India (June/ July 2019)

HAVING PLANNED INITIALLY JUST TO visit the mountains of Pakistan, I decided to extend my trip and also visit Indian Kashmir, booking a tour into the remote province of Ladakh. However there was a gap of ten days before it started – time for extra sightseeing on my own, starting with the Vale of Kashmir: famed for its idyllic landscapes but plagued for decades by political unrest and violence. I had been within 80 miles of Srinagar (principal city in the Vale) when I was in Skardu, but because of the political tensions it was impossible to cross the border there. In fact it was not even possible to fly directly from Pakistan into India – I had to make a detour via Abu Dhabi, over six hours of extra travelling time to reach Delhi. That city was sweltering in summer heat (already 30° at 8am), so I did no sightseeing – instead simply resting at the hotel until my flight north into the Himalayan foothills.

From the moment my plane approached Srinagar airport, I was aware of a far more tense political situation in Indian Kashmir than in the Pakistani section, partly because this was a Muslim enclave in an otherwise Hindu country. The trouble dated from 1947 when Britain left the Indian subcontinent, allowing the formation of Muslim Pakistan and Hindu India. Kashmir's leaders dithered about which country to join for so long that the situation turned violent. In 1948 the UN declared that there should be a plebiscite to decide the matter, once the military situation had calmed enough – three wars and multiple armed uprisings later, the plebiscite has still not been held. The situation had been calm for several years ... however just four months before my visit, a suicide bomber had attacked an Indian military convoy and killed 49 soldiers – in response, the numbers of soldiers in the Vale had been increased from 20,000 to 700,000. We were often held up by huge convoys of military vehicles processing along the highways; in every community, however small, there were armed soldiers watching from roofs and armed police standing on street corners. Two months after my visit, the Indian government revoked Kashmir's limited autonomy, then cut communication between Kashmir and the outside world – I was extremely fortunate to visit when I did:

"We are held up by convoy after convoy ... drivers become impatient, fanning out into a phalange of vehicles, creating a fourth, fifth, sixth lane, hooting more and more insistently. Anger against the Indian army is never far away, and frustration is building here. Finally the soldiers receive the order to release the flood of traffic. Though my guide keeps reminding me that 'Kashmir is safe for tourists', it is clearly VERY volatile."

Yet I consider myself so blessed to have had the opportunity to visit the Vale of Kashmir – one of the most beautiful landscapes in the world. Especially memorable was Dal Lake: once just a wide expanse of water but, in the 20th century, partly transformed by man-made islands holding fields of fruit and vegetables, or by enclosed patches of water used to cultivate water lilies and their valuable lotus-roots. Scattered among the islands were huge houseboats originally constructed as summer homes for British officials but given to Kashmiri families when the British left and run successfully for many decades as hideaway hotels. The unrest in the region has sadly destroyed this tourism industry and many of the houseboats were showing signs of decay, but I spent several idyllic nights in one stunning example – utterly tranquil hours watching dabchicks splashing among the reeds and kingfishers flashing past on fishing raids:

"I travel in a traditional 'shikara' canoe, surrounded by a silence broken only by the splash of the paddles (no motor-boats are permitted on the lake), till we reach a row of five ornate houseboats, all constructed of magnificently carved wood. Mine has an open porch leading to a large lounge then a dining room – all filled with beautifully crafted dark wooden furniture, lit by chandeliers and lined with splendidly carved wooden panels. I am introduced to my 'captain', who is also my chef and my housekeeper, who informs me that this is all for me ... there are no other guests. 'When do I want dinner? Can he

bring me some tea?' – the houseboat and shikara are mine to command! I am overwhelmed!"

My tour included visits to some of the elegant Mogul-style gardens which surround the town of Srinagar – each laid out in formal style around water channels and fountains, most packed with Indian tourists. Sightseeing also took me into the old town with its bustling bazaars and houses adorned with wooden balconies where the women dried vegetables for the winter. I was surprised to be allowed to enter the 14th century Jamia Masjid mosque with its forest of pine pillars supporting the roof, but Shah Hamdan shrine was the most impressive masterpiece of Kashmiri craftsmanship:

"This is an amazingly ornate building. As a woman I am not permitted inside, but I can peer through the doors and windows. Every inch of walls, ceiling and pillars is covered in papier mache decoration; even outside, the door and window-frames are gaudily colourful with designs of flowers and calligraphy."

I wanted to see more of the Vale of Kashmir than just Srinagar, so headed out along the broad valley, covered in rice paddies ringed by willow trees (regularly harvested to supply a cricket-bat industry). The vegetation turned to walnut and apple orchards laden with luscious fruit, as we started to climb into the hills which enclosed the valley, then changed again to thick pine forest as we drove higher. Here we began to see glimpses of distant Himalayan peaks and to meet groups of nomadic gypsy shepherds herding their flocks of sheep and goats up to alpine pastures for the summer. Arriving in the Aru Wildlife Sanctuary, I was introduced to a strapping young mountain guide who led me on a short trek into the mountains:

"I scramble along a rough path between the pines, stumbling over rocks and roots, high above a rushing green glacial torrent, until we emerge into a steep pasture filled with buffalo and sheep, guarded by gypsy women and children. They invite us into their shelter (built of raw tree-trunks and mud, roofed with turf) for tea and chapattis, squatting on an earthen floor freshly strewn with pine branches and divided from the stable by low wooden planks. Their life seems poor, yet this family is full of smiles and laughter."

We descended from Aru back into the Vale, then climbed up the opposite side towards the Pakistani border, to Gulmarg Meadow (2600m) – once an internationally popular winter and summer resort, now busy only with Indian tourists. I was looking forward to using the modern cable car (built in 2005, when hopes for tourism were bright) up to the top of the mountain at 3900m, but the weather was cloudy and windy, so I was only able to ascend to the halfway point, where shepherds guarded their flocks in waterlogged meadows. For the Indian tourists, the prime interest was in touching a tongue of old snow remaining from last winter – an exciting experience when your home is in the burning heat of lowland India!

From Srinagar I returned again to Delhi, now seeming even hotter after the fresh Kashmiri air. This time I did brave the climate for a short walk outside the hotel to Lodi Gardens, where a few Mogul tombs stood unappreciated amidst the lawns of a public garden – but with the temperature reaching 41° by 10am, I did not stay outside for long! My next destination was back in the Himalayan foothills at Shimla, this time travelling by train. I was rather apprehensive about Indian railways, but the first train was a businessman's express with comfortable seats, efficient air conditioning and regular (free) refreshments served directly to my seat. What was I worrying about? At Kalka I transferred to one of India's famous 'toy trains', the Himalayan Queen, which chugged slowly into the hills, taking over seven hours to cover the distance which I later travelled by car in three. I was travelling in First Class, which was roomy and comfortable – though very elderly, with worn plush seats and curtains at the windows. There was no air-conditioning of course, but with windows constantly open to catch the cooling air, the temperature inside remained bearable. I had hoped to see spectacular mountain scenery, but continuous scrub and forest beside the line obstructed most of the views, so the main highlight of the journey was the line itself:

"The engineering becomes more dramatic – hairpin bends inside mountain tunnels bring us back across the slope just above our previous line. We pass through the longest tunnel, taking five minutes to traverse it, then emerge near the top of the hills. The road which has accompanied us most of the way has now vanished and the views into the valleys are hazy with distance. Finally we reach Shimla, located at almost 7000ft above sea level."

The railway, like the town of Shimla itself, was built by the British to escape the unbearable heat of lowland India – in fact, Shimla became the summer capital of British India from the middle of the 19th century until independence in 1947. I was amazed at its location, sprawled over a series of exceptionally steep hillsides so that most of the upper town was accessible only by long flights of steps. I had expected to find a rather stuffy Victorian town – and certainly there were lots of architectural relics of British rule: the massive Viceregal Lodge, summer residence of India's viceroy and deliberately built to 'exude power'; Gaiety Theatre, its original hard seats still used for amateur performances; the austere Telegraph Office and Post Office, both also still in use; even Clark's Hotel (where I stayed), built in 1898 with its rooms cascading down the hillside from Reception on the principal Mall avenue. However the atmosphere in Shimla's streets was anything but stuffy – it seemed to have become the 'party town' for Sikhs from nearby Punjab:

"The Mall is buzzing with an atmosphere between a market and a funfair, its shops a mixture of tourist 'tat' and luxury Pashmina shawls. Everywhere there are people selling balloons, whizzers and light-sticks to young, trendy Indians wearing western dress. Up on the public square at the Ridge, Indian dance music is blaring from the top of the bandstand and Sikhs are dancing with broad smiles and gay abandon. Yet there is no frolicking for the heavily laden porters who push their way through the crowds, carrying on their backs all the city's goods, up the stairways from the transport depots far below."

It was time to join my next group tour, but first I had to take another train, and this time it proved the experience I had been dreading. The platform of Kalka station was covered in a human carpet of bodies sitting, sprawling, sleeping – a difficult task for me to pick my way across them (especially since I was still struggling after another vertigo attack the previous day) to reach the Paschim Express. Once aboard I found my reserved place – a hard, leatherette bunk in an unventilated sleeping carriage, from which all bedding and pillows had been stripped (this was meant to be a daytime journey). I comforted myself that it would be only a few hours' journey … but this so-called 'Express' stopped at every tiny station and also spent long periods stationary in the middle of nowhere. The 4-hour journey was transformed into almost eight long hours, and when I arrived at Amritsar station, my transfer driver was long gone. I emerged at 10.30pm on a dimly lit platform cluttered with sleeping bodies, fighting off insistent tuk-tuk drivers (who had no idea how to find my hotel) and struggling with my luggage over mounds of rubble to seek a taxi. What a relief next day to hand over the organisation of my onward journey to a professional escort!

Before leaving for the mountains, we had a few hours to explore Amritsar, unofficial capital of the Sikh people. I walked (in sweltering 40°+ heat) along a dusty road choked with traffic and littered with refuse, to visit the Jallianwala Bagh, site of a horrific massacre of Sikhs by British soldiers in 1919. Then a ceremonial gateway led me to a well-swept, smoothly surfaced street lined with elegant modern shops, leading to a marble-paved square in front of the complex of gleaming white buildings which surrounded the Golden Temple. In one corner, crowds of people were depositing their shoes before entering the complex – our guide Pema smoothly ushered us to the back of the square to leave our shoes in a less crowded depositary, then we waded through a footbath to enter the complex. A white marble promenade surrounded the sacred pool, which in turn surrounded a small building entirely covered with gold leaf, glowing in the sunlight – the Golden Temple, which houses the Sikh religion's holiest scripture:

"Everyone is dressed in their best outfits – women in gorgeous sparkling saris, men in smart tunics with neatly arranged turbans, always proudly wearing the small, curved knife which is obligatory dress for a Sikh man. Some people are kneeling in prayer; others are just relaxing beneath shady arcades; a few men are stripping off to bathe in the pool, carefully strapping their knives to their turbans first."

An interesting visit, but I was glad to leave the humid heat of Amritsar and head back into the Himalayan foothills. After a few hours crossing miles of flat paddy fields, growing the rice for which the Punjab is famous, we started to climb into thickly wooded, sandstone hills. We passed through the bustling city of Dharamsala to climb a series of tight S-bends up to the community of McLeodganj, founded as a summer resort by the British but now renowned as the residence of the exiled 14th Dalai Lama and many other refugee Tibetans. Sightseeing showed us the dour Christian church of St John and a sprinkling of tiny Hindu shrines scattered over the hillsides, though disappointingly the Dalai Lama's Buddhist temple was just an ugly concrete shell with little attempt at traditional Tibetan decoration – perhaps because the Dalai Lama has always considered his exile temporary and has no desire to create landmark buildings?

My time visiting McLeodganj was limited, since yet another attack of vertigo meant that Pema insisted that I visit the hospital in Dharamsala (fearful that it might be caused by blood pressure difficulties which would present problems at high altitude). It was an interesting addition to my Indian experiences: an A&E department where a single doctor presided over multiple beds tended by auxiliary nurses, then next day a return visit:

"We are offered the choice of two possible rooms – the first already has a huge queue waiting so we adjourn to the second and draw a numbered ticket before settling down to wait for a doctor to arrive. After a long wait, there's still no doctor in sight, so we move off to try the first room again – a doctor is now working there, and the queue is moving. After an examination and a visit to the hospital pharmacy, I am free ... and all for no cost at all!"

Our journey continued through the Himalayan foothills, thickly forested with skinny pine trees, massive eucalyptus and elegant clumps of mature bamboo. Along the route were tiny villages of slate-roofed houses, perched on the banks of rocky fast-flowing streams – I was reminded of the British Lake District, especially since the scene was bathed in thick grey cloud which occasionally exploded into torrential rain. Finally we reached the Hindu pilgrimage centre of Mandi, boasting over 80 temples and shrines dedicated to the god Shiva, part of the trinity (along with Brahma and Vishnu) which makes up the Hindu's Supreme Being. Pema attempted to give us a crash course in Hinduism, naming some of the many gods (including elephant-headed Ganesh and Hanuman the monkey god), but it was all too much: this faith is so complex! Yet I could appreciate the antiquity of Mandi's temples, some dating back to the 16th century – the heavily carved but sombre grey stone construction of the two oldest, contrasting with the brightly coloured plasterwork which usually covers Hindu temples. Most impressive for me, however, was a temple in the heart of the old town:

"This one is clearly still in regular use – bright carpets cover the floor and garlands of marigolds adorn the doorways and pillars. Someone chops bananas as an offering; others ring the bell energetically to attract the attention of the god, or tap the ceremonial drums. In the inner sanctum, ladies arrange flowers around a sacred well and light a candle in worship."

At last we could turn towards the high Himalayas, following the Boas River as it twisted and wound its way through thickly forested mountains, negotiating a road churned almost to destruction by major roadworks as the

Indian government worked to improve access to the sensitive Indo-Chinese border. We turned into the Kullu region, in the process of heavy development for domestic tourism, offering lowland Indians the opportunity to trek among its peaks or to raft on fast-flowing rivers: sadly, the result was that the mountain views were almost obscured by lines of teashops and souvenir stalls. There is such a delicate balance between developing tourist facilities and protecting the natural beauty which first attracted that tourism!

The large town of Manali was another example of over-speedy development: a rash of hotels and backpacker hostels, teashops and adventure tour offices – even a precarious zip-wire strung across the river's violent white water. Pema took us to view the last remnants of the old village – a group of houses built of stone and wooden beams (the traditional way of protecting from earthquake), with tiny windows and doors to keep out the winter cold. The courtyards were home to beautiful Jersey cows, while the upper balconies were piled with drying crops and flapping laundry – all very picturesque, though the few residents we glimpsed were clearly exasperated by the intrusion of constant visitors. We were made more welcome at the unusual pagoda-style wooden temple to the goddess Hadimba (uniquely worshipped in this area), set in the pine woods above the town, in a garden studded with blue hydrangea bushes:

"A queue of people waits patiently to duck beneath the low door to worship, the bell ringing constantly; garlands of marigolds hang from every possible ledge, tinsel ribbons (for wishes) festoon every fence and gatepost. There's certainly devotion here, though also curiosity from those who rush to ask us to pose with them for selfies!"

The Hindu world was left behind us as we departed from Manali, immediately starting the steep climb up to the Rohtang Pass (3978m), first of the high passes which guard the route into Buddhist Ladakh. The road swung uphill on continuous hairpin bends beneath soaring cliffs bathed in waterfalls – magnificent scenery, yet it was hard to look anywhere else except at the traffic! One of the most popular excursions for Indian tourists staying in Manali, was to ascend the Pass in search of snow – streams of cars were trying to drive upwards, frequently held up by descending trucks which required the entire road to negotiate the bends. There were so many long delays that enterprising traders had set up stalls beside the road, offering roasted cobs of corn to frustrated drivers, or (puzzlingly) lurid shell-suits. Finally we approached the summit:

"Still we climb, past great banks of old snow, in one place actually driving through a 'valley' of snow cut out by winter snowploughs. Just before the actual Pass, we reach the 'tourist summit' where the day-trippers come to frolic on the expanses of snow. Up here, at almost 13,000ft, it's like Blackpool on a mountain top! There are food stalls and wellie hire; pony rides and photo opportunities with yaks; inner-tube slides or just polished chutes where tourists can slide down wearing shiny shell-suits – so that's why they were for sale by the roadside!"

As we crossed the Pass, we left behind us most of the tourists – now we were into serious mountain landscapes, crossing range after range of the Himalayas via one high pass after another. The road deteriorated: often we were driving through deep mud – the downfall of the motorbikes which were now the most frequent vehicles around us (the 'road to Leh' is apparently one of the world's classic biker routes). They had roared past us in the traffic jams ascending the Rohtang but now were struggling to stay upright. Most of the other traffic was composed of trucks, especially oil tankers – this road was the only supply route to the major city of Leh. In one place, we met a huge stationary line of trucks – the road ahead had been entirely washed out by a rampant river and work was underway to lay a row of massive pipes to control the water. We walked from our vehicles down to the worksite, following local people as they hopped from pipe to pipe across the water into the village to wait out the delay in one of the cafes. Several hours later, a temporary surface of earth was laid directly on top of the pipes and the traffic began to move.

As our road scrambled over one ridge after another, we were gaining height quite rapidly, so our itinerary planned a couple of nights in the settlements of Keylong and Jispa (both at around 3000m) to acclimatise before going higher. There were no major sights to see, though Pema found us an ancient, crumbling castle (built of stone, wood and mud) overlooking the valley, bribing an elderly villager to open it up for us to explore. Though it was not on the usual 'tourist trail', I was impressed by its amazing 3-storey atrium bringing light and air into the heart of otherwise cramped and gloomy passages and chambers.

Refreshed and revitalised we continued our journey, following an unusually well-maintained tarmac road across increasingly dry and desolate hillsides where only a few of the most enterprising (or desperate?) families had tried to clear a patch of farmland from the stony slopes. The journey seemed to be going smoothly ... until suddenly we were halted by another huge traffic jam. Walking to the head of the queue, I found a large waterfall cascading across the road and partially washing it away. A truck had tried to cross but was grounded on a huge boulder on the edge of the abyss, and now everyone was waiting for an earthmover from a nearby military base to arrive to tow it clear – a delay of almost three hours this time:

"Meanwhile we wait. The other drivers are calm – the motorbike gangs turn back to find a teashop somewhere behind us; groups of men squat in the road in makeshift card-schools, joined by soldiers from the inevitable military convoy, while dance music pounds from one army truck. A convoy of Indian tourists even sets up a toilet tent for their ladies to use! No stress, no hooting – just part of the experience of driving this road."

There were more delays as we continued through increasingly desolate landscapes, where there were now no settlements at all. The winter snows were melting fast, gushing across the road and churning it into deep puddles and potholes – every vehicle was seeking the best route through the morass, and the bikers were struggling:

"The motorcyclists are in terrible trouble – dismounting their pillion passengers to wade through, revving their engines to try to prevent water from entering their exhausts. Many are poorly equipped, some only wearing blue jeans, many in trainers instead of boots. They sit on rocks just beyond the water trying to dry out, some riding on through the snow drifts with bare feet."

With no permanent settlements up here, tented service areas had sprung up, offering hot food and drinks and even simple dormitory beds for those needing them. When we stopped for lunch, I met a young British couple travelling on the local bus from Manali to Leh – they had left at 5am and had been held up for six hours at the blocked waterfall; their allocated seats were next to a pair of local ladies who had been trying to transport a window pane, but it had shattered on the rough road and now all were sitting amid shards of broken glass ... I later met them in Leh, learning that their journey had lasted 22 hours in total – the joys of youth! After lunch, we pushed on to cross the

Barocha Pass (4890m) – the watershed of the entire Himalayan range, but actually no more than an expanse of open snow littered with stone cairns and prayer flags. From here, we bumped down a series of dusty, gravel bends ever deeper into a barren stony valley. At the bottom we found a tented camp, our highest overnight stop at 4290m (14,500ft), nestled in an area of thin pastureland hemmed in by eroded mountains glowing with yellow, green and rusty red colours in the last of the evening sunshine. As the sun set, a bitter cold wind had us all snuggling down under thick blankets in our luxury tents (even provided with rudimentary private toilets and washbasins).

We left camp at 5.30am next morning, excited by the prospect of a day filled with high passes, initially accessed by the sequence of hairpin bends called the Gata Loops – 21 bends zigzagging across the face of the mountain. The earth around us was a glowing golden colour, with vivid orange rocky outcrops outlined against a cloudless blue sky – a perfect day for the mountains. The passes themselves were of limited interest, since the Gata Loops had already brought us to such an altitude that each pass was just a slightly higher ridge. We crossed the Nakela Pass (4738m) then continued over the Lachulung Pass (5060m) – such an anti-climax that we did not even stop. I was amazed at how little snow there was at these altitudes, but in fact the entire area was barren and arid – now on the northern side of the Himalayas, we were in the rain shadow where the precious monsoon rains could never reach. The valleys here were heavily eroded into pinnacles and towers thick with dust and scree – despite Pema's desire to avoid delay on this long day, we insisted that our driver stopped for us to admire one area where the valley sides were studded with exotically shaped hoodoos.

Finally we reached a high plain dotted with tufts of grass – the grazing lands of the Changpa tribes who lived a nomadic life reminiscent of Tibetan herders. We passed several large herds of yak mixed with sheep and pashmina goats, with clusters of the nomads' traditional black yak-hair tents nearby. The road was lined with boards bombarding us with inspiring messages from the Border Roads Organisation, self-declared 'Tamers of Mountains', exhorting us to abstain from drinking, drugs, excessive speed or gossiping while driving! Finally we were climbing again, back towards the snow line, and the boards declared 'Great Courage and Will of Steel is the Norm' – we were almost at the summit:

"And suddenly, with no fanfare, we are at the top of the Tanglang Pass (5360m/ 17,582ft). A sign declares proudly 'You are passing through 2nd highest pass of the world. Unbelievable is not it?' (actually the 2nd highest motor road in the world, but still exciting to reach this spot). Festoons of prayer flags, old and new, adorn a small Buddhist shrine – our drivers add a string of prayers for us. All around are snowy peaks and ridges, almost at the same level as us. The air is cool but not cold ... and so thin! I feel my head spinning as I take my photos, and for once I am glad to crawl back into my seat."

We had passed right through the Himalayas, descending now into Ladakh, sprawled across the valley of the River Indus on the edge of the high Tibetan plateau. The region is known as 'Little Tibet' and, as soon as we descended into the inhabited parts of the region, I could see why. The villages were composed of Tibetan-style square houses with prayer flags flying from corner turrets; stupas and chortens (large and small shrines) were scattered across the landscape; huge white monastery complexes crowned the tops of rocky outcrops along the route. We visited several of these monasteries in the succeeding days, including tiny Taktok, built around a cave where the 8th century founder of Tibetan-style Buddhism meditated: some of the worship areas were squeezed into the original caves, with roofs blackened by incense smoke and littered with white silk scarfs presented as offerings. Most impressive was Thiksey Monastery, resembling a smaller version of Lhasa's Potala, with temples perched high on a rock and the cells of the monks tumbling down the hillside below them. We climbed a long series of slate steps to view the Giant Buddha statue, three storeys high, with temples on each level from which we could admire his feet, mid-parts or head. The head was especially magnificent, made of delicately coloured terracotta enhanced with gold leaf, with a gentle soothing expression: the Dalai Lama had consecrated it in person in 1980, and declared it one of the loveliest representations of Buddha in existence.

The Buddhist faith in Ladakh was the most vibrant I had ever experienced – since we were in Himalayan India, where the Dalai Lama himself was resident, there seemed to be unlimited funds to maintain old temples and to create new ones. We visited Hemis Monastery, largest and richest in the region (supporting over 1000 monks) to attend one of their most important festivals. Among the crowds of tourists and excited chattering Ladakhis, I found myself a tiny corner on a stairway, tucked in between several local families, to watch the proceedings:

"Musicians begin a sonorous chanting accompanied by horns and clashing cymbals, then silence falls as the first masked dancers appear, almost invisible beneath flowing robes and huge spiked hats. They swirl a little, then start to balance from one foot to the other in stately fashion. Figures wearing huge masks process into the arena, while agile and barefoot dancers leap athletically around them. Some ferocious demons join the party, and for a short while the stage is full – then everyone leaves with a triumphant chorus of horn and cymbal: lunch break!"

We stayed several days in the bustling city of Leh, a traffic-choked sprawl of modern buildings housing the administration of Ladakh, military barracks ready to defend the nearby border with China, and hotels or guesthouses catering to the burgeoning tourist industry. The smoothly paved Main Bazaar, patrolled by beggars, western backpackers and a few local people, curved around the base of a rocky hill where narrow passageways meandered steeply upwards between original mud-brick homes to a looming fortress high above us.

For the last days of our tour, however, we left Leh and headed westwards along the Indus Valley to the much smaller and quieter town of Alchi. Along the valley were fascinating fortress ruins like 15th century Basgo Castle, reminders of the time when this valley was an important part of the Silk Road. Alchi town was a delightful spot, tucked into a quiet side valley away from the main road, alongside a sparkling mountain stream lined with willow trees, apple or apricot orchards, and terraced fields of vegetables. At the end of the valley stood Alchi Temple, oldest in Ladakh, dating from the 10th century and still a centre of intense devotion. Whereas most of the other temples in Ladakh were decorated by Tibetan artists with colourful but fairly crude designs, Alchi had been embellished by skilled Kashmiri craftsmen with magnificently carved woodwork and intricately delicate paintings:

"We bow to creep beneath very low carved door-lintels into each of the four temples. Most impressive is the temple housing three huge Buddha sculptures, dressed in dhoti skirts painted with innumerable detailed scenes from everyday life – I particularly like the tiny portrait of a man standing on one leg (perhaps dancing?), right on top of the Buddha's right kneecap!"

Our last day of sightseeing started as we scrambled up a loose scree path towards a hillside cave, marked as a shrine by a white painted ring around the entrance. Part of the crumbling cliff had broken away in front of the doorway, requiring a wide leg-swing and the faith that my balance would shift in time to move my body inside the cave – but I managed it, finding walls covered in intricate 10th century paintings. From here we turned into a narrow rocky gorge beside a delightfully clear mountain stream lined with poplar and willow trees, following it for miles until we reached the point where it came to a sudden stop at a steep cliff. Rizong Monastery sprawled across this cliff, its hidden location chosen deliberately to make it a centre for meditation. We visited the prayer halls, newly painted in bright, fresh colours – unlike so many of the temples we had seen, where the colours were muted by centuries of smoke and mould.

Finally we returned to Leh, again passing arid scree slopes backed by rocky snow-spattered ridges. This region was not as beautiful as I had expected but was certainly awe-inspiring – and the same could be said of the journey through the high Himalayas. What a privilege to have travelled that difficult but breath-taking route into the remote valleys of Ladakh!

Kashmir houseboat

Mongolian eagle hunter

Mongolian ger

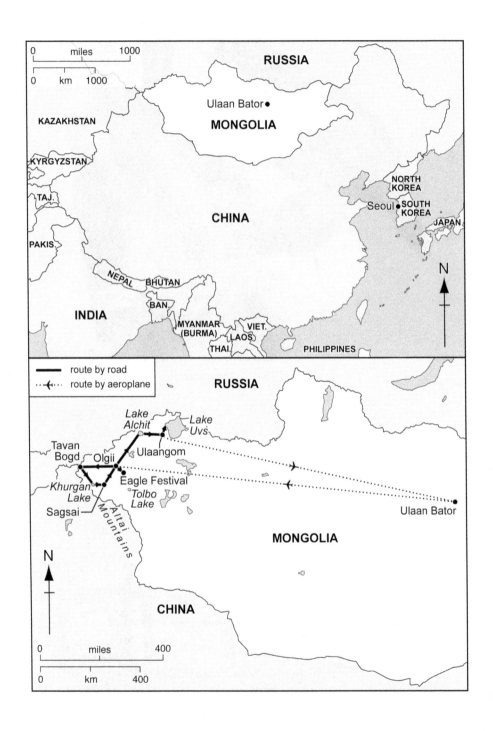

Western Mongolia (September 2019)

I DO NOT OFTEN CHOOSE to return to my travel destinations, but Mongolia is such a special country that I was keen to see more, especially the mountainous regions in Mongolia's far west. Once again I flew with Aeroflot, despite memories of peremptory service from them 40 years previously – would things have changed? Certainly, the air crew were much more helpful and friendly, but the ground staff in both London and Moscow were unsmiling, surly, rude and unhelpful: will they ever learn the principles of customer service? Mongolia's capital Ulaan Bator was transformed, however, even in the eight years since my last visit:

"A few low-rise communist apartments are still visible, but most are run-down or in the process of demolition, being replaced by gleaming high-rise accommodation. Even the Golden Buddha statue, built in 2005 to symbolise a renewed pride in national identity, has been almost swallowed up by luxurious homes – the young people of Mongolia seem now to have transferred their allegiance to materialism instead of Buddhist faith."

We made only a brief visit to the city, flying out next day on a tiny plane across miles of treeless, grassy plains crossed by serpentine rivers and scored by meandering dirt tracks – the Mongolia I remembered. After two hours we approached Olgii: what a surprise to find a fairly large town with broad avenues lined with battered grey housing blocks and modern, hastily erected hotels. Another change since my last visit – permanent settlements were springing up all across the country, housing the workers who ran the services for each region. Much of the town was quiet, though the bazaar bustled with shoppers:

"There's a mixture of peoples here – some slit-eyed and round-faced like typical Mongolians, but others with high cheekbones and wide eyes: the Muslim Kazakh people who form 80% of the population locally. A few men wear Mongolian 'del' tunics or embroidered Kazakh caps, but most are dressed in the international uniform of jeans and sweatshirts. Only their rosy wind-burned cheeks proclaim them to be people of the wide-open spaces."

Next day we boarded Landcruisers to head out towards the Altai Mountains which form Mongolia's border with neighbouring Russia and China. A gravel road carried us across golden grassy plains dotted with Kazakh gers (yurts), a little smaller than the Mongolian version. We also began to see small log cabins which the Kazakh nomads use as winter accommodation – most were still boarded up, but sometimes we saw ladies busily sealing the cracks with fresh mud in preparation for the arrival of the family for the winter. Unlike the Mongolian tradition of erecting their gers around communal service-centres for the winter, corralling their flocks with them whilst their herds of yaks fend for themselves on the open plains, the Kazakh people preferred to stay close to all their animals by over-wintering in these cabins scattered across the lower pastures. We passed many flocks of sheep and goats, and also herds of yaks and stocky, short-legged horses – Kazakhs are passionate horsemen, famous for their acrobatic skill on horseback.

We also encountered several communities of permanent wooden homes crowned by luridly coloured roofs, including the little town of Tsengel which seemed to exist mainly as a fuelling stop – small petrol stations lined the road above the town, and their owners rushed from their homes as we approached, in hope of a sale. Finally we reached the start of the Tavan Bogd National Park:

"The colours are amazing – yellowing grassland dotted with sorrel and green reeds, contrasting with the blue-grey scree of landslips and reddish rock of cliffs. And it's alive with wildlife – marmots standing to watch us or lounging on rocks, one running frantically for his burrow as our driver gleefully goes off-piste to chase him. A few scurries of movement and smaller holes must be suslik (prairie-mice), and a flash of black and white fur running on all four legs turns out to be a jackrabbit."

The valley became narrower, the road rougher ... at its furthest point stood our accommodation – a cluster of gers belonging to a family of ethnic Mongolians, who were camped a little further up the valley. Each ger contained three metal bedsteads topped by air-mattresses; part-way up the hillside stood a sawdust 'eco-toilet', plus an urn of cold water for washing; a communal ger acted as dining tent and lounge. No electricity, no hot water – but swooping flights of wagtails beside the river and soaring kites overhead, no sound except the wind and the water ... what more could I want? We spent a full day in this remote valley, enjoying the wildlife and watching the people going about their daily chores. Early in the morning I walked up to their encampment just as a man was rounding up a group of yaks and driving them toward his gers – two women emerged with buckets and stools and proceeded to milk them, enveloped in smoke from a newly lit fire in one of the gers, before the yaks were sent off again to their day's grazing by a few carefully aimed stones.

Later our guide Tulga took us to the head of the valley for a visit to the ger belonging to the family of our cook: spacious inside, with a huge iron stove in the centre and wooden beds on two sides; shelves and cupboards on the other sides, with a satellite box and small TV sitting on top of a painted chest, powered by a car battery which was charged each day from a small solar panel outside. Here we were treated to a feast of yak-milk delicacies, including chewy tasteless milk curds, hard tangy cheese and even clotted cream! Also on the table were freshly fried doughnuts and dishes of boiled sweets. Tulga explained that they eat virtually no fruit or vegetables, and use a lot of salt ... leading to serious liver and kidney problems in later life, and rotten teeth in the children:

"Visit over, we are free to amble home on foot. There is little wind today and we are far from the flocks ... I am surrounded by deep silence broken only by the occasional piercing scream of a hawk. On a distant rock I spot two rare saker falcons, national birds of Mongolia, and suslik scurry past, no more than a flash of movement in the corner of my eye. The rest of the group moves on ahead – I am left in glorious solitude."

We moved on to another location within the National Park, beside Khurgan Lake. While planning the tour, Tulga had made arrangements with a local family camped by the lake, to borrow two of their gers for our use. However, when he managed to make contact with them to check on their exact location, he learned that they had meanwhile moved their gers and livestock to a place with better grazing and less wind, but some distance from the lake – so Tulga decided to press on to the lakeshore where he remembered seeing some wooden cabins we might be able to use. The first group of huts was dirty and unheated – mutiny began to stir in some of our group:

"Tulga moves on, driving like a Top Gear presenter far ahead of the rest of our convoy, desperate to secure places for us in case there are other tourists around. Seeing a minibus ahead, he launches into a shortcut, hurtling over gravelly banks till finally he emerges on the main track just as the huts appear in front of us. He hastily claims a large hut for the kitchen and two gers for our accommodation, enlisting the Park Warden to chop wood for the fires our crew are lighting to heat the gers. In no time, our 'home from home' has been created from bleak nothingness!"

And what an idyllic site it proved to be, well worth all Tulga's stress! The night was illuminated by a huge, orangey-pink moon gleaming on the waters of the nearby lake. Next morning we woke to find a dusting of snow covering our gers and the lakeside pastures, with the Altai Mountains across the water freshly whitened. Fortunately it began to melt as we set off to see Turgen Waterfall, so our drivers were just able to follow faint tracks across the marshes which lined up correctly on wooden plank bridges crossing the streams. Finally we plunged into a narrow gorge slicing into the mountain range, bouncing along a rocky track before abandoning our vehicles to stumble onwards on foot, with an occasional slip knee-deep into the snow drifts. Then uphill, following the line of a small river running deep in a cleft, across steep larch-clad hillsides. The speedy younger members of the group surged ahead, outrunning our guide and going astray – so in the end I was first to reach the waterfall:

"I emerge high above the main river, which I can hear rushing far below. All around are snow-dusted rocky ridges, clear and sharp against the blue sky. Now the route becomes difficult and, with the snow, dangerous: the water flows down through a jumble of large icy boulders, many with sharp edges and ankle-twisting holes between them. I dare not go further, so content myself with a mere glimpse of the waterfall – but that's enough! The beauty of the walk has been the landscape itself."

Back at the vehicles we found our wonderful crew had been busy cooking up a hearty soup in the back of their van for our lunch, which we shared with an acrobatic Black Kite which swooped and soared around us, hoping for scraps. Then we drove along the shores of the twin Khurgan and Khoton Lakes before returning to camp on foot at our own speed. What a joy to stroll beside the water's edge watching lapwings and magpies skittering among the stones, then a cheeky ground squirrel which sprinted ahead of me, stopping at intervals to stand up like a meerkat to inspect my progress. I was sorry to leave this tranquil spot next day, turning our backs on the mountains to head east to the small community of Sagsai.

Just outside Sagsai we left our vehicles to cross a rickety bridge across marshy land to a Kazakh ger, home of an elderly eagle-master and his wife. Outside the ger, tethered to a rock, was a magnificent Golden Eagle. Its owner welcomed us to his ger, dressing in all his ceremonial finery before posing with his eagle … and then offering us the chance to lift the bird ourselves:

"It's amazing looking up at this powerful 2-year-old bird, not too heavy because she's not yet fully grown – gripping my arm confidently and peering at me, though hooded (for safety) so she cannot see me. The master encourages me to lift and drop my arm, so that she spreads her wings wide above my head."

Tulga began to tell us about the Kazakh eagle-hunters who lived in this part of Mongolia. These traditional hunters had for centuries been travelling high into the mountains to take fledgling eagles (always females, which are larger and easier to teach) from their nests, nurturing and training them for several years until they were able to use them to hunt hare or fox, or even (using two eagles together) wolves. They would fly the birds until they were 10 or 11 years old, then release them back to the wild for their remaining ten years of life, so that they would have time to breed. Traditionally the hunters gathered together each year at the start of the hunting season (in winter) to show off the prowess of their eagles and socialise. In 1999 a local entrepreneur had realised the potential of these gatherings and begun to market tours to the Eagle Festivals.

Eagle Festival day started with a total breakdown of so-called 'civilisation' in our hotel back in Olgii – no electricity and no running water: we were better off in the ger camps! But nothing could crush the excitement as we drove out to the shores of Tolbo Lake, where a ring of Landcruisers and ancient grey Russian vans was already gathered around a roped-off arena, enclosed within the cliffs of a small valley and surrounded by stalls of locally made embroideries and feltwork. Tulga had arranged for us to use, as our base, a couple of gers belonging to a group of eagle hunters from a single village, including a 15-year-old girl and a dramatically handsome young man of 24 – and for us to 'adopt' this group of hunters as our particular team. We were introduced to them and to their eagles, which were perched on a ring of rocks around the gers – each wearing blinkers and tethered just far enough from its neighbour to avoid fighting. Then we moved off to select a good spot on the rocks overlooking the arena to await the start of proceedings.

It was a slow start! Most of the morning was spent on photo opportunities as more and more hunters swaggered up to register with the officials, until finally sixty or so competitors assembled for a parade – mostly on foot, carrying their eagles on their arms, though a few were on horseback. Leading the parade was a young female hunter wearing pure white fur – Tulga hastened around to tell us that she was called Aysholpan, and had been the star of a documentary several years earlier (which I did remember seeing) which had made her an international celebrity:

"The hunters' partners climb up to a rocky spur with the eagles and, on command, release one bird at a time towards their handler standing in the middle of the arena – they will be awarded points for flying directly to their handler, as well as time points for the speed in which they do it. The first few birds soar low into the valley, directly on target, but then it all goes wrong! The air currents change (or perhaps the birds are just glad to be flying free?) so many of them start soaring around the valley, even landing on the opposite hillside for a rest – while their handler shrieks and yells and waves a hunk of meat frantically. The time penalties continue until the bird actually lands on his arm – oh dear!"

After all the excitement came the lunch break, when the hunters adjourned to their gers, fastening their eagles to rocks, fences or even car bumpers all over the site: a weird feeling to be picking my way between so many ferocious birds, stepping away from one to find myself almost falling over another! Meanwhile a competition of Mongolian archery was starting – the one traditional sport which I had not seen eight years previously, when I attended the Naadam festivals: I could not miss this! The archers (all dressed in Mongolian silk 'del' tunics and pillbox hats) were using blunt arrows and firing over a distance of 50 metres towards a row of wooden balls on the ground, partly hidden by low banks of earth in front of and behind them. The opposing team ensured that the balls were perfectly lined up, then caressed the earth banks with arcane gestures, before trying to distract the archer with howls as he took aim. Nearly every archer, however, managed to hit the balls, scattering one or two out of the line with a dull thud, then performing a little victory dance.

The afternoon brought traditional Kazakh competitions to demonstrate their masterful riding skills. First came Tiyn Teru, where riders tried to pick up 'flowers' (actually pieces of red plastic) from the ground while galloping at full speed – some managed to collect most of the pieces, others missed almost all, while one fell off (to the cruel laughter of the local crowd) and another turned his horse head over heels (to the horrified gasp of the watching tourists). Then it was Bushkashi, a horseback tug-of-war where two riders fought over a goat carcass (thoughtfully beheaded to appease the sensitivities of the watching tourists):

"The riders throw everything at it: one pair almost unseated in their efforts; another pair so desperate not to surrender that their battle leaves the arena and continues into the midst of the audience!"

Next day we returned to the festival site, passing en route a field where a bareback Mongolian horse race was being prepared – barefoot jockeys aged between six and ten were being dressed in shoulder-, arm-, knee- and leg-guards as well as helmets. What a difference from eight years previously, when I had watched children as young as four years old riding with no protection at all – Tulga told me that new laws were now protecting the children better. Their horses were being carefully groomed and their manes gathered together into a topknot, before setting off on races varying from 12 to 16km long – tests of endurance rather than speed.

Meanwhile at Tolbo Lake, the day's competition was for mounted eagle hunters, calling the eagles from the top of the cliffs down to a fox-skin lure dragged behind a horse. There were less competitors in this class, and they were far more successful than on the previous day – most birds soared directly down to the lure, though one took a circuitous route before finally locking on to the target. The celebrity Aysholpan was one of the contestants, with a minion to set up the lure and to disentangle her bird from it afterwards (so she did not need to dismount) – but her bird pounced swift and sure, clearly well-trained. As the day drew to a close, Tulga assembled us all back at our temporary base to meet 'our team' again – they had won 1st, 3rd, 5th and 6th prizes, and the overall prize of a new motorbike too. Well done to all!

The last days of the tour took us eastwards, out of the mountainous Kazakh region and back into the rolling grasslands which are typical of much of Mongolia. We passed tranquil Lake Achit, its surface carpeted with shelducks and mallards, then stopped for supplies in the tiny coal-mining community of Hotgur, a jumble of scruffy concrete homes loosely strung together by dirt roads – yet clearly a hub of local commerce with several grocery stores, a bank and a pharmacy. Spread across a vast plain, we discovered mysterious standing stones roughly carved into human shapes – 'bulbuls' thought to be over 1000 years old, some apparently marking ancient graves. Tulga told us that some of these graves had been opened by archaeologists, who had found gold jewellery inside – evidence of an ancient civilisation which had now disappeared.

Finally we reached the utilitarian town of Ulaangom, a functional but unlovely community of housing blocks and wide, dusty streets – I was grateful that Tulga organised an excursion to fill the time waiting for our delayed flight back to Ulaan Bator. He wanted to take us to the shores of Lake Uvs, but the dirt road led only to a government hay depot:

"From here we follow faint tracks across lush grazing lands, herding sheep and goats out of the way as we drive, but we still seem no nearer the water. So Tulga sets off cross-country, navigating by the colour of the vegetation (a reddish creeper grows on dry land, whilst the marshy hollows are thick with yellowy reeds) but finally the wheels begin to sink – we have to give up! We park on a dry mound amid tall waving grass seed-heads, where butterflies and dragonflies are flitting; the air is cool, the sun warm, the stillness broken only by the bleating of distant sheep and the chirruping of birds in the long grass."

For me, this is what Mongolia is all about: tranquillity and silence, abundant wildlife and an unhurried traditional way of life with plenty of time for reflection and dreaming. Though it is inevitable that the country will develop into a more modern, economically successful society, I hope that they will never lose those wide-open spaces where Nature dominates man's puny efforts to tame it.

Amazon -Parentins Carnival

The Amazon (January 2020)

I HAD NEVER BEEN ATTRACTED by the idea of cruising, but finally succumbed when I spotted a cruise to a fascinating part of the world, difficult to visit by any other means. For almost two weeks we had been calling at various ports and islands, followed by four full days crossing the vast empty Atlantic Ocean. The ship bustled with activities: quizzes, salsa lessons, ice-carving demonstrations – though there were also lectures on geology, history and wildlife. I was spending much of my time out on deck in the vain hope of spotting whales or dolphins, though the most common sight was ethereal, pale-grey flying fish. Finally the surface of the sea was transformed from its customary slate-grey into a yellowy brown colour, thick with river silt – though we were still miles from the South American coast. The flying fish disappeared, disdaining to live in such muddy water ... the air lost its freshness, becoming heavy and oppressively humid as thick clouds built up. We were approaching the mighty Amazon!

By next morning we were anchored at the mouth of the river, sitting for four hours as Brazilian immigration officials checked all the documents lodged with the purser, then finally taking on three pilots who would accompany us for as long as we cruised the river's channels. Meanwhile a constant parade of shipping passed us: ferries making the week-long journey to Manaus, with passengers sleeping in hammocks slung side-by-side along the decks (how grateful I was for my comfortable air-conditioned cabin!); freighters heavily laden with containers of imported goods, especially electronic components being taken to the tax-free haven of Manaus for assembly, before being re-exported; convoys of flat barges pushed by elderly tugboats, packed tight with vehicles bringing supplies to the riverside cities – there were no roads in this part of the world, so all transport was via the waterways. And there was wildlife to watch – swallows and ospreys soaring above our ship; vultures and egrets on the shore; cockroaches and crickets colonising the bulwarks around our decks; even occasional river dolphins surfacing briefly before sinking again into the opaque water.

As we moved off up the broad waterway, the distant banks were lined with thick forest running all the way to the water's edge, punctuated only by occasional wooden cabins and a few tiny fields. On board, a lecturer was telling us about the Amazon: the longest river in the world (a title disputed by the Nile) if its length is measured from Lake Titicaca in the Andes; a catchment area as large as Australia, carrying one fifth of the world's fresh water to the sea; temperatures up to 45°C in the dry season (July-December) and rainfall up to 3000mm per day in the rainy season, resulting in floods rising 10m on average (with the record being 29m in 2012). The land is naturally covered with tropical rainforest composed of an 'under-storey' of slow-growing hardwoods (like ebony) up to 30m high, then of 'canopy trees' (like mahogany) growing up to 40m, with 'emergent trees' (like balsa and kapok) rising above the main canopy up to 60m: a forest generating 20% of the world's oxygen.

24 hours later we reached our first stop, anchoring off the city of Santarem to allow us to make a landing using the ship's lifeboats. I had a glimpse of rather decrepit low-rise buildings and the powder-blue towers of a cathedral, but I was not planning to explore this city. Instead, I joined an excursion offering a walk in the Amazonian forest, though at first all we saw were large tracts of land cleared to grow soya, bananas or mangos. Finally we turned off the highway on to an earthen track reaching into the dense forest of Tapajos National Park, protected only because of draconian punishments for anyone daring to fell a tree – stricter even than the punishment for murder, our guide informed us:

"Leaving the coach, we launch into the forest, following a faint path which twists and winds its way over tree-roots and under fallen trunks, our guide easing our passage with his machete. Almost immediately the air under the trees is cooler, though still so humid that the sweat pours off me. The

vegetation absorbs the sound of our voices like a muffler. We walk silently on deep carpets of leaves which have fallen over the years yet have not rotted away, passing through a tangle of skinny trees, convoluted lianas and leafy shrubs, with occasional massive trees breaking through to soar skywards."

Our guide introduced us to many of the trees, stopping to hack small pieces of bark from a Quinine tree for us to sample (very bitter!); to remove a globule of sap from a Jactobar tree to light as a native candle; to hammer at an Ironwood tree, so dense and hard that it is impossible even to drive a nail into it; to chop open the huge pod of a Brazil-nut tree to reveal the familiar angular kernels inside. Most impressive was an ancient Samauma tree, third highest tree species in the world, its towering trunk supported by huge 'buttresses', each far taller than a man. We saw no birds or animals on our walk, but there were innumerable varieties of insect: brilliantly coloured giant butterflies, as big as small birds; tiny Honey Ants constructing strange black growths on the trunks of many trees; huge vicious Bullet Ants swarming from a hollow tree when our guide tapped it. Reddish growths at the base of some trees were the home of termites, while strange yellow pillars rising from the ground were the nests of cicadas; spiders of varying sizes spun webs among the twigs; tiny wild bees pestered us for our salty sweat. This was the Amazon jungle I had come to see!

The next stopover was the highlight of my Amazonian experiences. As dawn broke, we approached a clear stream flowing into the main river through wide water meadows. On its banks was the tiny fishing village of Boca da Valeria, a cluster of simple wooden homes raised on stilts for protection during times of flood, with a large stone church built on the highest point of the village. The entire population turned out to welcome us, with fireworks greeting our arrival … and even rare pink dolphins (Botos) frolicking around our tenders as they shuttled us ashore. At first, to avoid the crowds, I hired a local canoe to take me up the Valeria River, admiring egrets and cormorants sitting on the riverbanks, while vultures and swallows soared overhead. Back in the village, I again turned away from the crowds to walk towards some of the outlying houses. A lady greeted me as I passed, pointing out to me a sloth crawling with languid haste through the branches of a tree, then invited me to visit inside her home – simply built of wooden planks and roofed with corrugated iron, yet boasting a fridge and a tiny TV powered by a small generator and linked to a rusty satellite dish on the hillside above. Outside she showed me her garden of herbs and onions growing in boxes and buckets on her verandah, and her flock of chickens which she explained (in Portuguese with a few words of Spanish) provided eggs to sell in exchange for fuel on her monthly trips to the nearest town, several days journey away by river.

Back in the village most of the passengers were returning to the ship, so I was finally able to meet the village children who had brought their pets (mainly parrots or parrakeets, but also a small cayman with his mouth taped shut and a very bored bandicoot) to show us – in exchange for small gifts of pens and notepads. I was almost the last to leave the village, sad to leave this idyllic spot:

"Back aboard, cruise life has recommenced with bridge games underway and a raucous singalong around the pool. But I stand on deck reflecting on Boca da Valeria and its delightful people. OK – they wanted to be given gifts, but they deserve something for allowing over 1000 nosy people to peer into their lives for five hours. There were lots of smiles and they seemed genuinely glad to see us. As we leave, music strikes up – they are gathering to swap stories of their unusual day."

Our Amazon stopovers were filled with contrasts – none more so than between that peaceful village and the city of Manaus. For over an hour before our arrival, the banks of the river were lined with huge oil refineries and factories, then docks filled with bright red and yellow cranes lifting mounds of containers to and from innumerable moored freighters. The surface of the river was mottled with streams of the Amazon's normal muddy water, now thick with clumps of vegetation washed down by the start of the rainy season, and parallel streams of clear black water – the 'Meeting of the Waters' where the biologically dead, acid water of the Rio Negro flows into the Rio Solimoeus to create the Amazon, running side-by-side for 8km before they blend together. Manaus itself was a shock – a huge city bustling with traffic and humanity, blending poverty-stricken shacks and shoddy modern apartments with magnificent (if often run-down) palaces built during the 19th century rubber boom which ended dramatically in 1910, leaving the city bankrupt. Most imposing of all was the Opera House, a pink and cream baroque confection with a grand colonnaded facade and incongruously gaudy golden dome – the first public building to be constructed when the city was establishing itself as 'Paris in the Jungle', with every piece of stone and decorative glass brought upriver by ship and laboriously carried into the jungle by slaves.

We spent long enough in Manaus to also take an excursion across the Rio Negro to visit Lake January, an open meadow in the dry season which fills with floodwater up to 10m deep from January onwards. It was already several metres deep when we visited, so we could clearly see the ingenious floating homes of the residents – built on rafts of massive logs which lift the houses as the waters rise:

"Motorised canoes take us deeper into the lake, picking our way through tall grasses and deep reedbeds. The trees are already partially submerged, though a 'tide-line' high on their trunks reveals where the water will eventually reach. At the end of the lake we find some giant Victoria water lily pads several metres wide – pairs of jacanas (Jesus Birds) noisily defend their nests, built on top of the leaves. In the trees nearby are kingfishers and herons, while on a rickety wooden walkway in one of the villages, I encounter a troupe of golden Capuchin monkeys."

Our ship was too large to continue any further than Manaus, so we turned back, stopping in different places on the return journey. Parentins was a smaller, quieter town which apparently comes to life just once a year, when it hosts the second largest carnival in Brazil – the BoiBumba. Our arrival was again a highlight for the local population, and we were greeted by smartly dressed scouts and guides who stood all day in the heat and humidity to salute us whenever we passed by. The wharf was besieged by bicycle-taxis offering tours of the town's (very few) sights. I rented one and was carried in style past the ugly modern cathedral and the huge stadium where the carnival floats are paraded, then on to a massive warehouse where last year's floats were stored ready to be used again. I was amazed at their size and complexity: an anteater taller than a double-decker bus; luridly coloured dragons; an eerie snake-headed goddess. The town boasted a special theatre where they presented a regular show to out-of-season visitors, giving a flavour of their carnival … and they had arranged a special performance exclusively for our ship:

"Non-stop, loud samba music beats the rhythm to which group after group of dancers gyrate, full of energy and enthusiasm. Figures costumed in paint and feathers, who stamp and twist beneath strobe lighting and weird green

illumination, represent the Indian tribes; girls in full skirts whirl in the style of Rio's carnival while their male partners leap athletically beside them; massive floats slide in from the sides of the stage, articulated so they can throb in time to the beat."

Another stop provided yet another contrast: the resort of Alter do Chao, a community of comfortable hotels and luxurious holiday villas clustered around white sandy beaches beside a deep green lagoon. Popular with city-dwelling Brazilians for the beaches, for me its main delights were the abundant brightly coloured birds and other wildlife living in the lush gardens:

"I am surrounded by gorgeous black and yellow Oriole Blackbirds, so shy everywhere else but here flocking like starlings. The bushes are full of fluttering blue or orange finches, while in a tree I spot a small white animal with a pink face – a Silvery Marmoset resting on a branch. A bright green iguana sits in the roadway, fearlessly watching the visitors walking by."

For the next two days we cruised back out into the ocean, far enough to escape the Amazon's thick mud so that the ship could scoop up cleaner water to desalinate for showers and toilets, without the risk of clogging the filters. Then we returned to the estuary for one more visit: the city of Belem, vaunted as the most historic community in Amazonas. What a disappointment! We anchored at the nearby port of Icoaraci, boarding coaches for the drive into the city, past lines of scruffy factories and jumbles of poor housing festooned with wiring, covered with graffiti and surrounded by festering litter. Belem itself still showed signs of a wealthy past, with grand public buildings and churches, though most were blackened with mould and crumbling into ruins with shrubs rooting themselves in crannies in roofs and walls. The harbour was filled with battered fishing boats, their owners gutting their catch and strewing detritus across the wharfs to be devoured by swarms of black vultures. We explored a vast riverside market, interesting for the variety of unfamiliar fruits and roots on sale, but unnerving when we realised that we needed to be accompanied by a guard to watch over us as we walked. Armed police with dogs were securing the small tourist enclave around the restored fortress and cathedral:

"Belem is not what I expected – clearly run-down and scrabbling for a living. There have been some efforts to restore a couple of historic buildings, but most is rotting with mould, hidden behind trailing wires and engulfed by clouds of vultures. The streets are jammed with traffic, the pavements rife with

pickpockets. What a contrast to the relaxed and welcoming towns and villages we have seen deeper in the jungle."

I could have done without visiting Belem, but before we left South America there was one more highlight to come. We sailed north along the coast to French Guiana, anchoring in the open ocean close to a group of islands called the Iles du Salut (the Isles of Safety) – such a misnomer in view of their history! From 1852 till 1953, France used these islands as a penal colony where at least 80,000 prisoners were incarcerated in horrible conditions from which very few ever managed to return. The former accommodation of the guards was now transformed into simple tourist lodgings, but the remains of the prisoners' cells were still visible:

"Claustrophobically narrow cells with no room to walk around: some have barred windows for light and fresh air, though the punishment cells have no opening except a thick wooden door – the darkness of solitary confinement. Even the isolation hospital consists of a large hall divided by iron bars to which the prisoners' chains could be attached, with a row of stone-faced holes as the only latrines."

Yet despite their history, the islands were now a tropical paradise! Dense vegetation inland was enlivened by flowering hibiscus, bougainvillea and African flame trees, while coconut palms lined the shore. Frequent signs warned against swimming because of strong currents and sharks – effective guardians to prevent the escape of prisoners, though now there were several artificial stony swimming ponds close to the sea. Everywhere there was wildlife: reddish agouti scurried silently among the bushes while lizards crackled noisily through the leaf litter; tiny hummingbirds darted from flower to flower and ospreys hovered overhead; turtles browsed just below the surface of the sea, lifting their heads occasionally to take a breath; adult Capuchin monkeys were digging industriously into piles of rotting wood for grubs, undisturbed by our presence, while their infants swung wildly from lianas above them. I would have loved to stay for a while in this idyllic setting … perhaps one day?

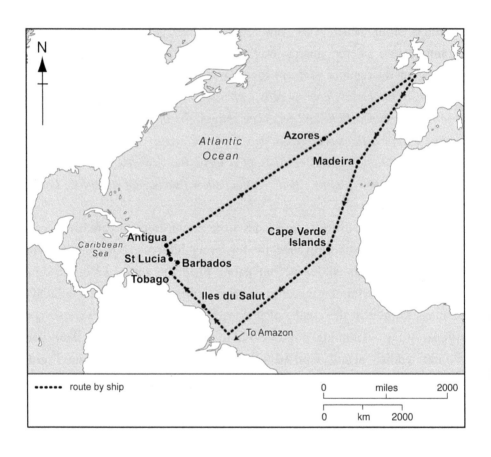

N

Atlantic
Ocean

Azores

Madeira

Cape Verde
Islands

Caribbean
Sea

Antigua

St Lucia Barbados

Tobago

Iles du Salut

To Amazon

••••• route by ship

0   miles   2000

0   km   2000

Atlantic and Caribbean Islands (January/ February 2020)

THOUGH THE AMAZON WAS THE principal reason for choosing an extended cruise out of London, it also allowed a taste of other worlds – exploring islands which would be difficult to visit except by ship. They introduced me to the early Portuguese navigators: while the Spanish were heading west to strip the wealth of South America, skilled Portuguese seamen were searching out new trade routes to the Far East, settling islands and ports along the way. In 1494 the two kingdoms signed a treaty dividing the newly discovered lands, along a line reaching down the western side of the Atlantic Ocean. It put most of the Americas into Spanish control, but the easternmost tip of Brazil was in the Portuguese zone – so they claimed the whole of Brazil: I had always wondered why Brazil was the only South American country to use Portuguese as their official language.

First port of call was the volcanic island of Madeira, uninhabited until the Portuguese arrived in the 15ᵗʰ century and still part of Portugal – thus benefiting from generous EU subsidies. In 2016 I had made a brief visit to the island, enjoying its lush vegetation and densely planted gardens; amazed by the engineering of modern roads which laced together the different corners of this precipitous lump of rock via bridges and tunnels … and by the older engineering of 'levadas' (irrigation channels) cut from the steep hillsides and still running with fresh water today. This time I decided to remain in the capital city Funchal, exploring streets and squares patterned with typically Portuguese black and white designs and visiting the Collegiate Church:

"Though neat and elegant outside in its black and white livery, inside it's

an over-abundant feast of patterns and colours. Every inch of the walls and ceilings is decorated – the ceiling pretends there are three cupolas above us, the walls are painted to represent tiles and niches. But there is nothing imaginary about the ornate altars, adorned with gold leaf."

Two days sailing further south, we reached the Cape Verde Islands, lying almost 400 miles off the African coast. We approached at dawn, cruising gently into a complex jumble of islands, each surmounted by a sharp jagged peak – the remnants of volcanos which exploded through a 'hot spot' in the earth's crust, gradually drifting east as the geological plate moved, to allow a new volcanic island to bubble up through the crack. We visited the island of Sao Vicente, discovered in the 15th century by the Portuguese but not settled until the 19th century when it became the principal coal-fuelling station for ships preparing to cross the Atlantic. By the 20th century that industry had died, and the island was left with little income; after independence from Portugal in 1975, even the EU subsidies disappeared. By the time we visited, the main town Mindelo was run-down, its port crumbling for lack of investment. In the countryside were arid hillsides with a few deserted terraces where farmers had given up trying to eke a living from desperately dry land. The island has no natural water supply and for the past three years even the rainy season had failed, so the land was littered with abandoned homes.

What a contrast between the Cape Verde Islands and the Azores: both strings of isolated volcanic isles formed over 'hotspots' in the earth's crust; both discovered and settled by the Portuguese; both established as refuelling stops on the long journey across the Atlantic. Yet the Azores were regularly immersed in thick cloud (giving the nickname 'islands of mist') with frequent rainfall giving abundant supplies of water. The Azorean port of Horta had adapted to service ocean-going yachts in place of Portuguese treasure galleons or coal-burning steamers and was still drawing an income as a vital stopover port. More importantly the Azores had remained an autonomous region of Portugal, still benefiting from European wealth. I wonder whether the population of Cape Verde has ever regretted demanding independence?

We visited two Azorean islands in the middle of our six-day return journey across the Atlantic, first calling at Faial on the western side of the group. The main town, Horta, was neat and attractive with the black and white facades of imposing baroque churches sitting amongst gleaming white houses. Most of the land was covered by forest or lush grassland, where fat beef cattle were grazing in windswept fields enclosed by hedges of blue hydrangea bushes. However, this was still an actively volcanic island, frequently shaken by earthquakes and blighted as recently as 1957/58 by an eruption which buried several villages, leaving many homes roofless and abandoned:

"We descend to the sea where the tiny whaling village of Comprido once stood, till it was entirely buried by ash and lava bombs. Now the road passes through acres of grey dust, barely beginning to grow new vegetation. A few broken walls still show through the ash; the top of the former lighthouse rises above the layers of volcanic detritus which have buried its lower floors."

Overnight we moved east to the island of Sao Miguel, largest in the Azores and first to be settled by the Portuguese in the 15th century. Once again, our visit was accompanied by thick cloud and light drizzle which made the landscape lush and green – allowing the cultivation of a range of crops including super-sweet pineapples, as well as a thriving dairy industry. This island is famous for its landscape of volcanic craters (all now extinct as they have gradually drifted away from the 'hotspot' in the west of the archipelago), including one vast caldera three miles across which contains seven separate craters. An island tour took us to various viewpoints over the caldera, but usually the view was lost in thick cloud:

"We have one more viewpoint in our itinerary – veils of mist dull the view, then drift away for a tantalising glimpse towards the north coast, sparkling in brilliant sunshine, and the bright green mounds of volcanic cones which last erupted 50,000 years ago. It's a voluptuous landscape, rolling and heaving beneath a thick, velvety green cover of vegetation. What a joy to actually see something!"

To the far west of the Atlantic Ocean, enclosing the Caribbean Sea, is an arc of islands renowned for their gleaming beaches and luxuriant tropical climate. My cruise called at four of these islands and I was excited to see why the West Indies have become such a magnet for tourism – but they were spoilt for me by the hordes of tourists which swamped almost all the places we visited. Everywhere our ship went, disgorging its 1000 passengers, we were accompanied by three or even four other much larger cruise ships with up to 5000 passengers each – all visiting the same tourist venues, all at the same time, all with the same desire to see everything within a limited time ashore. Yet I should not complain, since I was one of those tourists myself!

Our first port of call was Tobago, less popular than many of the islands – only one other ship was in port with us! And what a delight to find a less humid climate than we had experienced in the Amazon area – for the first time in weeks, I was able to walk the streets without streaming with sweat. The people seemed reserved rather than openly friendly, but very relaxed and easy-going. An excursion took me out into the rainforest for which the island is famous, walking along a concrete path beneath tall trees hung with bromeliads, and past immense stands of bamboo alive with birds. Our goal was Argyle Falls, where a small river leaped over a cliff in three successive stages, tumbling into a deep pool. Some decided to swim there, but I was content just to dip my feet into the cool water to be inspected by shoals of tiny fish.

Next stop was Barbados, a limestone rock distinct from all the other volcanic islands and set outside the main chain of the Lesser Antilles; belonging to Britain until 1966 and still part of the Commonwealth. My excursion here took me through open pastureland and sugar-cane plantations to visit Harrison's Cave, boasting several high domed chambers and beds of stalagmites. The most memorable feature of the visit, however, was the electric tram which transported us alongside the underground river, with a guide who was determined to keep us entertained with non-stop anecdotes and jokes. I also had time to explore the city of Bridgetown, wandering through the 'historic town' past churches and imposing public buildings dating from its time as a British colony, and along streets of shops filled with luxury duty-free goods. Yet it was the people I found most interesting, and especially their hairstyles:

"Clearly hair is a big issue here. Most of the women have tamed their curls with tight plaits, either hanging free or piled into a bun. Some men also have long hair, often matted into dreadlocks; others have pushed their bushy manes into huge caps, some 2 ft high, balanced on top of their heads."

Most attractive of all the Caribbean islands we visited was St Lucia, its skyline a jumble of thickly forested, jagged mountain peaks, looking so enticing as we battled our way into harbour, dodging three other huge cruise ships which were attempting to moor at the same time. Sightseeing took me first high into the hills to an old plantation house almost hidden by its luxuriant garden – it was now run as a B&B … what a delightful place to stay for a relaxing holiday! We descended to the picturesque fishing village of Anse-le-Ray, its main street lined with brightly painted wooden homes festooned with souvenirs – yet in the side streets I encountered local people still living a normal life away from the tourists: ladies sitting on their doorsteps to chat as they peeled their vegetables and even a young man laundering his clothes in an ancient (leaky) twin-tub plumbed in to a standpipe. Down on the beach groups of chattering men were skilfully gutting their catch of flying fish, or mending nets under a rough awning. We continued into the hills to the Aerial Tram, a series of continually moving, open metal cages (modelled on a Swiss cable-car) which carried us up into unbroken rainforest, at first on a lower wire passing between the trees and then returning on a higher wire running through the canopy:

"Our onboard guide points out interesting trees along the way, some draped with lianas and colourful creepers, while beneath us are beautifully shaped tree-ferns. At first the landscape seems entirely silent, but as we become attuned to forest noises, we begin to hear the occasional crash of a falling branch or fruit, the distant song of a tree-frog, the twitter of an unseen bird."

One more island to go … but I was tired of crowded tourist coaches, so as we disembarked at Antigua, I headed for the swarms of taxi drivers touting for business at the port gates. I chose a friendly young man (Johnnie) who drove me around his island for three hours, showing me the sights which he felt I should see, whilst also regaling me with stories about his life – a wonderful way to explore! We drove up into the hills to viewpoints overlooking millionaires' homes and Englishman's Bay, a sprawling natural harbour filled wall-to-wall with yachts of every size and description, then continued through orchards of mango trees, groves of banana palms and fields of pineapples. In all the islands I had so far visited, I had failed to find that classic image of gleaming palm-fringed seashore for which the Caribbean is famous – so I asked Johnnie to take me to his favourite beach:

"We turn to drive along the Caribbean side of the island and now we are passing pure white beaches and calm turquoise sea. Johnnie chooses to stop at Jolly Beach, a line of sunbeds dotted with beach umbrellas … but no shady

trees, so the sun beats down relentlessly, dazzling my eyes on the white sand. Tourists lie baking in the midday sun – are they mad? How can they stand this heat? I cannot wait to return to our air-conditioned car!"

Though I was fascinated by the Atlantic islands we visited, especially the Azores, and would love to visit most of them again, my diary records disappointment in the much-vaunted West Indies:

"The Caribbean has not met my expectations – but why? The climate has generally been fresh and far less humid than the Amazon; there have been tropical flowers and hummingbirds to enjoy; the people have been helpful and pleasant. Yet I could not escape the over-developed tourist industry: crowds of trippers pouring off the ships; tacky souvenir stalls everywhere; officious tour guides marshalling their groups with unsmiling discipline. I loved the lush gardens and silent forest of St Lucia ... but Antigua's white sand beaches seemed just barren overheated wildernesses to me. It is time to leave!"

St Lucia - Pink Plantation

Uzbekistan – Bukhara

Antarctica - Orne Harbour

Acknowledgements

OVER THE YEARS, FRIENDS HAD asked whether I was planning to write a book about my travels and my answer was always 'perhaps one day' – but that day would never have come without the enforced leisure time provided by the Covid lockdowns in 2020. Even then I might never have started, without the encouragement (and nagging) of my friend Mary Kerslake – for which I am very thankful!

Thanks also to many other friends for their encouragement to continue writing, especially those who eagerly bought the first volume of my book and then regularly contacted me to say how they were enjoying travelling with me, chapter by chapter.

Without the expertise of local guides throughout my journeys, my experiences would have been much poorer – thanks to them all, especially Tashi in Tibet and Handa in Mongolia: shining stars of their profession!

I am again grateful to Mirador Publishing, and especially my editor Sarah, for leading me patiently through the arcane mysteries of publication, with continuing enthusiasm and encouragement. And to Cath d'Alton for producing clear and informative maps to guide my readers through each chapter.

Most of all, my eternal thanks are due to my God, who created this wonderful world and who has allowed me to see so much of it – Praise Him!

Lightning Source UK Ltd.
Milton Keynes UK
UKHW022018200221
378988UK00005B/82